# South Africa-China Relations

# South Africa-China Relations

## Between Aspiration and Reality in a New Global Order

Phiwokuhle Mnyandu

LEXINGTON BOOKS
*Lanham • Boulder • New York • London*

Published by Lexington Books
An imprint of The Rowman & Littlefield Publishing Group, Inc.
4501 Forbes Boulevard, Suite 200, Lanham, Maryland 20706
www.rowman.com

86-90 Paul Street, London EC2A 4NE

British Library Cataloguing in Publication Information Available

**Library of Congress Cataloging-in-Publication Data**

Names: Mnyandu, Phiwokuhle, author.
Title: South Africa-China relations : between aspiration and reality in a new global order / Phiwokuhle Mnyandu.
Description: Lanham : Lexington Books, 2021. | Includes bibliographical references and index.
Identifiers: LCCN 2021036026 (print) | LCCN 2021036027 (ebook) |
    ISBN 9781793644503 (cloth) | ISBN 9781793644527 (paperback) |
    ISBN 9781793644510 (epub)
Subjects: LCSH: South Africa—Foreign economic relations—China. | China—Foreign economic relations—South Africa. | South Africa—Foreign relations—China. | China—Foreign relations—South Africa.
Classification: LCC HF1613.4.Z4 C6 2021 (print) | LCC HF1613.4.Z4 (ebook) |
    DDC 337.68051—dc23
LC record available at https://lccn.loc.gov/2021036026
LC ebook record available at https://lccn.loc.gov/2021036027

*For Nomathamsanqa Maureen Carol-Dawn Mnyandu (1944–2000).*
*No son had a better mother.*

*To Professor Olayiwola Abegunrin (1944–2020).*
*Thank you for your* ubuntu.

# Contents

# Acknowledgments

I am indebted to my wife and best friend, Desaray "Kiri" Wilson-Mnyandu, MS, for her support. During the course of this research, she not only helped me with her intellect but also gifted our family with a daughter, Thembani, and sons, Mazwe and Sakhile. The successful completion of this work is not my victory but hers, for she bore the brunt of the sacrifices research often imposes on family life.

I am grateful to my ancestors—my great-grandfather, James Mnyandu; my grandfather, Donald Mnyandu; my grandmother, Thembani Mnyandu—all of whom form a line of dignified Africans who dedicated their lives as educators who also had a sense of civic duty, a heritage that set me on a path to academia two generations later.

I am thankful to faculty colleagues at Howard University: to Professor Mbye Cham, for his fatherly and upright mentorship; to Professor Emeritus Robert Edgar, for offering constructive critique whenever I needed it; and to Professor Wilfred David, for his valuable contribution to my academic thinking. I am immensely grateful to Ms Sarah Oni Spratt, to Professor Krista Johnson; to Professor Alem Hailu; to Professor Almaz Zewde; to Professor Msia Clark, to Professor Mohamed Camara (Chair), to Dr Anita Plummer, to the late Professor Sulayman Nyang, to Professor Flordeliz Bugarin, and to Dr Esther Lisanza for their insights, friendship, and collegiality.

I am very grateful to my eldest brother, Ellis Muziwandile Mnyandu (Gedeza) for his support when I began my studies in the United States. I am grateful to the Ryochi Sasakawa Foundation for the Fellowship that helped me meet some of the cost of this research.

This research would have been impossible without assistance of certain individuals in South Africa and China. I am grateful to Professor Siphamandla Zondi (Gagashe) at the University of Johannesburg, Ms

Penelope Masenamela at the Institute for Global Dialogue, and Mr Greg Munyai at the Department of International Relations and Cooperation, for valuable academic and logistical assistance; to Professor Liu Hongwu, Chair, Ambassador Shu Zhan, Senior Fellow at the Institute for African Studies at Zhejiang Normal University, as well as Ms Shen Hong for her excellent interpretation and patience; to Professor Li Anshan and Professor Liu Haifang at the Center for African Studies at Peking University, for being generous with their time and academic resources.

I am also grateful to Dr. Yoon Jung Park, Associate Director, China-Africa Research Initiative at Johns Hopkins University, for her constructive evaluation of this research.

I am grateful to Nigerian scholar, Alaba Ogusanwo, whose pioneering work, *China's Policy in Africa 1958-1971*, published in 1974, the first by an African scholar, inspired me to pursue research on this subject.

Finally, I am grateful to the Institute for African Studies at Zhejiang Normal University, Jinhua; the Center for African Studies at Peking University in Beijing, China; the National Library of South Africa; the Government of the People's Republic of China; the Department of International Relations and Cooperation of South Africa (DIRCO); the library of the Thabo Mbeki Africa Leadership Institute; the Library of Congress' African and Middle East Division; and the US Archives II in College Park, Maryland. This research was enriched by the up-to-date data found in the following platforms: the United Nations Conference on Trade and Development (UNCTAD), the United Nations University World Institute for Development Economics Research (UNWIDER), the Department of Trade and Industry of South Africa (DTI), Forum on China-Africa Cooperation (FOCAC), and Statistics South Africa.

*Ukwanda kwaliwa umthakathi, ngiyabonga kakhulu* (Sincerely, thank you very much).

# List of Abbreviations

| | |
|---|---|
| ANC | African National Congress |
| BBSDP | Black Business Supplier Development Program |
| BRI | Brazil, Russia, and India |
| BRICS | Brazil, Russia, India, China, and South Africa |
| CIS | Co-operative Incentive Scheme |
| FDI | Foreign Direct Investment |
| FOCAC | Forum on China-Africa Cooperation |
| G20 | Group of 20 |
| NEPAD | New Partnership for Africa's Development |
| OAU | Organization for African Unity |
| PAC | Pan Africanist Congress |
| PRC | People's Republic of China |
| ROC | Republic of China |
| SACP | South African Communist Party |

# List of Figures and Tables

## FIGURES

## TABLES

# Introduction

On March 14, 2013, Xi Jinping became the president of China. Eight days later, he went on his first presidential visit abroad, to Russia, Tanzania, and finally South Africa. The historical symbolism was clear in the first two stops—Russia is a neighbor and long-standing ally; Tanzania, the first country in the greater southern Africa region to establish relations with Beijing (on December 9, 1961), is also an old friend. There was little historical rationale, however, for the South Africa visit. After all, South Africa had been one of the last countries in the world to recognize the People's Republic of China (on November 27, 1996), having held off together with a dozen others ranging from Kiribati to the Solomon Islands. Also, each of Xi's two immediate predecessors (Hu Jintao and Jiang Zemin) had visited South Africa only once as presidents.

But by 2020, Xi had made three visits to Pretoria and managed to hold bilateral meetings with his South African counterpart at least once a year. By contrast, it had been almost ten years since an American president had last visited South Africa. At the conclusion of Xi's 2013 visit, the two countries upgraded their relations to "comprehensive strategic partnership," the highest level of classification. This took place just four years after China surpassed the United States as South Africa's largest trading partner, and two years after South Africa, upon China's invitation, was accepted as the newest member of BRICS (Brazil, Russia, India, China, and South Africa). It soon became apparent that the Chinese leader's first trip abroad had culminated into something beyond historical gestures. It had turned into a strong symbolic embrace for Beijing's newest strategic ally.

The deepening of South Africa-China relations, since they were formally established in 1998, introduces a new player in the make-up of forces that have a real effect on South Africa's developmental trajectory. In 2019, the

1

volume of trade between the two countries stood at $25.9 billion, a dramatic increase from 1998 when it was just $1.01 billion.[1] In 1998 only 1.8 percent of South Africa's total trade was with China; trade with the United Kingdom alone (at 8.9 percent) was a percentage point shy of combined trade with BRI (Brazil, Russia, and India) and all African countries, which was 9.9 percent.[2] Two decades later, in 2019, trade with the United Kingdom had fallen to roughly a quarter (3.5 percent), the United States half (from 11.6 to 6.8 percent), and Japan a third (8.3 to 4.5 percent) of the 14.5 percent trade South Africa enjoyed with China. Trade with other economies hitherto considered "traditional" partners also saw a marked decrease.[3] South Africa's trade with the EU (excluding Germany) decreased from 27 to 17.9 percent, while trade with Germany shrank from 11 to 9.1 percent. Notably, South Africa's trade with the African continent grew from 7.8 to 19 percent in the same period.[4]

The relative speed with which cooperation has deepened between the two countries has, however, often overtaken a reflection on the developmental outcomes likely to emanate from it or how such close relations affect South Africa's endemic developmental problems. Since the dawn of multiparty democracy in 1994, South Africa has pursued its economic policy under pressure from a myriad of domestic and international forces as well as their often-constraining interests influencing which and how policy gets implemented. South Africa has an acute need to achieve certain developmental goals that remain largely unfulfilled, notwithstanding the immense potential.[5] Widespread economic dissatisfaction has continued to give rise to organized

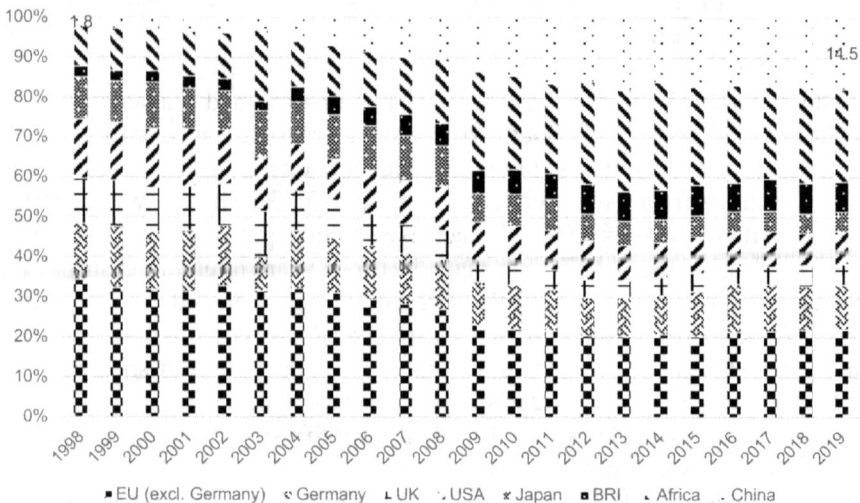

**Figure I.1   Top Countries' Share of Trade with South Africa, 1998–2019.** *Source*: Department of Trade of South Africa Department of Trade and Industry of South Africa, "Trade Reports," http://tradestats.thedti.gov.za/ReportFolders/reportFolders.aspx?sCS_referer=&sCS_ChosenLang=en (accessed February 4, 2015).

and spontaneous demonstrations regarding a coterie of issues, all of which concern development and lack of quick-enough service delivery by the state. It is possible that in the deepening of relations with China, South African policy makers, not unlike those in other parts of the developing world, have sensed an opportunity to overcome some of these constraints. A comprehensive strategic partnership with China, viewed through the prism of a South-South renegotiation of policy autonomy space sufficient enough to enable South Africa to achieve its developmental imperatives through a diversified portfolio of developmental partners, may be seen, therefore, as having made closer relations inevitable.

A further change in global dynamics affecting the pace and nature of South Africa-China relations has also been apparent on the multilateral front in bodies such as the Group of 20 (G20), BRICS, and the Forum for China-Africa Cooperation (FOCAC), where both China and South Africa have become important interlocutors. Since China's own recent economic success makes it an increasingly dominant player in this new global dynamic where consequential partners in trade and sources of foreign direct investment (FDI), the essential elements for developmental progress, are no longer confined to Western economies alone. This has increasingly placed China in a mentorship position with South African policy makers wont to solicit and receive lessons on developmental best practices from Beijing.

## OBJECTIVES OF THE STUDY

The first objective of this work is to look at the historical elements of the earliest Chinese-African contacts and how these have evolved to find expression in contemporary patterns of relations between South Africa and China at a bi- and multi-lateral level. Secondly, it examines the ways in which systemic problems, rooted in the asymmetrical power dynamics of the global political-economic system, have contributed to the de-acceleration and acceleration of the pace of South Africa-China cooperation between the Mbeki and Zuma administrations. Thirdly, the role played by Chinese export and import trade *patterns* and *hubs* is examined to ascertain the intended and unintended effects of China on South Africa's developmental trajectory. Lastly, the book undertakes an analysis of the prospects for a developmental state in South Africa, given the advanced nature of South Africa-China cooperation at bi- and multilateral levels. By studying the various interactions between China and South Africa over the years of their relatively short formal relations, this book also hopes to contribute toward improving mutual understanding between the Chinese and the South Africans, as well as contribute to the conversation on helping (South) Africa extract optimal returns from its engagement with a power such as China.

## THEORETICAL FRAMEWORK

The developmental state is used as the framework through which South Africa-China relations are examined in this work. South Africa remains "one of the few governments in the world that has expressly committed itself to the construction of a developmental state."[6] The ruling African National Congress has often touted its aspiration for a developmental state which it defines as a state-of-affairs where the state, "whilst acting effectively to promote growth, efficiency and productivity, it must be equally effective in addressing the social conditions of the masses of our people and realizing economic progress for the poor."[7] This book engages with this framework to the extent that developmentalism prioritizes policy autonomy and the role of policy-making elites in accessing it to re-structure capitalism and accrue incremental agency on an incremental basis for developmental outcomes.

Chalmers Johnson was the first to coin the term "capitalist developmental state" in his groundbreaking work on Japan, *MITI and the Japanese Miracle*, in 1982. According to Castells, a developmental state is one that

> establishes as its principle of legitimacy its ability to promote and sustain development, understanding by development the combination of steady high rates of growth and structural change in the productive system, both domestically and in its relationship to the international economy. . . .Thus, ultimately for the developmental state, economic development is not a goal but a means.[8]

Thus emerges a definition of the developmental state which takes into account the dynamic and fluid context of the international economy in which the development must take place, not in an unaffected vacuum. Another definition, by Peter B. Evans, highlights a need for the "21st century developmental state" to conform with certain realities and standards that obtain in the global system; its building must be a "continually reflexive, 'learning by doing' process"; it "puts robust, competent public institutions at the center of the developmental matrix"; it must pay attention to "local institutional starting points to succeed"; and, to fail, it must be applied "unreflective imports of ready-made models"[9]. Chang, while he does proffer the definition that a developmental state "derives its political legitimacy from its record in economic development" which it achieves through industrial policy, hastens to make a distinction between the "'classical' developmental state"—like Japan—and current aspiring ones, emphasizing that the latter can and should learn from the former but should not copy it wholesale.

What has continued to be an abiding concern for the policy-making elites in South Africa is how to transform a hitherto "esoteric" developmental state, whose immanent *apartheid* structure was designed to benefit a white minority at the expense of the black majority, and how to turn this state into an inclusive developmental one catering to a population of 58 million. This book engages with this framework to the extent that developmentalism prioritizes policy autonomy and the role of policy-making elites in accessing it to restructure capitalism and accrue agency on an incremental basis for developmental outcomes.

## SIGNIFICANCE OF THE STUDY

This study is significant for three reasons. First, the need for South Africa to find lasting solutions for its developmental problems and China's role therein, the latter having become a new strategic ally, makes it important to understand these relations in a comprehensive way. This work is the first monograph to do so vis-à-vis South Africa and China exclusively. Second, China is Africa's largest trading partner and South Africa's biggest export destination. While there is a dominant narrative of extractive industry-oriented trade patterns that have typically dominated China's relations with African countries, certain assumptions may be difficult to sustain regarding South Africa and are in need of nuance. Through data, this study will contribute to this ongoing and important conversation about China's trade make-up when it comes to African countries, using the case of a regional power, South Africa. Third, by identifying dominant, unique, and enduring features in the relationship, this study will introduce a new dimension to the African Studies literature by analyzing developmental challenges to African states when ascendant powers are concerned.

## METHODOLOGY

For analyzing a comprehensive gamut of South Africa-China relations, which spans historical, political, economic, and socio-cultural spheres, this study applied a mixed-method approach using the *concurrent triangulation* (CT) strategy to conduct semi-structured interviews and documentary surveys. First, qualitative and quantitative primary data was sourced from the United Nations Conference on Trade and Development (UNCTAD); the United Nations University World Institute for Development Economics Research (UNWIDER); the government of the People's Republic of China; South Africa's departments of Trade and Industry (DTI), International Relations and Cooperation (DIRCO) as well as Statistics SA; and finally, the FOCAC. Second, semi-structured interviews were conducted with South African scholars; Chinese scholars; current South African government officials and former Chinese government officials; lastly, African traders located in Yiwu, Zhejiang province. All shall remain anonymous.

For the interviewees, a series of questions were asked. Following is a sampling of the questions asked for a selected category of interviewees:

1. South African and Chinese academics. What is the major difference between the Jiang, Hu, and Xi presidencies, as well as Mbeki and Zuma administrations vis-à-vis relations between the two countries?
2. Former Chinese government officials. According to your experience, what are some of the unique challenges in dealing with your South African counterparts compared to those from other African countries?
3. South African and Chinese academics. What would you say are South Africa and China's paradigms for development, and are they compatible?
4. South African government officials. According to your experience, what are the operational challenges you have experienced which are unique to the China-South Africa dynamic?
5. South African and Chinese academics. What is the historical explanation, if any, for the current accelerated rate of South Africa-China engagement?
6. African traders in Yiwu, Zhejiang. What, if any, are some of the barriers to doing trade in Yiwu and which of these, if any, do you think you experience because you are African?

## REVIEW OF LITERATURE

The question of whether China is a "friend" or "villain" has often dominated the narrative of the country's relations not just with South Africa but the rest of the African continent. This binary, which is reminiscent of Cold War–era narratives, has given rise to what Dot Keet sees as "highly selective and self-serving analyses of China," one that has a little nuance of opportunities as well as challenges.[10] It is important for a researcher to make a distinction between "declarations of intent and 'principles,' on the one hand, and actual practice and changing forces on the ground in China, and Beijing's subtly changing policies on the other."[11] Studies of Chinese relations with South Africa must, therefore, as an integral feature of their analyses, seek to discern between stated developmental ends and their actual manifestation as affected by Chinese presence on the ground, where the outcomes of policy actually take place. Borrowing from Keet, this section assesses writings on Africa-China relations using three of the major topics that often dominate the contemporary conversation about China and (South) Africa: China as a neo-imperialist; China and (South) Africa's compatibility; and prospects for building and sustaining a South Africa-China alliance.

## A Chinese Neo-Imperialism?

This critique emanates from perspectives that locate China in a political-economic space not far removed from other world powers that have visited domination and exploitation upon Africa. This view sees a danger in the involvement in Africa of an external country whose pursuits of its interests are not linked to normative concerns, at least in an expressed manner; and when expressed, are still contradicted by action on the ground. On July 2019, China's ambassador to South Africa, Lin Songtian, opined during an interview that newly elected president, Cyril Ramaphosa, who had come to power after the ruling ANC recalled Jacob Zuma, was "the last hope for [the] country" and that the country's state-owned power utility company, ESKOM, was a "debt trap" lacking in "management capacity."[12] Observers would have been forgiven for being shocked at such views coming, uncharacteristically, from a Chinese ambassador. Further utterances recurred, including all-out spats on Twitter with US politicians. Less than a year, the ambassador was recalled and re-assigned, perhaps out of Beijing's sensitivity about what might be grounds for accusations of "neo-imperialist" tendencies. But to some, this instance illustrated a China that is increasingly emboldened to pronounce on issues the country has in the past taken care to avoid: the internal affairs of other countries. Questions may be asked if this was an isolated incident or the beginning of a more assertive Chinese foreign policy posture in Africa.

Either way, according Campbell, if there is any element of imperialism surrounding China in Africa it is, conversely, a positive one characterized by a "consolidation of African independence and the challenge to the hegemony of the dollar and US imperialism."[13] If anything, he continues, the recent African struggle against apartheid is enough a memory tool to effect "the kind of organization necessary to maintain self-determination," and Chinese corporations do not yet have the "kind of self-confidence and track record to act with imperial impunity."[14] But incidents such as in 2009, 2011, and 2014 when South Africa denied a visa to the Dalai Lama in fear of upsetting Beijing, many argued, may well be one of the incidents giving rise to a critique which sees a worrying trend in China's increasingly activist foreign policy.[15] However, the extent to which South African agency is curtailed, as a direct result, as opposed to a prudent South African decision to enhance strategic relations with Beijing, becomes important to establish, especially regarding the economy.

## China-(South)Africa Compatibility

While the particulars of the skeptical arguments of China's forays in Africa have been different with different Chinese political epochs, its main objectives seem to have remained constant throughout the twentieth century.

Long-time American scholar of China George T. Yu, back in the 1960s attributed China's "failure" in Africa to a "basic incompatibility between Chinese foreign policy objectives and the goals of the African states."[16] But this historical sentiment assumes easy compatibility of African ideals to other outside powers such as the United State or European nations and their foreign policy objectives, which can hardly be taken for granted.

But in many ways, South Africa and China indeed are markedly different countries, with equally different economic means. South Africa is the fifth-most populous country on the continent, but its population of 58 million is roughly equivalent to only one of China's 34 provinces and territories, Zhejiang. China has a population of 1.4 billion people.[17] Although South Africa is the ninth largest country in Africa, its total area of 1.2 million square kilometers is only the size of Tibet. China, with an area of 9.6 million square kilometers, is the third largest country in the world.[18] Politically, South Africa, while older as an oppressive apartheid republic (of 1948), even older as a British-protected Union (of 1910), is a young democracy approaching its third decade as a multiparty system of governance; China, although still widely—if not contestably—considered an "authoritarian" one-party state, is over 71 years old as a singular communist "People's Republic," older as a contested nationalist "Republic" (declared in 1912), and even older as a civilization.[19] Socially, South Africans are generally free to move about the country in pursuit of whatever economic opportunity their means may afford, and still access certain state benefits. China has, until late 2015, strictly enforced a *hukou* system of population registration that restricts the movement of people around the country by tying access to entitlements such as education and healthcare to the place of each citizen's original domicile, leaving large numbers of rural immigrants to cities without social benefits.[20] South Africa's birth rate stood at 2.4 per woman in 2017 and its citizens are free to have as many children as they wish; China had, until 2013, a strict one-child policy.[21]

On the November 5, 2006, the FOCAC took place in Beijing where an unprecedented 48 heads of states from Africa assembled at the Great Hall of the People for a two-day summit. According to Nigeria-American scholar, Olayiwola Abegunrin, this summit served as a "pointer of several Sino-African dynamics": aid to Africa was doubled; a "strategic partnership" for international cooperation was established; the China-Africa Development Fund was established with $5 billion in starting cash; opening up African exports to China by increasing from 190 to 400 the number of good receiving preferential treatment; and "pledges for 30 hospitals, 30 malaria treatment centers, and 100 rural schools in African countries," among other things.[22] In December 2015, in Johannesburg, the FOCAC II Summit took place where a $65 billion package of aid, investments, and loans was announced by President Xi Jinping. FOCAC III took place in September 2018, in Beijing

and resulted in a $60 billion pledge by China. Where questions of develop-
ment are concerned, therefore, and the latter is used as a benchmark for
gauging compatibility, doubts have tended to be dismissed by South African
policy makers and some scholars based on these practical outcomes that have
proven to be difficult to replicate by other world powers.

## Whither an Alliances?

Much has been made about how China's foray into Africa is part of a grand
strategy of maximizing its strategic advantage in which it invested for
decades.[23] Taylor locates China's focus on Africa around a need to "rational-
ize" what he identifies a "general inability to project into the international
scene. . . . [A] major feature of China's informal national ideology . . . is that
somehow China has been 'cheated' of its place in the sun by the imperial-
ists of the nineteenth century, and that this prevention of China assuming
its 'rightful place' . . . has continued, even to contemporary times."[24] Like
its foray into other developing regions of the world, its engagement with
Africa—and as a corollary, South Africa—is consistent with China's "vocal
opposition" to a "hegemonism" (*ba quan zhu yi*) China sees as emanating from other powers' expansionistic growth throughout its ancient and
contemporary history.[25] A "fairly consistent foreign policy" to prevent this
"hegemony" and at the same time open up economic space has therefore
been China's long response to this.[26] From this then emerges the strand of a
critique, which concerns South Africa being used as China's tributary in its
game of grand African strategy. Chinese scholar and former diplomat avers
that what may appear as tributary-building is in effect a Global South-centric
infrastructure upon which solid alliances may be built that have "important
implications for international negotiations and multilateral agenda setting . . .
over a wider spectrum."[27] It is important, therefore, to view South Africa as
"maturing" into this global dynamic rather than a hapless regional power.

The placing of South Africa-China alliance prospects on Pretoria's ability
to play a conduit role for a greater China-Africa alliance may also be seen
as undermining South Africa's agency to be able to act in their own interest,
including forming alliances. Indeed, South African scholar, Garth Shelton,
argues that there is a wide enough "range of common interests" between
the two countries, including restructuring the Bretton Woods system for a
"more equitable, fair, balanced, and stable global financial system."[28] These
are enough motivations to build and sustain a comprehensive, developmental
alliance. On the questions of being a conduit, since many African countries
have enjoyed relations with China for a far longer time than South Africa,
they may well possess sufficient capacity from their experience in dealing
with China without needing assistance from Pretoria.

But criticism also emanates from what some see as China's "tangible, if yet unquantifiable 'Middle Kingdom' (*Zhongguo*) mentality, which sees China as central to the world," and whether or not this may manifestation in relations with South Africa.[29] Here then is a paradox found in China's identity: on the one hand, a nation that holds profound feelings of victimhood under dominance and invasions from outsiders throughout its history—and the accompanying sensitivity this carries; on the other hand, a nation which has perpetually held a sure sense of its centrality to the world—and the attendant superiority complex. It is in this context, in what Steven Levine has called an "international affirmative action," that China continues to call itself a "developing country" and thus create common aspirational ground with African countries while at the same time seeking restitution of its position central to the global system and power.[30] And it is in this explanation that the debate in the literature concerning China's benefit to South Africa is located.

On April 14, 2011, with the support of China, South Africa became a fourth member of BRICS (Brazil, Russia, India, and China, and South Africa), signifying a further consolidation by major developing countries toward a strategic partnership and influence. Western views, however, saw South Africa as a small economy that was "sneaked" into a body of large emerging economies undeservedly.[31] But a global context must be identified where mutual bilateral interests seek to effect structural change at a multilateral level through cooperation. Before such developing-country alliances and their global impact can be analyzed, however, Vom Hau et al. argue that it is "crucial to unpack how these global changes interacted with specific economic and political contexts at the national level."[32] Before the influence of BRICS itself can be analyzed, a gap has to be filled in a comprehensive way between key county-to-country relations and their developmental impact on the contexts mentioned above. To date, no study has done this beyond book chapters and journal articles.[33] This is the aim of this research, to put in a developmental context China-South Africa relations as they have played out in multiple levels of state-to-state interactions.

Ultimately, regarding the friend-villain binary, instead of asking if China is a friend or villain for South Africa, the following question is more helpful to our understanding: how well is South Africa prepared for its high-level, multifaceted and comprehensive engagement with China?

## THE QUEST FOR AGENCY IN CHINA-SOUTH AFRICA RELATIONS

In the ongoing conversation around issues of decolonization, it is often noted that in much of the published mainstream history of foreign relations between Africa and the world, contact with Europeans is often the first frame of reference. Where it has been verifiably documented, however, contact with the Chinese has tended to contradict this dominant narrative insomuch as it exposes an African agency in foreign affairs before European colonialism, one which is gradually gaining attention as China-Africa relations have come under the world's spotlight. Chapter 1 looks at these earliest contacts between Chinese and black (African) people. Names such as *heirein* and *kulun*, associated with people generally considered black since before the Ming era are discussed, as well as these terms' evolving connotation from positive to negative in correlation with the spread of slavery. The Kingdom of Mapungubwe in present-day South Africa is also examined as holding promise for further studies on the early Chinese forays into southern Africa. The historical mystery surrounding the site is also illustrative of the academic toll *apartheid* rule exacted on knowledge production about the early foreign relations of the Africans of South Africa, which effectively censored what we would eventually come to know (or not know) about the totality of Chinese-(southern) African contact. Prominent figures of these early contacts are also examined. One is Chinese admiral Zheng He, who managed to reach the east coast of Africa on his fourth (1412–1415), fifth (1417–1419), and sixth (1421–1422) of seven voyages. From these early encounters, salient features of Chinese-African diplomacy emerge, such as the use of tribute. Another figure is Dutch colonialist, Jan van Riebeeck, and his plans, documented early and frequently in his diaries, to indenture Chinese laborers into the Cape colony. Early contacts were therefore allusive, reduced to fanciful stories in Chinese literature and imperial records, replete with the exaggerations and racial stereotypes of the times. Later, these contacts were attenuated by colonialism and outside domination such that there was little either the Africans or the Chinese could do of their own volition to effect much of the outcomes of their encounters. The indentured Chinese laborers in the mines, for instance, in late 1800s, came from foreign-dominated parts of China, through foreign interlocutors, to foreign-dominated South Africa, whereupon they and their black African counterparts were consigned to labor in the mines under debilitating conditions imposed by colonial commercial interests.

Chapter 2 looks at the second historical period (after 1949) and the mutuality of struggles that had a major impact on contacts—the People's Republic of China's struggle for international recognition as the sole representative of the Chinese people at the UN; black South Africans' struggle for liberation from oppressive apartheid rule. The chapter also deals with the little-known interaction between communist China and (apartheid) South Africa between 1951 and 1953, during the Korean War. It looks at the Sino-Soviet split and China's role in another split between South Africa's two main liberations organizations, the African National Congress (ANC) and the Pan Africanist

Congress (PAC), in 1959. Lastly, the issue of post-apartheid South Africa's relations with Taiwan is examined. Although Mandela's government inherited these relations from the previous apartheid government, the Taiwan issue proved to be a foreign policy fiasco with which the inexperienced ANC government struggled.

There is a single thread running through all these historical events which have influenced when and how Chinese encounters with South Africans have occurred: almost none of them are of the making of the vast majority of Africans in South Africa. If Chinese contact with South Africans was attenuated by colonial domination, it was later attenuated by apartheid, and in the contemporary period, remnants of the two. These elements have bequeathed a unique set of challenges to the foreign and economic policy responses of the South African government even as relations with China have blossomed.

## Changing Dynamics

One of the challenges that continued to confront post-apartheid policymakers as South Africa established relations with Beijing in the late 1990s was that this was an era of unparalleled dominance of the Washington Consensus, replete with structural adjustment programs and other austerity measures. Chapter 3 examines the effects this political-economic environment had on the Mbeki administration's initial relations with China, and how Mbeki's own plans to lead an African *renaissance*, through an African economic growth program overseen by peer review mechanisms, served to constrain certain overtures by South Africa to Beijing. The persistent Western reticence to invest in Africa, and the extent to which it constituted a major "push" factor for what would later be closer SA-China relations, are also examined. Data is evaluated for indicators of this "de-naissance" whereby the African fidelity to the neoliberal order and multilateral institutions was largely unrequited by sustained Western investment capital.

In chapter 4, data of South Africa's participation in the Group of 8 (G8) is analyzed in contrast to participation in the Group of 20 (G20), the FOCAC and the BRIC (Brazil, Russia, India, China) bloc. South Africa stopped attending the G8 as an "invited non-member" in 2011 (37th G8, Deauville, France), the same year it began its formal participation as a member of what became BRICS (3rd BRICS, Sanya, China). Tellingly, Brazil, China, and India had stopped attending the G8 as "invited nonmembers" as well, in 2009, when 1st BRICS took place in Yekaterinburg, Russia. The chapter further traces the evolution of Pretoria's approach from being a reticent participant in Beijing-centric FOCAC, under Mbeki, to being a facilitator of Chinese multilateral engagements with the rest of the region in BRICS, under Zuma. Instead of being isolated events, these are identified as forming an incremental strategic calculation by South Africa. It constitutes a response to a change in the global dynamics where the developmental wherewithal (capital) was no longer confined to the Global North, a fact made stark by a diminution of Western demand for South Africa's exports following the crisis of capitalism that began in 2007.

## INTERSECTING IMPERATIVES

If this section looks at the extent to which closer strategic relations between South Africa and China were seemingly made inexorable by global dynamics, chapter 5 looks at South Africa's unique developmental state-of-affairs and the effect closer relations have had on it. South Africa's total population growth, urban population, and inequality have continued to contribute to factors that make the developmental indices of the country worse year after year. The country's inequality and unemployment have barely improved since 1994. Moreover, the manner by which unemployment has manifested itself in South Africa—through gender (it is worse among women); race (it is worse among Africans); and youth (it affects African youth the worst)—continues to haunt relations between South Africa and China. The chapter analyzes the intersection of the Chinese imperative of economic growth through, among other things, merchandize trade, with the South African imperative of fighting unemployment. It focuses on the manner by which these imperatives find expression through on-the-ground Chinese-(South) African interactions in the arena of trade. It takes a comparative look at the role contemporary migration from China and other major "contributor" countries has (or has not) played.

Besides migration's impact (if any) on employment rates, China-South Africa relations have had to contend with a series of concerns bordering on the make-up of trade itself. First is the question of whether or not trade between the two countries is balanced or not; second, whether it is too concentrated, especially on raw materials export; and third, whether or not South Africa simply exports raw materials to China and imports finished goods. Chapter 6 evaluates South Africa's trade balance with China in comparison to the latter's trade with Germany, EU, and the African continent; analyzes the Concentration Index for South Africa's imports from China; and looks at the Trade matrix of top eight products exports and imports. From quantitative data as well as field research was done at the Yiwu International Trade City, a picture emerges for South Africa's trade with China, which contradicts dominant narratives about the make-up of Chinese trade with African countries in general, even as it confirms some in counterintuitive ways, regarding South Africa. Furthermore, certain export industries are identified as holding more promise for South Africa to focus on if the country is to begin making a dent on its unemployment. It is with unemployment in mind that the book concludes with an evaluation of the developmental state prospects in chapter 7. A qualitative documentary survey of data is examined for the extent to which a "policy dissonance" between stated and manifest developmental policy has taken root in South Africa and China's role, if any, in this dynamic.

Hopefully, in the totality of this work will emerge a better understanding of the manner by which a quest for agency, changing global dynamics, intersecting strategic imperatives, and a convergence of paradigms regarding development, together form the backdrop of a rapidly evolving partnership between China and South Africa, as well as how this increasingly constitutes a significant facet of an emerging global order.

## NOTES

1. "Trade Reports," *Department of Trade and Industry of the Republic of South Africa*, accessed February 15, 2020, http://tradestats.thedti.gov.za/ReportFolders/repo rtFolders.aspx?sCS_referer=&sCS_ChosenLang=en

2. Ibid.

3. Ibid.

4. Ibid.

5. "Carroll: Mine Violence Caused by Legacy of Apartheid," *Mail and Guardian*, December 05, 2012.

6. Omano Edigheji, "Constructing a Democratic Developmental State in South Africa: Potentials and Challenges," in *Constructing A Democratic Developmental State in South Africa: Potentials and Challenges*, ed. Omano Edigheki (Cape Town: Human Sciences Research Council Press, 2010), 11.

7. Ibid., 1.

8. Manuel Castells, "Four Asian Tigers with A Dragon Head: A Comparative Analysis of State, Economy, and Society in the Asian Pacific Rim," in *States and Development in the Asian Pacific Rim*, ed. Jeffrey Henderson and Richard P. Appelbaum (London: Sage Publications, 1992), 56–7.

9. Peter B. Evans, "Constructing the 21st Century Developmental state: Potentialities and Pitfalls," in *Constructing A Democratic Developmental State in South Africa: Potentials and Challenges*, ed. Omano Edigheji (Cape Town: Human Sciences Research Council Press, 2010), 37.

10. Dot Keet, "South-South Strategic Bases for Africa to Engage China," in *The Rise of China and India in Africa: Challenges, Opportunities and Critical Interventions*, ed. Fantu Cheru and Cyril Obi (London; New York; Uppsala, Sweden: Zed Books; Nordic Africa Institute, 2010), 22.

11. Ibid.

12. Alexander Winning and Joe Bavier, "Ramaphosa is 'Last Hope' for South Africa, Chinese diplomat says," *Reuters*, July 29, 2019.

13. Horace Campbell, "China in Africa: Challenging US Global Hegemony," *Third World Quarterly* 29, no. 1 (2008): 92.

14. Ibid.

15. Richard Lapper, "Furore as South Africa Bans Dalai Lama from Peace Conference," *Financial Times*, March, 24, 2009.

16. George T. Yu, "China's Failure in Africa," *Asian Survey* (1966): 468.

17. "The CIA World Factbook 2012," accessed February 4, 2015, https://www.cia .gov/library/publications/the-world-factbook/.

18. Ibid.

19. Gavin Lewis, "China's Success is Limited," *Financial Mail*, December, 10, 2010.

20. Tiejun Cheng and Mark Selden, "The Origins and Social Consequences of China's Hukou System," *The China Quarterly* 139, no. 1994 (1994): 644–668.

21. In 2013 the policy was amended from a one- to two-child restriction on condition that both parents must have had no siblings.

22. Olayiwola Abegunrin, *Africa in Global Politics in the Twenty-First Century: A Pan-African Perspective* (New York: Palgrave Macmillan, 2009), 120.

23. Baogang Guo, *China's Quest for Political Legitimacy: The New Equity-Enhancing Politics* (Lanham, MD: Lexington Books, 2010); David M. Lampton, *The Three Faces of Chinese Power: Might, Money, and Minds* (Berkeley: University of California Press, 2008); Sarah Raine, *China's African Challenges* (New York, NY: Routledge, 2009).

24. Ian Taylor, *China and Africa: Engagement and Compromise* (New York: Taylor & Francis, 2006), 1.

25. Ibid.

26. Ibid.

27. Zhan Shu, "China and Africa: The Chinese and the African Dream," in *Perspective on South Africa-China Relations*, ed. Funeka Yazini April and Garth Shelton (Pretoria: Africa Institute of South Africa, 2014), 109.

28. Garth Shelton, "China and South Africa—Common Interests and Global Objectives," in *Perspective on South Africa-China Relations*, ed. Funeka Yazini April and Garth Shelton (Pretoria: Africa Institute of South Africa, 2014), 11.

29. Taylor, *China and Africa*, 2.

30. Steven Levine, "Perception and Ideology in Chinese Foreign Policy," in *Chinese Foreign Policy—Theory and Practice*, ed. Thomas Robinson and David Shambaugh (Oxford: Clarendon Press, 1995), 44.

31. Ibid.

32. Matthias Vom Hau, James Scott and David Hulme, "Beyond the BRICs: Alternative Strategies of Influence in the Global Politics of Development," *European Journal of Development Research* 24, no. 2 (2012): 194.

33. David Shinn and John Eisenman, *China and Africa: A Century of Engagement* (Philadelphia: University of Pennsylvania Press, 2012); Taylor, *China and Africa*.

# Chapter 1

# Dynastic Era–1949

## *From Allusive to Attenuated Contact*

To understand China today, American sinologist Jonathan Spence wrote, "you have to understand its past."[1] This chapter traces the history of Africa-China contact and these two territories' policy responses to one another with the purpose of contextualizing contact as far as South Africa is concerned.

### PRE-MING DYNASTY PERIOD (UP TO 1368)

Since the imperial era, contact between Chinese and African people can be divided into two types. The first is a marginal contact which took place as a result of explanatory allusions in Chinese literature and language when descriptions of skin tones considered comparatively darker were employed. These concern the basic-yet-salient idea that goes beyond the spatial confines of continental Africa—the idea of blackness itself or black people. These *allusive* contacts, at first positive and fantastic, later descending to derision and giving rise to negative and long-lasting stereotypes still found in China today, constitute a meta-narrative of what has proven to be an evolving idea of what it means to be black or African in the collective Chinese psyche.

In Chinese literature, one of the very first instances where reference is made to a black person is in work *Mozi*, a philosophical text by Mo Di (ca. 280–390 BCE) in which the sage discusses the appropriateness of "taking what is black and what is not black about a man to be the extent of [being a] 'black man (*heiren*),' and taking the [acts of] cherishing some men and not cherishing others to be the extent of 'cherishing men.'"[2] The second mention of *heiren* is around the first century in *Classic of Mountains and Sea* where the anonymous author writes that "there are also black people. They have the heads of tigers and the feets of birds. Clutching a snake in their two hands,

17

they are constantly chewing on them."[3] Here we are introduced not just to the black complexion but also its association with a people considered alien and debased in their existence.

Another word found its way into the vocabulary. In a seminal work, *The Blacks of Premodern China*, American scholar Don Wyatt traces the existence of the idea of "black people" in the Chinese lexicon through a historical survey of imperial texts from various dynasties and offers an explanation of the one word that came to denote a black person in China: *kunlun*. The term has been traced to the *Jinshu*, an imperial chronicle of the history of the Jin Dynasty (265–420 CE) in which the biography of Empress Li is found. It states that "given that she was tall in stature and her complexion was dark, the [other] concubines called her Kunlun [or *kunlun*]. Alarmed by this, the ministers referred to her [instead] as 'precious,' . . . and she subsequently gave birth to Emperor Xiao Wu [r. 373-96]."[4] Initially, the term was not at all a reference to people's skin color, but when it first appeared between 976 and 922 BCE, but it came to refer to the Kunlun mountains in the south of China.[5] By the fourth century, however, the term's use had changed and the Chinese began to use *kunlun* to when specifically referring "all peoples they distinguished from themselves primarily on the basis of their culturally undesirable and stigmatizing complexions."[6]

Whereas before, allusive contact was in works of fiction, or written accounts of rehashed, second-hand tales of fantastic detail, over time, with more enslaved people coming to China, the term became a reality. With this transformation of the term, its connotation of *kunlun* servants or slaves also turned negative. What had been tolerance and wonder for almost supernatural *kunlun* strength had evolved into derisive contempt for his child-like helplessness. The reasons for this change in Chinese tone from that of "awe to bleak realism" regarding *kunluns*, who were "no longer either heroic or magical" but "displaced nomads, tragically ill-adapted to their Chinese surroundings," may be found in Europe's own experience with Africa in the pre- and post-slavery eras, and how Europeans generally viewed Africans in each epoch.[7]

According to Phillip Snow, in his comprehensive treatment of early China-Africa relations,

these slaves in Canton [Guangzhou were] no longer being glimpsed through the blurred fancy of a short-story writer but scrutinized, for the first time, by the ordinary citizen. To understand his reaction we need only recall the impact of large-scale slavery in Europe. Europeans in medieval and early modern times looked on Africans respectfully as inhabitants of hazy but imposing lands. When the African slave trade reached its peak in the seventeenth and eighteenth centuries they ceased to feel that respect. They saw at close quarters African victims of slavery, helpless and therefore contemptible; and they extended their contempt in due course to Africans in general.[8]

This evolution from grand tales of powerful and magical *kunluns*, who were still considered alien and gross, suggests an early comfort with, lack of sympathy for, and general acceptance of, the domination of persons deemed extremely different and therefore, perhaps, not so undeserving of their fate at the hands of other more nobler men. It may be said that this first type of contact has often provided the language by which the main narrative of China-Africa encounters was sustained henceforth.

*Attenuated* contact is the second type of contact between Africans and Chinese and was initially as a result of the presence of darker-skinned slaves in China, including those from Africa. Whereas the first type of contact constitutes a meta-narrative, and this type is the main narrative of Chinese-African encounters, both still have one characteristic in common: their evolution over time. Like allusive contact, it has imbued present contacts with certain stereotypes, both negative and positive. One of the first instances, said to have taken place in 1071 and also between 1081 and 1083, was that of a leader from Zengjan (present-day Zanzibar), who made his way to the Song court where he was treated much differently than the *kunlun* slaves of Canton. He was lavished with 2,000 ounces of gold and given the title Lord Guardian of Prosperity.[9]

It may be puzzling why the visitor from Africa was not referred to as *kunlun*. According to Wyatt, whereas the term *kunlun* enjoyed "widely accepted if poorly defined usage" long before the first documented encounters of Chinese and Africans took place, it came to extend to Africans "only after the fact."[10] Up until the Ta'ang dynasty there was no term for "identifiable people of African heritage" in the Chinese lexicon.[11] If what is found here is proof that in seventh century Guangzhou existed black and invariably foreign enslaved people who came to be known as, "*kunlun* slaves," it is still, however, not a link to Africa itself.

The link of the *kunlun* slaves to Africa is made by the term's appearance in the literature of the T'ang Dynasty. In his obscure work, "The Importance of Negro Slaves to China under T'ang Dynasty (A.D. 618–907)," translated by Wyatt, Chinese scholar, Zhang Xinglang concluded that *kunlun* slaves were from nowhere else but Africa. Although most were "often enslaved and delivered into Chinese hands by Arabs—doubtless via the conduit of the Melakan (Malaccan) Strait and its surrounding islands—*kunlun* slaves were not (as was often supposed) of any part of Arabia."[12]

They were from Zinj, the island of Zanzibar, in present-day Tanzania. But because Arabs used the name Zanzibar ("region of the blacks"), the geographical area this name denotes most likely extended far beyond the island, to include areas "from South of the Juba River [modern-day South Sudan] to Cape Delgado," modern-day Mozambique.[13] Adekunle seems to verify the probability of this by citing the Indonesians who had arrived in Madagascar in the first century AD, who between the third and sixth century were "found along the coast of East Africa" and were involved in trading various goods to Iraq—including slaves.[14] Thus did Zinj slaves make their way into China, though from these records there is no evidence of the Chinese themselves being involved in the intercontinental trading of African slaves. What is clear is the extent to which contact between the people of China and Africa was from these early stages beginning to be calibrated significantly by people, entities, and other phenomena other than the Chinese of Africans themselves.

We get the first indication of contact during the T'ang Dynasty (618–944) from the text *Youyang zazu* (Youtang Mountain Miscellanies), written by scholar Duan Chengshi (d. 863), in what Dyvendak sees as the "first definitive information" on east Africa.[15]

> The country of Bobali lies in the southwestern seas. Its inhabitants eat nothing of the five grains but consume only meat. They often pierce the veins of cattle with needles, and draw forth blood, which they drink raw, intermixed with milk. They wear no clothes—except for covering themselves below the loins with sheepskins. The women are without disease and chaste. The land produces ivory and ambergris. . . . Since ancient times they have not been subjugated by any foreign country. . . . Yet, even though they possess 200,000 foot-soldiers, the Arabs still make frequent raids upon them.[16]

This is in today's Somalia. While it is likely second hand, Duan Chengshi's account still is in effect the "first piece of writing in Chinese literature to describe conditions as they contemporaneously existed" anywhere in Africa.[17]

Later on, in the Xin Tangshu (New Tang History) by scholar Ouyang Xiu (1007–1072), published posthumously in 1077, we find a Chinese description of another east African city-state, "Molin" or Malindi, in present-day Kenya.

> The southwest of Fulin (Baghdad [present-day Iraq]), once one has traversed the desert for two thousand *li*,[18] one arrives at the country called Molin. . . . Its people are black, and their nature is fierce. The land is pestilential—without herbs, without trees, without grains. Horses subsist on dried fish; people sustain themselves on Persian dates. They are unashamed in debauching the wives of their fathers and chiefs. Thus, they are barbarians at their worst, calling their actions "seeking out the proper master and subject." In the seventh lunar month [Ramadan], they rest completely. During this time, they neither send out nor receive any items but sit drinking throughout the night.[19]

Later, in 1348, during the Yuan dynasty era, another work introduces us to another city-state, "Zinj" or Zanzibar. Written by Wang Dayuan, the *Daoyi zhilue* (Annals of Island Barbarians) speaks of

> the country southwest of the Arab countries. Its coasts are treeless; most of the soil is brackish. The arable land is poor, such that there is little grain of any kind, and yams are grown in its place. Any ship travelling there to trade makes immense profits. The climate is irregular [but] in their habits the people preserve the rectitude of olden times. The hair of the people is tied up in knots (*wanji*); they wear short seamless shirts. Their livelihood consists of netting birds and beasts for food.[20]

This work by a Chinese scholar is thought to be as close to a first-hand account pre-Ming descriptions could get, since its author was a known traveler. However, some scholars still do not rule out his simply receiving his knowledge while travelling elsewhere other than Africa itself.

Early mastery of seafaring was an important factor in enabling Chinese contact with faraway peoples often regarded as "outer barbarians." Italian scholar, Teoboldo Filesi, notes that China's first ventures far from its shores were "peaceful" and were a "product of [Chinese] national propensities, of commercial interests, of technical ability and of nautical knowledge."[21] But even as some scholars admit that China's feat of the time "evokes profound admiration," they dispute whether the China of the earlier Han and T'ang eras constituted a "maritime nation," because it did not have enough of a "naval force able to maintain control and supremacy in the oceans, . . . notwithstanding its use of naval fleets for coastal warfare and for invasion of Korea and Indo-China."[22]

But such an argument reduces the accuracy of bestowing a "maritime nation" status to its ability to dominate and subjugate, and do it the farthest from its shores. Though China did dominate the seas at some point in this era, according to this argument, it was too close to home; where it did sail far from home, it did not dominate and subjugate, which means China could not have been a "maritime nation" on both seemingly contradictory counts. Interestingly, the same scholars consider China a "maritime nation" in the later Sung (960–1279), Yuan (1280–1368), and Ming (1368–1644) dynasties although the country still did not subjugate or dominate any more than the accounts of earlier sojourns claim.

There seems to be some consensus, however, that during the Sung dynasty (960–1279) trade between China and Africa was taking place. Shwarz points to various sources for proof:

> There is the Catalan Atlas of 1375, but earlier editions existed; this shows Chinese ships sailing about the Indian Ocean, with meticulous regard to details

of construction and rigging. . . . The trade with East Africa began certainly during the Sung dynasty, 960–1280, if not before; there is mention in the "Book of Marvels of India" of a fleet that sailed in 945 . . . Al Biruni was on the Arabian coast and saw the fleets of junks, which he describes in his "Geography," 1040. Idris, 1154, is equally explicit; he states that the Chinese transferred their trade to the island of Zinj (Zanzibar), which is of the coast of Zinj, and by their equity, mild ways and accommodating spirit, soon came into very intimate relations with inhabitants. Those "intimate relations" produced a fine crop of half-caste children up and down the coast. . . . They can still today be recognized by their yellow skins and other Mongoloid characteristics. Mas'udy, in his "Golden Meadow," says that to the south of the country of the blacks (Zinj) there were the Ma-Kwakwa, Gog and Magog . . . Magog is the Bantu plural for Gog.[23]

Although there appears to be a general consensus regarding Chinese presence in Africa during the Ming Dynasty (1368–1644), as is discussed in the next section, contact in earlier T'ang (618–905) and Sung (993–1278) dynasties remains a subject of dispute in twentieth and twenty-first-century studies.

According to Joshua Potter, the problem is that studies, almost all by Western scholars, have "neither categorically asserted nor dismissed" direct early contact between China and Africa.[24] He attributes this to the tendency of Western scholars to "cling to the most easily available information," leading them to conclude that Chinese trade in these early periods "existed only with the Arabs."[25] It does not help that Chinese court records, known for their thoroughness, have often been found to be ambiguous, leaving scholars to rely on nuggets of information. The bigger problem is that from these records, the "few" Western scholars who have written on early Chinese contact have, Potter argues, often not only "concentrated only on one source" but have also "added a great deal of interpretation." Therefore, a better proposition may be that "there *could have been* direct" albeit "limited" contact.[26]

## The Kingdom of Mapungubwe and Possible Chinese Contact

The Kingdom of Mapungubwe is one example where the possibility of any evidence of a southern African contact with the outside world, including Chinese people, fell victim to the politics of the time. Located in the Limpopo province to the north of South Africa, the Mapungubwe Cultural Landscape was declared a World Heritage Site by UNESCO in January 2002. However, for decades, the existence of an ancient, sophisticated African kingdom, and the anthropological proof of the vitality of life there and this city-state's relations with the outside world, remained shrouded in mystery and state-sanctioned secrecy.[27] The city-state of Mapungubwe is said to have existed within a 30,000-hectare area with a further 100,000 hectares buffer area.[28] Most importantly, according to UNESCO,

> Mapungubwe's position at the crossing of the north/south and east/west routes in southern Africa also enabled it to control trade, through the East African ports to India and China, and throughout southern Africa. From its hinterland it harvested gold and ivory—commodities in scarce supply elsewhere—and this brought it great wealth as displayed through imports such as Chinese porcelain and Persian glass beads.[29]

This Bantu civilization first came to the attention of scholars on December 1, 1932, when a "prospector" convinced a local African to lead him to it. Although the locals, who called it "Mapungubwe," knew of the area's existence, they had always considered it a "place of dread" to which "they would not so much as point."[30] After a two-year excavation, from February 1933 through June 1935, a civilization emerged, together with artifacts strongly suggesting contact with foreigners, including Chinese.

News of the Mapungubwe location, and its implications for an advanced and dynamic African civilization, did not however find wide dissemination. Soon after its discovery, the South African government acquired the site (in 1933) and barred access, delaying further studies by decades. To some scholars, this is understandable in the context of apartheid rule that followed not too long after the site's discovery. Proof of an African civilization that had foreign relations with people from faraway lands, and the agency this would imply, contradicted in a fundamental way the racist narrative of the apartheid regime concerning the capabilities of Africans. The government "certainly did not want to glorify any native delusions of grandeur" about a prehistory involving functional statesmanship and a thriving livelihood.[31] The South African government wanted to perpetuate the perception that nothing much "happened in southern Africa until the Europeans arrived in the 1500s."[32]

Whatever the motivation of the government of the time, the reports that surfaced still did not dispute the findings of foreign objects that signified Sino-African contact:

> Two small fragments of porcelain were found in the occupation layers on the hilltop. . . . They were at once forwarded to the British Museum where they were examined by Mr Hobson, who identified them as Chinese Caledon, and dated them definitely as late Sung Period [960–1279 AD]. . . . They are the earliest datable objects found. . . . It is very likely that it was kept with great care for a long period, as is the case to-day in the Malay Archipelago, where the Natives possess very old Chinese porcelain, which they carefully preserve.[33]

Debate is still ongoing on whether the Chinese porcelain was indeed from the Song or the later Yuan and Ming dynasties. Some scholars have suggested that it is more likely to be from a later period.[34] There are various reasons why the task of providing certainty remains difficult for scholars. First, the people, unfortunately, did not keep written records. We are left to rely on what is either yet-to-be discovered anthropological evidence, or an equally undiscovered record of Western sources or perhaps the apartheid government's archives. It is not implausible that the latter may well have had an overwhelming incentive in making sure records with definitive proof are either destroyed or expunged. Additionally, it is not beyond the realm of imagination to consider that what was found in the excavations of the 1930s may well have been remains of other more complete artifacts that had long been looted.

What also emerges and is difficult to quantify is the sheer intellectual cost that the apartheid system exacted on the production of knowledge regarding African people in South Africa. As a result, the story of Mapungubwe and the possible Chinese-African contact therein, is one of another possible contact that was attenuated by apartheid and its indifference to collecting or preserving affirming knowledge about Africans.

## MING (1368–1644)–QING DYNASTY (1644–1911)

The Ming Dynasty was a restorative emperor for China. Following the foreign domination of preceding Mongol rule, China gained "renewed independence and pride, political and social stability, and previous unparalleled preeminence."[35] As an integral part of the restorative mandate of Ming rule, outward exploration was inevitable if not desirable for the projection of power abroad as well as a domestic consolidation of it through the acquisition of prestige granted by tributes to the Ming court as far afield as possible.

In the spring of 1404, Ming emperor Yongle (1360–1424) commissioned a series of explorations of lands of the Western seas. Zheng He (1371–1435), a Muslim Admiral and a Ming "Grand Eunuch," would lead a total of seven such expeditions to the "lands of the Western seas." On the fourth expedition (1413–1415), he met Africans for the first time. At Zheng He's persuasion, after an encounter in Hormuz and Kozhikode, the African merchants, likely from the city-states of Barawa, Mogadishu, and Malindi, accompanied him back to the Ming courts to meet and pay tribute to Emperor Yongle. According to Wyatt, this singular event of Africans journeying to "distant China and their entrance into the empire as the free representatives of what the Chinese regarded as sovereign, if subordinate, countries stands as a historical watershed."[36] It also demonstrates a "psychic distance travelled" from thinking of and encountering Africans as slaves to meeting them again as free people.[37]

In addition to his fourth expedition, Zheng He also visited Arabian and African locations in the fifth (1417–1419) and sixth (1421–1422) of his seven voyages. In the first (1405–1407), second (1407–1409), and third (1409–1411) voyages, he had only reached areas closer to the Indian sub-continent. In Africa proper, existing official records reveal only Mogadishu, Brava, and Djubo (in present-day Somalia), as well as Malindi (in present-day Kenya) as being in Zheng He's itinerary. But looking to other sources, such as reports by his companions, other destinations find themselves into the list, such as Zinj, today's Zanzibar. Thus it would appear that the record of Chinese exploration of the east coast of Africa has not yet been explored enough to exclude other locations south of this region.

The fifth voyage (1417–1419), in which Zheng He accompanies Africans back to their home, makes this, according to Wyatt, the first time in history that "Chinese can be said with certainty to have purposefully set direct sail for Africa, and . . . set foot firmly on African soil."[38] Because almost all official records of Zheng He's expeditions were likely destroyed, accounts by the eunuch's companions such as Ma Huan's (1414–1451) *Yingyai shenglan* (Captivating Visions at the Ocean's Limits), Fei Xin's (1388–1436) *Xingcha shenglan* (Arresting Views from a Raft Guided by the Stars), and Gong Zhen's (1413–34) *Xiyang fanguo zhi* (Record of Barbarians States of the Western Sea), are all we have left to rely on. It is in the record of Fei Xin, who was on the fifth and seventh voyage, that we find Chinese arrival in and first impressions of and African location in Mogadishu (Somalia):

> Journeying south of Weligama (Bieluo) in Ceylon [Sri Lanka] (Xilanshan) for twenty-one days and nights, one can reach this country, which is near Mogadishu. Its mountains and lands abut the sea, and the lands are broad and salty. . . . The customs are somewhat simple. There is no agriculture of any kind, and the people eke out a living by fishing. Both men and women have hair of knotted "fists" (*quanfa*), and wear short shirts that they sash with strips of cotton. Onions and garlic they have but they lack any kind of gourd. . . . In trading with them, we use gold; silver; satins; silks; rice; beans; and porcelain. In exchange for the gifts of grace [that are conferred by the empire, their leaders] have come forth to offer tribute with their local products.[39]

These gifts included animal products and animals including zebra ivory, and other indigenous products including frankincense.

Another east African city-state the Chinese reached is Juba, the record of whose visitation also found its way into the official record, *Mingshi* (Ming History).

The country of Juba, for its part, abuts Mogadishu. During [Emperor] Yongle (1403-24), it once submitted tribute. The population of this land is sparse, and its customs are somewhat pure. Zheng He went to this place. The land itself lacks vegetation, and the rocks are piled up in making places to dwell. For many years there can be droughts; thus, Juba entirely like Mogadishu. That which this country produces may be subsumed under such categories as lions, gold coinage, leopards, ostriches, ambergris, frankincense, amber, and the like.[40]

Despite the diversity of the places where contact was made, dispute continues regarding the earliest verifiable point of contact. Differences in Western scholarship emanates from what some twentieth-century scholars see as a "scarcity of first-hand sources."[41] Duyvendak relegates past accounts of Chinese contact with Africa to "hearsay" since we have not yet found proof that the Chinese "themselves ever reached the African shores."[42] The Ming Dynasty–era expeditions of Zheng He, therefore, are to him the first proof of an instance when the Chinese "discovered Africa for themselves."[43]

But illustrations of maps existing in China do suggest a substantial pre-Ming familiarity with east *and* southern Africa that make early possible contact not improbable. A surviving map which identifies with reasonable accuracy not only the shape of the bottom of the African continent, where the country of South Africa is located today but also physiological features may offer some clues.

On November 5, 2002, the Parliament of the Republic of South Africa put on display a life-size copy of the Ming-era map known as the *Da Ming Hun Yi Tu* ("The Amalgamated Map of the Great Ming Empire," a gift from the Chinese government. South Africa remains the only country outside China where the official copy exists.[44] Created in 1389, it contains the names of various continents as well as details not before accurately mapped, especially about southern Africa. For the territory now known as South Africa, like Chi Ssu Pen's map decades before, it identifies "Mountains of the Moon," what to some cartographers may be the mountain range known of the Drakensberg, as well as "a river that may correspond to the Orange River."[45] This is important because Africa's "triangular shape, or at least the typical southern tip of the continent appears on European maps not before 1500."[46] In both the European and Arabic maps produced at the time, the southern African landmass is deformed, facing outward to the right instead of downward. This casts doubt on the argument that Chinese cartographers produced these maps from second-hand Arab sources.

This *Da Ming Hun Yi Tu* has further important implications for scholars of South Africa-China relations. First, it is the first map to display the southern tip of the African continents with reasonable accuracy, far more accurately than the European maps of the time did, and did so more than a hundred years before the first documented arrival of Europeans in the southern African region. For scholars seeking to verify early Chinese contact with the peoples of the southern region of the continent, this map raises more questions than answers. Most importantly, it leaves the matter whether or not Chinese voyagers, including Zheng He, ever reached as far as the Cape far from being closed. If evidence of cartography has proven the navigation skills of others, including Arab travelers, this detailed map, together with artifacts such as Chinese porcelain found in the Limpopo province may well be reason enough for further inquiry by scholars.

The second reason for the significance of the *Da Ming Hun Yi Tu* is where it locates China, which is at the center of the world. This is in keeping with the perpetual Chinese self-image already discussed earlier, one that played a determining role not only in the manner of Chinese advances in Africa but her retreat as well. It is also instructive that centuries after these maps were made, China would choose no other country than South Africa as the location of the *Da Ming Hun Yi Tu*. Perhaps this promised not only to be the most visible location for this treasure, but also symbolized the role China envisages South Africa would play as a conduit to relations with the greater region and continent, built on demonstrably primordial relations.

These factors about the Chinese record by itself point to state whose self-awareness may be traced to its earliest times of existence. Indeed, in the very name of China in Mandarin, *zhongguo*, which is "Middle Kingdom," is found no abundance of deprecation concerning the country's locus in the geography of the world, and by extension in the politics of it. Thus it becomes easier to see how in the Chinese perspective, its ventures into the African continent, from the time the country established diplomatic relations with the first independent African country in the twentieth century—Nasser's Egypt in 1956—China seeks to contradict the common narrative of its relations as a "venture." To China, later-day relations with Africa are a return to re-visit relations it once either had, attempted to have, or, owing to the whims of a superiority complex of the time, abandoned in peace. By the time China would have liked to return to forge relations with city-states of Africa, thanks to colonialism, it was no longer for the Chinese or Africans to decide.

## Imperial China's Negative Racial Stereotypes: A Mixed Blessing?

In 1435 emperor Zhengtong came into power. A year later, he put a ban on seafaring. The consequences were swift and devastating: "by the early 1500s only one or two warships was left of every ten that were supposed to be present, and the largest warships were . . . crewed by 100 men."[47] This was a far cry from Zheng He's days where a large ship could carry "1,000 sailors and marines, plus passengers, in conditions of comfort."[48] After Zheng He's seventh (1431–1433) and last expedition, shorn of the new technology of war, stuck in an autarkical stasis, the Chinese were "no longer in a position to compete with [Europeans] for mastery of the seas, with fatal consequences to their own future."[49] Times had changed and China had become weak.

A number of reasons have been attributed to this Chinese turn inward, such as a highly self-sufficient nature of the country's economy. Some have cited an additional factor embedded in China's Confucian ethics that pervaded Ming-era foreign policy responses. A "Confucianized racism," which has always been a part of the way premodern China sought to make sense of the diversity of the world while maintaining primordial confidence, accounts for the Chinese reticence to engage faraway peoples on a plane of "formal equality."[50] This view holds that Ming Dynasty China had not rid itself of a "basic contempt for barbarians who did not observe Chinese mores."[51]

An account from Fei Xin, one of Zheng He's companions, of Mogadishu, is instructive in its description of the prevailing sentiment: "The land is a stony desert whose fields do not yield much. . . . The customs of the people are bigoted and insincere."[52] Dreyer notes that the use of the word *wanyin*, which also mean "stupid" makes this "the most pejorative description of any foreign country on the Zheng He circuit."[53] Some of these descriptions may well have made their way into the Chinese lexicon and terminology of various geographic features associated with this part of the world including the name of the continent of Africa itself. Named *feizhou*, it means "land of nothing." To be fair, it is important to note that further south in Brava, a different impression was left on the Chinese. In much smaller Zhubu, the Chinese encountered a people they conclude to be "'also' honest," like those in Brava."[54]

It remains, however, that the issue of China's foreign exploration had become a "moral" one for Ming court officials who "like good Confucians, despised trade and luxury and foreign barbarians."[55] Besides, according to this perspective, a self-sufficient China could do without products, deemed to be "nothing but curiosities," from these foreign hinterlands.[56] Here we find an indication of an early Chinese reticence in its foreign policy, a country reluctant to engage too closely with foreigners; the farther away they were, the more this propensity seemingly manifesting itself. This may explain why China, a naval power of this period, with ample manpower, did not seek to colonize the people it encountered in east Africa. To the Chinese, however bountiful the lands were and as welcoming as the people of east Africa may have been, they were still alien.

Some see this Chinese reticence to acquire in-depth knowledge about Africans as being responsible for long-lasting distorted images of Africa among Chinese people. According to Wilensky, the brevity of time the

Chinese spent in Africa, even among Zheng He's companions, only left them with "brief impressions added to a collection of enduring stereotypes about Africa and people with dark skin."[57]

The Chinese were, however, not alone in being prisoners of their time, in their superiority complex of viewing with relative contempt people and cultures they deemed foreign. That unflattering and sometimes downright contemptuous views of Africans were pervasive among *all* foreigners that came into allusive and attenuated contact with Africans before and after the Ming-era contacts has been widely documented. Some examples are worth mentioning. The words of the sixteenth-century Arab traveler Ibn Battutah, who would have shared the same faith with a majority of east Africans in the city-states he had visited, illustrate: "The Negroes are brutes without reason, without intelligence or knowledge. They have no notion of anything. They live like animals, without rules or laws."[58] This indicates that negative stereotyping of Africans as unrefined, undesirable and lacking in intelligence was common even intra-religiously. According to Portuguese navigator Alvise Camadosto, the same Africans were "'exceedingly idolatrous, have no laws, and are the cruelest of men.'"[59]

At around the same time as Camadoste's sentiments, Frenchman Alphonse de Santiago, in his *Cosmographie de l'Europe en 1544*, gave his description of the people of east Africa: "And inland there are people who have no heads and whose heads are in their chests while the rest is formed like a man. And further east there are those who have only one eye in the forehead. And south of the Mountains of the Moon there are others who have feet like goats and still others with the face of a dog."[60] In 1649, French explorer Vincent Le Blanc, who had travelled as far south the Cape, would also broach the realm of fantasy when he described the Africans of these territories as "so savage that they hardly know how to speak, so dirty that they eat intestines of animals full with manure without washing them, and so brutal that they resemble more hungry dogs than men who use reason."[61]

Ultimately, racist tropes notwithstanding, where the Ming Dynasty Chinese explorers halted, the Portuguese would less than 100 years later not only go further but exact a violent subjugation and dispossession on east Africans. But to some, the Chinese reticence, even incapacity to colonize, and the mystifying withdrawal from east Africa, emanating not from goodwill but most probably disdain and feelings of superiority, albeit not exceptionally, is a demerit to any case for the Chinese latter-day insistence of never having been a "colonizer" in Africa. Although the reason is still cold comfort to those who observe the negative stereotype behind the Chinese disengagement, we are however left to deduce that it is not that the Chinese were unwilling to colonize, but they, in their conservative estimation, found any colonization of "barbarians" in distant lands, and the resources this would require, not worth it for the "Middle Kingdom."

In their final analysis, a would-be colonization of Africa would have served no defensive purpose at home for China, thus failing the supreme watermark of feasibility used in foreign policy calculus before, during, and long after the Ming Dynasty. Today as it was then, it is, to a large degree, in its defensive anxieties that China's foreign policy objectives are extractable. Thus is the observer of early China-Africa encounters left with two perspectives when comparing Chinese engagement with that of Europe: the negative (Chinese) stereotypes that saw east African city-states left alone with their agency or the negative (European) stereotypes that virtually became a centripetal force for the colonial domination of east and southern African city-states.

## Colonialism and Attenuated Encounters in South of Africa

On April 21, 1652, Dutch colonist, Jan van Riebeeck, upon seeing the "broad, fertile soil" in the Cape, made mention of how it would be "suitable if some industrious Chinese were to come here" for the purpose of plowing the land.[62] On the 27th of the same month, he lamented the hardness of the soil but concluded that

> judging by the deep tracks made by the cattle, it should be soft enough in the wet season and suitable for cultivation; if only there were enough men for the purpose, for which we require some married Chinese and other Mardijckers [liberated slaves from outside] or even also Hollanders, who could be allowed on some condition to occupy some plots of land.[63]

On the 28th he wrote of having found a fort and encountering

> so much flat country, stretching right across from the one mountain to the other and from the shore of Table bay . . . , that it would take a whole day to cover it by foot. . . . It is 10 miles wide, traversed by the loveliest fresh rivers one could desire; even if there were ten thousand of Chinese or tillers they could not take up or cultivate a tenth part of the land.[64]

On the 29th van Riebeck again observed that "not one thousandth part of the suitable earth and valleys . . . could be ploughed or sown by the few men we have, and a large number of Chinese or other industrious people or families would be required."[65] Five months later, on September 18, the issue of prospective Chinese labor came up again: "It is a pity that the land in that vicinity [along the Salt River] cannot be cultivated owing to lack of labor. Chinese or other free men could easily work it and comfortably earn a living."[66]

That the labor, through Malay slaves, was soon forthcoming to the area "within a few years" after van Riebeeck's landing, is well-established.[67] But the record of whether in this intervening period he did follow through on his serious intentions regarding the Chinese or how soon his stated wishes were fulfilled, remains scant if inconclusive. The first documented Chinese influx into South Africa did begin between the mid to late-1600s when a relatively small number of Chinese came to the Cape "either as banished convicts or ex-convicts, who had been exiled by the Dutch East India Company to serve their term of sentence there."[68] No batch of these immigrants was ever found to be more than 50 at a time. A second group, coming after the Qing emperor's lifting of bans on outside travel and "opening up'" of China, albeit under (Western) duress, was another small number of "contract laborers and artisans" arriving between the late 1700s and the early 1800s.[69] Cape population records registered about 215 Chinese in 1891.[70] But by 1904, Cape records would register 1,308 Chinese.[71]

Thanks to mining in the Transvaal, this number would not remain small for long and would lead to a third group of Chinese. South Africa-China relations, in what could be said was to be the "formal beginning," of a semblance of relations, passed a milestone when the Qing emperor Qianlong's beleaguered government opened a consulate-general in Johannesburg in 1897.[72] Possibly in anticipation of an impending Chinese influx, the post seems to have served little other purpose than see to the expatriate Chinese labor in the mines, the third group of the early Chinese influx into South Africa.

From the mid-nineteenth century onwards, the domination of Qing-era China by various outside powers would continue in one form or another until the mid-twentieth century. This humiliating episode was formalized in a series of "unequal treaties" forced upon the country. British scholar Robert Gilbert has observed that "no one that takes even casual interest in news from China can be ignorant of the persistent outcry raised by that country against the so called 'unequal treaties.'"[73] Taken as a whole, these treaties stand as a singular sore point in the collective memory of the Chinese, and remain a potent frame-of-reference in China's narrative of its contact with the world.

One of the treaties is the Convention of Peking (1860), signed with Russia, France, and Britain. Among other things, it forced China to pay reparations, to open up a number of its ports including Guangdong, and granted extra-territoriality to Europeans. It also opened up the way to export Chinese labor to far-flung locales, mainly colonies, where colonial powers would benefit from cheap, mostly indentured Chinese labor. British sinologist, Martin Jacques has observed that

although China was not colonized, in effect it became a semi-colony, with foreign troops free to roam its territory, the treaty ports resembling micro-colonies, missionaries enjoying license to proselytize Western values wherever they went, and foreign companies able to establish subsidiaries with barely any taxation or duties. China was humiliated and impoverished.[74]

The British colony in South Africa was one of numerous African territories throughout Africa which received indentured laborers whose movement emanated from this and similar treaties. In 1904 the Transvaal legislative Council decided to fix a shortage of black labor in the mines by approving the importation of indentured laborers from China. In two years, over 50,000 Chinese were working in the mines in Witwatersrand, and there was an "understanding" that they would be confined only to unskilled positions.[75]

Like other indentured laborers before them, including the Indians imported to work the sugarcane farms of Natal in 1860, the Chinese were not immune from discriminatory labor practices already in place in South Africa. They took the place of black laborers, but not white. This separation was comprehensive and enforced by a list of "over fifty separate skilled trades and occupations from which the Chinese were specifically excluded."[76] The Chinese found themselves, as Yoon Jung Park argues in her seminal work, *A Matter of Honor: Being Chinese in South Africa*, virtually in between the white privilege and black disenfranchisement in the economy.[77]

Figure 1.1   **Chinese Mine Laborers and South Africa Circa 1897.** *Source*: Courtesy of US National Archives, College Park, MD.

These first encounters between the Chinese and Africans in South Africa amounted to attenuated encounters because they took place under relative duress, in periods of relative domination where both groups of people lacked sufficient political agency and economic franchise for meaningful, equitable, and mutually beneficial relations to develop. Attenuated encounters between Chinese people and Africans in South Africa, where one would be socioeconomically disempowered by the presence of the other while neither was an agent unto themselves, were not a new phenomenon entirely.

On Chinese soil, much earlier, in 1573, Ming emperor reluctantly cedes control over the island of Macau to the Portuguese. No sooner had this happened than African slaves were brought in large numbers. Forced to participate in various colonial suppression campaigns against the Chinese population. By 1635, of the 7,000 inhabitants of Macau 5,100 were said to be slaves, most of whom were from Africa.[78] Oddly enough, in 1622 it is the African slaves who decisively helped the Portuguese defend Macau from a Dutch attack in what is "the only battle ever fought between Europeans on Chinese soil."[79]

On South African soil, a similar, less-violent violent scenario would take place four centuries later in the mines of the Transvaal, only this time, *vice versa*. The presence of Chinese people seemed to present more problems than solutions for the colonial authorities. The Chinese had a sure sense of themselves, which often pitted them against other groups, including Africans and Indians, who had demonstrated more subservience to the harsh and often violent treatment they routinely received from whites. To the (white) South African public observing with contempt, from simple infractions of the color code, such as using "whites-only" rickshaws, to belligerent acts of self-assertion such as pursuing Indian traders who cheated them, the Chinese "simply did not 'know their place' within the Transvaal racial and class hierarchy."[80]

Another more consequential effect of Chinese labor was that of decreasing the bargaining power Africans had assumed regarding their labor. Whereas before, mining agents had struggled to convince blacks to come to the mines, the colonial powers viewed the Chinese labor presence as having taught the natives a "lesson" regarding the perceived value of their labor. In the view of the colonial elites, "with the perverseness of children, the natives, seeing that they were no longer indispensable, began to offer their services to the white man with increasing readiness."[81]

Thus it is that one of the first encounters between Africans in southern Africa and the Chinese, having taken place through the institution of slavery in seventeenth-century Macao, to the Chinese disadvantage, would later take place in South Africa proper, through the institution of colonial-era mining, and make no less a contribution to defining if not limiting the boundaries of contacts and relations the Chinese would have with the African people of South Africa.

By 1906, widespread rumors of Chinese public attacks, riots, criminality, violent disputes with Africans over (African) women, reactions to "corporal punishment," "unnatural" sexual practices, to mention a few, had become widespread and escalated into white panic and a political nightmare that saw most of the indentured Chinese repatriated by the beginning of 1910.[82] Yoon Jung Park notes the conundrum they faced: "How this tiny immigrant population from an ancient civilization should be categorized and treated often confounded white politicians and commentators over the years;" their very existence in South Africa, although brought about by the white minority capital-state matrix of power, seemed to increasingly fly in the face of the "social imperative of creating a state sculpted by racial domination" [83]

In an ironic twist, over a century later, on June 18, 2008, the Pretoria High Court gave a landmark ruling that classified Chinese-South Africans as "Colored." This instance of early Chinese discrimination likened to that of their Indian counterparts, would be cited as a basis for declaring that Chinese-South Africans fell under the "formerly disadvantaged group" designation, making them eligible to fall under the broad group of "black" and thus benefit from the country's vigorous affirmative action and other remedial stipulations of the country's Broad-Based Black Economic Empowerment (BBBEE) Act and the Employment Equity Act.[84] However, in a demonstration of tension and discomfort among black-Africans, South Africa's main business group was vocal in its objection to what it saw as a negation of a special place of remedial privilege that should be reserved for black-Africans. Thus it is that more than a century later, certain rivalries around questions of access to scarce opportunities to participate in the economy, the Chinese found themselves once more pitted against Africans in South Africa through no fault of their own.

Because of the times, the early Chinese presence in South Africa and Chinese contact with black South Africans has from its earliest periods not taken place with the full agency of either side. It could not prevent being calibrated by colonialism, and it took place under the disempowered auspices of the system of colonial domination and capitalism. As far as the Africans in South Africa may be concerned, at best, these were attenuated contacts. Unlike in the early Ming encounters further north when Admiral Zheng He and his expedition met the Africans of East Africa in the fifteenth century, Africans of the South had negative first encounters with Chinese in tragic episodes of neither side's making.

## REPUBLICAN CHINA (1912–1949) AND SOUTH AFRICA

On May 31, 1910, the Union of South Africa was founded. It united the English-speaking Cape and Natal territories with the Afrikaans-speaking

Transvaal and the Orange Free State. Nineteen months later, another event took place with the aim of charting an African reacting. This culminated in the establishment of the South African Native National Congress, later the ANC, on January 8, 1912.

In the same year, the Republic of China came into being, effectively bringing to an end the imperial rule which had lasted over 2000 years. What followed, however, was a succession of nationalist rulers, like Sun Yat-Sen in 1912, as well as warlords. Mainland China's attempts to achieve unity would remain in dispute until 1949. During the republican period, owing to colonial rule in most of Africa, the continent and its people played a negligible role in international affairs, let alone have notable contact with China. In any event, not only did China have plenty of pressing problems to deal with within its borders, it also was in a position of relative "inferiority in international affairs. The unequal treaties still existed. The foreign concessions and the leaseholds, essentially imperialist colonies spread all over the country, were still in place, and the foreigners retained considerable economic power."[85] What was important to the new republic at this time was the consolidation of power and building a semblance of a modern, united, sovereign nation-state under civilian rule.

Sun Yat-Sen acknowledged the exogenous nature of China's problems, and the "economic oppression" that this had brought.[86] But to him, any recovery from this state lay in China not only seeking education and advancement, but also cultivating nationalism, which he argued remained "that precious possession by which humanity maintains its existence. If nationalism decays, then when cosmopolitanism flourishes we will be unable to survive and will be eliminated by other races."[87] To him, relations were worth pursuing with any state abroad, so long as those relations "elevate China to an equal position among the nations, in international affairs, in government, and in economic life, so that she can permanently exist in the world."[88]

Thus legitimacy for China and Chinese people, through international peer-recognition, away from the middle kingdom-outer barbarian prism of the imperial period, began to emerge as an evolving post-imperial foreign policy imperative. This is a significant shift away from isolationism to a willingness to adopt best practices from the world. What was taking place in China was different from what was happening in Africa, including South Africa. In the latter, a process of economic marginalization of the African majority was in full swing, as was their massive displacement. The Land Act of 1913 saw millions of African communities lose their land to settlers.

It is easy to see what put South Africa in the crosshairs of late-nineteenth to early-twentieth-century China such that importation of labor to the southern-most tip of the faraway continent of Africa would be seen as a viable option to the Chinese. By the time China became a republic, white minority-ruled

South Africa was a "full participant" in the world trade system.[89] By 1913, South Africa was ranked 12th in the world by per capita GDP. While this was far behind other dominant (mainly Western) economies, compared to Latin America, Asia, and other African countries, only Argentina, Chile, and Mexico ranked ahead of South Africa's GDP of $1,600.[90] While this does not show the extent of socio-economic conditions endured by South Africa's African majority, it does illustrate how the country had moved "significantly ahead of many colonial and semi-colonial economies" including China.[91]

This, in no insignificant way, played a role in China's notice of South Africa. To republican China, as it was to Japan, the Union of South Africa was, at least politically, not part of "dark Africa" but a "civilized" country of statesman such as Jan Smuts, with which, from this vantage point, relations could be as progressive as with any other. Formal relations between republican China and the Union of South Africa began in 1931.[92] Ironically, whereas the period from the beginning of the twentieth century through 1949 saw relative inactivity in China-Africa relations, there was no lull in China-South Africa relations; whereas from 1949 onwards, communist China would reach out to and enjoy a cumulative flourish of relations with Africa, there would be a virtual lull in relations between Beijing and Pretoria.

In 1948, the National Party won elections and took over the reigns of government in South Africa. What soon followed was a series of legislative maneuvers which culminated in *apartheid*, the system of institutionalized racism and economic displacement of nonwhites based on comprehensive and violently enforced segregation. This system, and the liberation movement that would attempt to defeat it, played a dominant role in attenuating the contact South Africans would have with the Chinese for half a century to come.

## NOTES

1. Jonathan Spence, "Confucian Ways," *BBC Reith Lectures*, accessed August 21, 2020, http://www.bbc.co.uk/radio4/reith2008/transcript1.shtml.
2. Yujiang Wu, *Mozi Jiaozhu* [Collated commentaries on Mozi] (Chongqing: Duli Chubanshe, 1944), 10A/42.19.98, quoted in Don J. Wyatt, *The Blacks of Premodern China* (Philadelphia: University of Pennsylvania Press, 2010), 23.
3. *Shanjiang* [Classic of mountains and seas] (Shanghai: Shanghai Shudian, 1989), 18.86, quoted in Wyatt, *The Blacks of Premodern China*, 25.
4. Quoted in Wyatt, *The Blacks of Premodern China*, 68.
5. Wyatt, *The Blacks of Premodern China*, 18.
6. Ibid., 19.
7. Phillip Snow, *The Star Raft: China's Encounter with Africa* (London: Weidenfeld and Nicolson, 1988), 19.
8. Ibid.

9. Snow, *The Star Raft*, 21.

10. Ibid., 132.

11. Ibid.

12. Quoted in Wyatt, *The Blacks of Premodern China*, 69.

13. Ibid., 70.

14. Julius, O. Adekunle, "East African States," in *Africa Volume 1: African History Before 1885*, ed. Falola, Toyin (Durham, NC: Carolina Academic Press, 2000), 198–9; on continuous African presence in Iraq, numbering over a million by 2013, see Jalaj Dhiab, "Black Iraqis: Scarred Memory and Recovered Identity," in *Minorities in Iraq: Memory, Identity and Challenges*, ed. Salloum, Sa'ad (Beirut, Baghdad: Masarat for Cultural and Media Development, 2013), 102–11.

15. J. J. L. Duyvendak, *China's Discovery of Africa* (London: Arthur Probsthain, 1949), 12.

16. Chengshi Duan, *Youyang Zazu* (Taipei: Taiwan Xuesheng Shuju, 1975), 4.3b; cited in Wyatt, *The Blacks of Premodern China*, 84–5.

17. Wyatt, *The Blacks of Premodern China*, 85.

18. Chinese unit of distance equivalent to approximately 0.3 mile; 2000 *li* would be equivalent to 621.4 miles.

19. Xiu Ouyang, Song Qi, et al., *Xin Tangshu* [New Tang History] (Taipei: Dingwen Shuju, 1976), 221B26I; cited in Wyatt, *The Blacks of Premodern China*, 87.

20. Dayuan Wang, *Daoyi Zhulie* [Annals of Island Barbarians] (Taipei: Dingwen Shuju, 1975), I.30; cited in Wyatt, *The Blacks of Premodern China*, 89.

21. Teobaldo Filesi, *China and Africa in the Middle Ages* (London: Routledge, 1972), 12.

22. Ibid., 12.

23. E. J. L. Shwarz, "The Chinese Connections with Africa," *Journal of Royal Asiatic Society of Bengal (Calcutta)* 5 (1938): 176–8; cited in Filesi, *China and Africa in the Middle Ages*, 1–2.

24. Joshua Potter, "Chinese-East Africa Trade before the 16th Century," *Ufahamu: A Journal of African Studies* 5, no. 2 (1974): 113.

25. Ibid.

26. Ibid.

27. Sian Tiley, *Mapungubwe: South Africa's Crown Jewels* (Johannesburg: Sunbird Publishing, 2004).

28. UNESCO, "Mapungubwe Cultural Landscape," accessed August 21, 2015, http://whc.unesco.org/en/list/1099/

29. Ibid.

30. Leo Fouche, ed., *Mapungubwe Ancient Bantu Civilization on the Limpopo: Reports on Excavations at Mapungubwe (Northern Transvaal) from February 1933 to June 1935* (Cambridge: Cambridge University Press, 1937), 1.

31. David Fleminger, *Mapungubwe Cultural Landscape* (Pinetown, South Africa: 30° South Publishers, 2008), 12.

32. Ibid.

33. Ibid., 26.

34. Linda Prinslo et al., "Re-dating of Chinese Celadon Shards Excavated on Mapungubwe Hill, a 13th Century Iron Age Site in South Africa, Using Raman Spectroscopy, XRF and XRD," *Journal of Raman Spectroscopy* 36, no. 8 (August 2005): 806–16.

35. Charles O. Hucker, "Preface," in *Chinese Government in Ming Time*, ed. Charles Hucker (New York: Columbia University Press, 1969), vii.

36. Wyatt, *The Blacks of Premodern China*, 99.

37. Ibid.

38. Wyatt, *The Blacks of Premodern China*, 100.

39. Xin Fei, *Xingcha shenglan* [Arresting Views from a Raft Guided by Stars], in *Shuofang beisheng* [Complete Historical Records of the North], vol. 3, ed. He Quitao (Shanghai: Guji Chunbanshe, 1999), 4.4a–b; quoted in Wyatt, *The Blacks of Premodern China*, 104.

40. Tingyu Zhang et al., *Mingshi* [Ming History] (Beijing: Zhonghua Shuju, 1974), 326.8449–50.; quoted in Wyatt, *The Blacks of Premodern China*, 105.

41. Filesi, *China and Africa in the Middle Ages*, 1.

42. Duyvendak, *China's Discovery of Africa*, 26.

43. Ibid., 13.

44. Carol Kauffman, "Patterns of Contact: Designs from the Indian Ocean World: A Curator's View," *The East African Review* 51 (2016): 7.

45. "Kangningbo," *Cartographic Images*, accessed August 21, 2015, http://cartographicimages.net/Cartographic_Images/236_Kangnido.html.

46. Walter Fuchs, "Was South Africa Already Known in the 13th Century?" *Imago Mundi: The International Journal for the History of Cartography* 10, no. 1 (1953): 50.

47. Ibid., 171.

48. Ibid., 109.

49. Witold Rodzinski, *The Walled Kingdom: A History of China from Antiquity to the Present* (New York: The Free Press, 1984), 150.

50. Christopher A. Ford, *The Mind of Empire: China's History and Modern Foreign Relations* (Lexington, KY: University of Kentucky Press, 2010), 88.

51. Ibid.

52. Edward L. Dreyer, *Zheng He: China and the Oceans in the Early Ming Dynasty, 1405–1433* (Upper Saddle River, NJ: Pearson, 2006), 88.

53. Ibid.

54. Ibid., 89.

55. Jeannette Mirsky, *The Great Chinese Travellers* (New York: Pantheon, 1964), 248.

56. Ibid.

57. Julie Wilensky, "The Magical Kunlun and 'Devil Slaves': Chinese Perceptions of Dark-skinned People and Africa before 1500," *Sino-Platonic Papers* 122 (July 2002): 42.

58. William B. Cohen, *The French Encounter with Africa: White Response to Blacks, 1530–1880* (Bloomington, IN: Indiana University Press, 2003), 3.

59. Ibid., 4.

60. Alphonse de Santiago and Georges Musset, ed., *Cosmographie de l'Europe en 1544* (Paris, 1904), 342; cited in Ibid., 5.

61. Vincent Le Blanc, *Voyages Famieux de Vincent le Blanc* (Paris, 1649), 2; quoted in Ibid., 6.

62. H. B. Thom, ed., *Journal of Jan van Riebeeck Volume 1: 1651–1655* (Cape Tow: A.A. Balkema, 1952), 33.

63. Ibid., 35.

64. Ibid., 35–6.

65. Ibid., 36.

66. Ibid., 61.

67. Peter Richardson, "Chinese Indentured Labor in the Transvaal Gold Mining Industry, 1904–1910," in *Independent Labor in the British Empire: 1834–1920*, ed. Kay Saunders (London: Croom Helm, 1984), 260.

68. Karen L. Harris, "Sugar and Gold: Indentured Indian and Chinese Labor in South Africa," *Journal of Social Science* 25 (2010): 150.

69. Yoon Jung Park, *A Matter of Honor: Being Chinese in South Africa* (Lanham, MD: Lexington Books, 2009), 10.

70. Harris, "Chinese Indentured Labor," 151.

71. Ibid.

72. Liang-Tsai Wei, *Peking versus Taipei in Africa: 1960–1978* (Taipei: Asia and World Institute, 1982), 362.

73. Robert Gilbert, *The Unequal Treaties: China and the Foreigner* (Arlington, VA: University Publications of America, 1976), viii.

74. Martin Jacques, *When China Rules the World: The End of the Western World and the Birth of a New Global Order* (New York: Penguin Books, 2009), 103.

75. Charles H. Feinstein, *The Economic History of South Africa: Conquest, Discrimination and Development* (New York: Cambridge University Press, 2005), 54.

76. Ibid., 75.

77. Park, *A Matter of Honor.*

78. Snow, *The Star Raft*, 39.

79. Ibid.

80. Rachel K. Bright, *Chinese Labor in South Africa, 1902–10: Race, Violence, and Global Spectacle* (New York: Palgrave Macmillan, 2013), 102.

81. Basil Worstfold, *The Reconstruction of the New Colonies under Lord Milner Volume I* (London: Keegan Paul, Trench, Tubner and Company, 1913), 367; quoted in Ibid., 176.

82. Bright Ibid., 95–131, 176.

83. Park, *A Matter of Honor*, 9, 11.

84. "Black Business Criticizes Ruling on Chinese South Africans," *Mail and Guardian*, June 02, 2008.

85. John E. Schrecker, *The Chinese Revolution in Historical Perspective* (New York: Greenwood Press, 1991), 131.

86. Yat-sen Sen, *San Min Chu-I* [The Three Principles of the People], trans. by Frank W. Price (Taipei: Sino-American Publishing, 1953), 10.

87. Ibid., 17.

88. Ibid., 1.

89. Feinstein, *The Economic History of South Africa*, 5.

90. Ibid.

91. Ibid.

92. Wei, *Peking Versus Taipei in Africa: 1960–1978*, 362.

*Chapter 2*

# 1949–1998

## *Contested China, Contested Liberation*

On October 1, 1949, Mao Zedong declared the founding of the People's Republic of China (PRC). At the time, it was Chiang Kai-shek's Guomingdong government on the island of Taiwan that was internationally recognized as "China." It took twenty years for the United Nations to recognize the PRC as the sole representative of the Chinese people on October 25, 1971. Early in its existence, therefore, the imperative of changing this virtual persona non grata status in the international political system dominated China's foreign policy and had a lasting effect on its relations with Africa.

### 1949–1970: TO BANDUNG AND BEYOND

Beijing's preoccupation with raising the country's international profile was evident in 1955 when the Afro-Asian conference of "non-aligned" countries was held in Bandung, Indonesia. Western opinion of the conference was negative. In the United States it was characterized as a "Babylonic cacophony ending [that wound end] up in a rising crescendo of confusion and indecision."[1] Nevertheless, the conference provided a platform for the PRC to kick-start relations with numerous nations, including the five African countries in attendance (Egypt, Sudan, Ethiopia, Liberia, and Libya) as well as with various independence formations, including the African National Congress (ANC). From April 18 through 24, the Africans sought to use the conference to drum up solidarity for their independence struggle away from the constraining loyalties of the capitalist West-communist East ideological schism.

A year earlier, China had signed the *"Panch Sheel"* (Sanskrit for "five virtues") agreement with India, following border skirmishes. They agreed to the following: (1) mutual respect for each other's territorial integrity and

41

sovereignty, (2) mutual nonaggression, (3) mutual non-interference in each other's internal affairs, (4) equality and mutual benefit, and (5) peaceful coexistence. The warm reception these same tenets received at the Bandung conference led to their incorporation into its 10-point declaration at the end. Beyond Bandung, China canonized these as the "Five Principles of Peaceful Co-existence" and made them the gold standard of its foreign policy posture for the world and Africa until the present period. After the conference, still under the aegis of the "Five Principles," China moved quickly to establish diplomatic relations with more African countries. In 1956 alone, a Chinese cultural mission paid an official visit to Egypt, Sudan, Morocco, Tunisia, and Ethiopia; China's first commercial contracts with African countries took place with the purchase of cotton from Egypt (contracts with Morocco and Sudan were also signed); and Nasser's Egypt formally recognized Beijing on May 30, marking the first diplomatic relations between the PRC and an African nation.[2]

## China and South Africa's Liberation Struggle

For South Africa, China's involvement in the Bandung conference and what would come to be known as the "Bandung spirit"—the internationalist commitment to fight for liberation, sovereignty, and development for nations of the global South—was significant. At the conference, the South African Communist Party (SACP) was represented by its secretary-general, Moses Kotane. A message was read from the ANC president, Chief Albert Luthuli, who failed to attend due to an apartheid government travel ban. In October of 1955 Kotane paid a visit to Beijing, following an invitation to the sixth anniversary of the PRC. He noted that "everybody seemed happy and determined and they were very clear about their political line."[3]

Kotane was not the first prominent leader in the South African liberation movement to seek relations with China through a visit. Earlier, in October 1953, ANC secretary-general Walter Sisulu, accompanied by Ismail Bhoola and Duma Nokwe, had paid a six-week visit to China where he met Mao Zedong and Chou Enlai. Having decided on the inevitability of the armed struggle, Nelson Mandela had asked Sisulu to make a request to the Chinese for arms. But the Chinese were "weary and cautious," questioning Sisulu whether the liberation forces had "matured enough to justify such an endeavor."[4] According to Sisulu, the Chinese insisted that the armed struggle was a "very serious affair," with which the ANC were not to "play," and must first "analyze the situation before [making] a decision about what to do."[5] Sisulu returned, as Nelson Mandela would later recall, "encouraged but [with] no guns."[6] This visit caused a storm within the ANC. Albert Luthuli and Z.K. Mattews decried the visit to a socialist country, which expose the long-standing divide in the ANC between the Marxist/socialist and national-ist/anti-communist bloc. To further complicate matters, the anti-communist bloc was not entirely Africanist either nor were the anti-Africanists entirely pro-communist.

The roots of the friction also lay in another event in 1955. From June 25 through 26, emanating from the "spirit of Bandung," the groundswell of enthusiasm the conference concluded just weeks before had elicited, the Congress of the People took place in Kliptown, South Africa. A multira-cial configuration of political and civic groups met to chart the course of the liberation struggle. Its final declaration, the "Freedom Charter," which stated that South Africa belonged to "all who live in it, black and white," while seen as progressive by many, was also seen as a capitulation to the non-African minority by some.[7] Critics saw the charter as a departure from what the ANC's founding objectives regarding the preeminence of Africans. Also, they charged it was too socialist and bemoaned what they saw as too much influence from white liberals in crafting the historic document. While the "Freedom Charter" has been largely venerated in post-apartheid South Africa, and retains as iconic status to most South Africans as the US constitution to most Americans, this was not the case at the time of its craft-ing. The vocal descent from Kliptown culminated in the formation of the Pan Africanist Congress (PAC) on April 6, 1959, which became not only an Africanist splinter from the ANC but later, during the Sino-Soviet split, China's ally in the South African liberation movement.

The split in the liberation movement manifested itself in three ways: mate-rially, ideologically, and racially. First, it made it easy—in a material and deterministic way—to ascertain, at any given time, who between China and the Soviet Union was the sponsor of the main South African liberation groups. Ideology is the second form in which intra-party splits manifested them-selves. Not all who supported the ANC were Communists or even Socialists. Nationalists among the ANC's ranks tended to take a hard anti-communist line and would often than seldom base judgment of leadership capabilities on the individual's ideological bent, real or assumed. Thirdly, some believed that the struggle was against white rule in favor of black majority rule, and the struggle could therefore not include other races. Post-Bandung divisions notwithstanding, China was determined to project a significant presence by establishing contact with any liberation organization it could.

This was the case when Mao Zedong received a group representing various Arab and African countries' independence organizations on April 28, 1961. South Africa's ANC was represented by Tennyson Makiwane.[8] Mao voiced his concern that China had "no clear understanding of African history, geography, and the present situation," and asked that an "institute of Africa" be established to study these subjects.[9] According to Chinese scholar, Li

Anshan, this was the impetus for the establishment of an institute for African Studies soon afterward.[10] In the PRC's quest for more diplomatic relations with Africa, the country also had to contend with global events that had an effect on the fate of its people as well as the Africans, but over which it had little control.

## The Korean War: Faraway Lessons, Local Message

Between 1950 and 1953 The Korean war between the North and South unexpectedly drew South Africa into indirect contact with the PRC. As part of the UN coalition's air unit, apartheid South Africa's air force flew over 12,000 sorties bombing positions occupied by Chinese "volunteers" in the North.[11] It would seem that this was yet another event which inserted itself into the relations between the Chinese and (South) African people, attenuating their contact. While there may have been some surprise that apartheid South Africa would commit its air force to a dangerous mission over 7,000 miles, in an alien land whose war it had virtually nothing to do with, some saw this as Pretoria seizing a chance to exhibit military strength. Indeed, in an unprecedented "first time in the history of the Union of South Africa," all white political parties agreed to this overseas combat operation.[12]

According to apartheid government's calculations, participation in the Korean War had three benefits for Pretoria: first, it helped the country contribute "to the repulse of an act of Communist aggression"; secondly, it demonstrated a "will to resist"; thirdly, South Africa scored political points with Western powers and solidified its anti-communist standing.[13] According to Thomas Bertelsmann, this not only cemented the United States-South Africa alliance against communism, but it also "confirmed military ties" between the two.[14] But another audience was the southern African region, the African continent at large, as well as liberation movement leaders contemplating armed struggle against Pretoria. Ironically, in one event, Chinese people, far away from South African shores in Korea, fell victim to the same apartheid military apparatus their black counterparts would in the not-so-distant future also try to survive. This is because sorties by the apartheid air force would also be conducted closer to home in frontline states such as Mozambique, Angola, and Namibia.

## The Sino-Soviet Split and Contested Paths to Liberation

Almost a year after Bandung, in February 1956, the twentieth congress of the Communist Party of the Soviet Union took place at which new leader, Nikita Khrushchev, denounced Stalin' personality cult. Mao took exception and a schism ensued, one that dragged liberation groups in and forced them to navigate a tightrope in all their external dealings. In 1958 China promulgated a slogan imploring people to "struggle against blind faith in established technical standards and regulations and in foreign experience."[15] In Moscow this was taken as a denigration of the same Soviet technical expertise that aided China's throughout the 1950s. In August 1960 the Soviet Union withdrew 1,390 specialists from China.

The Sino-Soviet split did not affect relations with the liberation movement immediately. Some members of the ANC's armed wing, *Umkhonto weSizwe*, such as Milton Mkwayi, Joe Gqabi, Andrew Mlangeni, and Raymonds Mhlaba, had been sent to the PRC in June 1962 as part of Operation Mayibuye, a plan for infiltrating pre-selected rural areas and scoping them as targets for sustained sabotage against the apartheid government's infrastructure.[16] This was at a time when the Sino-Soviet dispute was beginning to escalate. Russian scholar, Vladimir Shubin, notes the following: "Initially, Beijing was very active in Africa and the ANC delegation headed by Oliver Tambo was warmly received in China in September-October 1963, but the relationship soured when the ANC (and SACP) failed to side with China in the growing" dispute.[17] At first the ANC was reticent toward Moscow, not wanting to be seen to be taking sides in the East-West schism of the time. If ideology was responsible for the reticence, the temporal vagaries of waging a liberation struggle soon helped their decision. In 1962, after a trip to more than four African countries, Nelson Mandela had been able to raise only 25,000 pounds. On April 5, 1963, Oliver Tambo visited the Soviet Union and requested 250,000 pounds. Later that year, 300,000, over 40 percent of the ANC's needs, was provided.[18] This helped the ANC weather the financial shortfall caused by the decline of Chinese support owing to the former being seen to be taking the Moscow side.

By 1963, things had become complicated within the ANC-SACP alliance. China was considered a "security threat and ideological challenge to the Soviet Union's leadership of world communism," including communist leadership within the liberation movement.[19] Thomas sees South Africa as "one of the most clear-cut examples of the way the Sino-Soviet split divided political groups."[20] Some, especially those who had been part of African revolts against whites, such as those in Mpondoland, were more convinced of the benefits of a rural-based armed struggle led by the peasantry. This put them into the camp sympathetic to Beijing's line within the alliance. Indeed, some of the earliest offer to train uMkhonto weSizwe had come from China wherein Nanking, some had completed armed training. Things got worse within the ANC. Anyone who voiced displeasure was labeled a "Maoist and revisionist, or alternatively and imperialist, and branded a fifth column who was against the liberation of South Africa."[21] China stopped accepting uMkhonto weSizwe trainees, and those in exile camps who were Chinese-trained were monitored for "traces of Maoism."[22]

But if taking the "Soviet line" was strategically good for the ANC alliance, it was proving difficult tactically, especially in the armed struggle. On this, Mao's guerilla tactics remained widely appealing and were seen to be bearing fruit in liberation battles of neighboring Rhodesia. There, Chinese-trained Josiah Tongogara, had implemented the Chinese "fish-in-water" tactic of infiltrating the countryside and mass mobilizing for an "organic" guerilla effort full of recruits who were self-sufficient and locally based. This was contrary to what the ANC's uMkhonto weSizwe was doing. Former ANC leader Ronnie Kasrils explained that "small units would infiltrate the country, carry out operations, and withdraw back to the neighboring states," which left ANC leaders still "not satisfied with the progress."[23]

Liberation front organizations were not spared. Here, a convergence took place between the Soviet Union's "goal of limiting China's influence and the ANC's goal of eliminating the PAC in world affairs (and gaining exclusive international legitimacy for itself)."[24] This manifested itself whenever the ANC and the PAC at international summits, such as when the Afro-Asian Peoples' Solidarity Organization (AAPSO) held its meeting in Moshi, Tanzania in 1963. Oliver Tambo, leading the ANC alliance delegation, lobbied and failed to get an impending plenary meeting of another summit, soon to be held in Beijing, to be canceled. Joined by the Cubans, the Chinese successfully lobbied instead for the broadening of AAPSO's reach to include Latin America, through the Afro-Asian-Latin American People's Solidarity Organization (AALAPSO) to be held in Havana. This has been cited as the first instance when Beijing "openly tried to split political movements in the Third World" and ensure the split continue unabated.[25] Another front organization for writers, the Afro-Asian People's Permanent Writers Bureau (AAPWB), was formed in 1966. It too soon found itself split between its Cairo-based branch, which was pro-Soviet, and another based in Beijing. Although the ANC assisted the Soviet Union's side in these meetings "by simply attending," the split still left a bitter taste in the organization, as well as a feeling that the Moscow-Beijing schism had "diverted" the liberation movement from its serious ends.[26]

For all their differences, the Soviet Union and China did share the same analysis of what South African liberation leaders needed for a guerilla campaign against the apartheid regime. Like all guerilla forces, they needed a reliable base close to the territory they seek to besiege. According to this rationale, exiled South African guerrillas would be well-served by helping in Rhodesia, Mozambique and Angola's own wars "as a prelude to attacking South Africa at close quarters" as well as gaining useful combat experience.[27]

## The Conduit of Tanzania

Having established formal relations on the same day it became a unified republic, in April 26, 1964, Tanzania was able to play a role as a forward base and in circumventing the de facto embargo apartheid that South Africa had imposed on regional countries and their mostly landlocked economies, by being a window to the world and a staging ground for liberation movements. Tanzanian president Julius Nyerere visited China in February 1965 and 1968. Chou Enlai visited Tanzania in 1965. It was during this visit that the Chinese Premier harkened back to the centuries-old history as a backdrop to what should be excellent relations, stating that "although this is our first visit . . . my colleagues and I do not find ourselves in a strange land" as "intercourse between our countries dated back to 900 years ago."[28]

But the Sino-Soviet split still loomed in the background. It was also during this visit that the Premier said, "The present situation is very favorable to the African people. As long as they maintain firm unity and fight perseveringly, they will surely be able to defeat all the intrigues of the old and new colonialists."[29] Reflecting the Sino-Soviet split, this has come to be seen as a Chinese breach of its "nonalignment" stance and an attempt to assume leadership in the third world community of states, a point made more strongly by the frequent mention in the speech of the imperialism, colonialism, and neocolonialism in the same breath as triplets of domination to be fought. For its part, China was simply broadening the definition of what national liberation meant, to include in it not just "opposition to imperialism, colonialism," but also "superpowerism."[30]

Whatever their causes, the disagreements among liberation ranks, and the ensuing splits posed existential problems for China's support of the liberation struggle as a whole. They gave the impression that China had to choose sides or at least tread an ideological and ethnic minefield. Either organization the country chose to align itself with, Beijing was still would still displease the other. The country changed tack and began to support "any national liberation organization and if there were rival movements, Beijing attempted to keep friendly relations with all of them as a means of keeping open the channels of communication."[31] By trying to be strategic in cultivating "free-ranging" relations, and using Tanzania to facilitate them, China began an attempt to bridge the ideological and trust gap among Soviet-aligned liberation organizations.

## 1970–1980: SINO-SOVIET SPLIT AND THE LIBERATION MOVEMENT

Although China tried, by 1970, it was still unsuccessful in its attempts to eschew choosing sides between the liberations organizations. The 1970s still began as a decade of promise for relations between China and the South African liberation movement, especially the ANC. In 1970 Tambo accepted an invitation to Beijing where he met Vice Premier Chen Wu Kei. By January 1979, another meeting had taken place this time with Vice Primer Li Hsien Nien. Here China voiced a willingness to "normalize relations with the ANC on the basis of a common commitment to the liberation struggle and opposition to 'imperialism.'"[32]

The fact that the relations were not as strong between Beijing and the ANC at this time, while the latter was considered firmly in Moscow's circuit, did not preclude the ANC deriving marginal benefit from aid forthcoming to the broad frontline liberation movements as a whole. Arms are an example. From 1965 onwards, Chinese military personnel continued working in Tanzania, training guerillas from regional armed groupings, including ANC armed wing, uMkhonto weSizwe. One night in September 1971, a discussion took place between Samora Machel, representing FRELIMO, and Chinese Premier Chou Enlai. Lasting the entire night, the meeting concluded with Chou's announcement that 10,000 tons of weapons had left Shanghai for Dar es Salaam. Samora Machel had often warned the ANC leadership to be wary of the SACP because of its proximity to Moscow. He saw the Soviet Union as ultimately "not genuine friends of the African people, . . . racist and interested in dominating Africa."[33] That Machel was close to China, even while FRELIMO was still encamped in Tanzania, had already been common cause after his visit to Beijing in 1975 where he was received "virtually as a head of state" after arriving on an airplane provided by Beijing.[34] Thus did the aid meant for FRELIMO begin to make its way to other groupings including ZANU and the ANC, itself a "reflection of close co-operation between Beijing and Tanzania."[35] Tanzania became a rear base for virtually all frontline liberation groups and became an indispensable logistical link to the world.

By 1975, the Moscow-Beijing schism had managed to manifest itself in various liberation battles and other geopolitical events in earnest, and, with the hindsight of history as benefit, would to many observers be found deleterious to the liberation movement.

An example is a discussion between US president Gerald Ford and Mao Zedong on the former's visit to Beijing, concerning Angola where apartheid South Africa was embroiled in a battle with Soviet- and Cuban-backed fighters from Angola's MPLA and other armed wings of "sister" liberation organizations.

*Mao:* "I am in favor of driving the Soviet Union out [of Angola]."
*Ford:* "If we both make good effort, we can."
*Mao:* "South Africa does not have a very good reputation"

**Figure 2.1    Samora Machel with Chinese Military Adviserduring War for Independence.**
*Source*: Author; Courtesy of the US National Archives, College Park, MD.

*Ford:* "But they are fighting to keep the Soviet Union from expanding. And we think that's admirable"

*Deng:* "You mean you admire South Africa?"

*Ford:* "No. They have taken a strong stance against the Soviet Union. And they are doing that totally on their own, without any stimulation by the United States."[36]

Whether this was a spectacular miscalculation by the Chinese leadership or an expression of the wishes of Beijing is not known. But what is known is that it put fuel to the fire and made China look reactionary. For Angola and their South African allies, "only one socialist country remained in the 'unnatural alliance' (of Angola's enemies)," and it was China.[37] In Mozambique, while Machel was trying to implement his own interpretation of Maoism, "the same literature was being cleared off the bookshelves in uMkhonto weSizwe camps;"[38] and the same splits and purges were also occurring among the political prisoners in Robben Island who saw China as having "lost interest in African affairs."[39]

Although the Sino-Soviet split played a significant role in the tenor of the debate, intra-African views were equally as strong and the Africans were driven by their own motives emanating from their respective countries' political environments. Contrary to what has often been put forth, not all African dissent was a proxy ideological debate. Most important for contemporary studies of Africa-China relations is the realization that the debate on whether or not the accelerated pace of relations with China is good for Africa still persist among scholars even, if not especially, in the present period. Ultimately for China at the time, the Sino-Soviet split, acrimonious as it was, still did not prevent the former from having unanimous African support when it mattered the most, at the United Nations.

## China, (South) Africa, and the United Nations

The 1970s also saw more African countries receive independence, which in turn increased member states of the United Nations, and the consequences were soon apparent. On October 25, 1971, the UN General Assembly passed Resolution 2758 to admit the PRC as the sole representative of the Chinese people and drop recognition of Taiwan. Of the total 128 countries that voted, 76 (60 percent) voted for the PRC, 35 for Taiwan, and 17 abstained. Of the countries that voted for Beijing 26 or 1/3 were African. This was a far cry from 1952 when only four African nations—Ethiopia, Liberia, Egypt, and apartheid South Africa—were members of the UN, and all voted for Taiwan. When it came to it, the "steady increase of [independent] African nations" in turn increased the value of Africa as a voting bloc at the UN.[40] Moreover, China's diligent public diplomacy in Africa, indeed the near-completion of the Tan-Zam railway, formed a set of circumstances that gave the Chinese a favorable report among the Africans.

Later that month, the *Christian Science Monitor*, in an article on October 27, 1971, would report on the reaction of African delegates following the vote as "a frenzy of delight—their arms swooping above their heads and jumping up and down in their seats as wild applause engulfed the circular chamber."[41] Chairman Mao Zedong would directly credit Africa when he pointed out that "it is our African brothers who have carried [us] into the UN."[42] The extent to which this matter had been unresolved for over two decades pointed to the need on the part of Beijing to increasingly have a secure source of partners, and in this Africa played a part. This also sowed the seeds for the mutual cooperation that became the benchmark of China's approach to Africa decades later.

China's UN seat had been an intractable issue. In 22 years, the UN had voted on it 21 times, every year but two since 1945. There was another strategic implication that made the issue more important. Taiwan had been a founding member of the UN in 1945 and belonged to the Security Council as one of the five Permanent Members with veto-power. It had been more favored than communist Beijing and had encountered little Western resistance—indeed was encouraged—as it gained support for permanent Security Council membership. But the specter of Beijing's membership at the United Nations, and the former's all but inevitable assumption of a Permanent Seat on the Security Council, presented a strategically undesirable state-of-affairs to Western leaders—that of a second contrarian, Communist, veto-wielding country on the Security Council in addition to the Soviet Union.

From an anti-apartheid standpoint, this welcomed event meant another sympathetic country on the Security Council to which South African liberation organizations could look for support. This was manifested three years later when, after previous failed attempts, both the ANC and PAC were granted observer status at the UN General Assembly through a unanimous 111-0 vote on December 16, 1974. What emerges here is the inability of both the Chinese and the ANC leadership at the time to look at the big strategic direction and then maneuver around imminent disagreements for tactical advantage in their respective spheres of struggle. For the ANC, that sphere was now at the United Nations but also increasingly back home where the organization sought to demonstrate international authority and gravitas to the increasing pool of black supporters. For China, the multilateral forum of the United Nations was the sphere where the country sought to turn its sight on economic development. In a way, there existed a mutual quest for legitimacy between China and the ANC-PAC rivalry. For either of the latter, it was to be recognized as the primary representative of the liberation movement in South Africa, a quest that would continue until the 1994 elections, which saw the ANC's status formalized in political power. For China, it was a quest to be recognized as the sole representative of the Chinese people, a quest that would continue past the turn of the millennium, and would, save for the few countries holding out by formally recognizing Taipei, be a major success.

In the 1970s, the formal Chinese recognition at the UN and the attendant rise in profile this meant for Beijing contributed to drive the apartheid to seek to cultivate better relations with Taiwan and to drop any inhibitions of not antagonizing Beijing it may have before held.

The major reason for this was that as long as the ROC had any hope of winning and retaining influence in black Africa, it could not afford to display friendship for the apartheid white minority regime in Pretoria. Conversely, South Africa did not seek friendship with the ROC because that might provoke Peking into more active support of South African dissident movements. After the 1971 ouster of the ROC from the United Nations, both governments had reason to reevaluate their earlier policies. Abandoned by most of its black African friends, Taipei felt isolated by the PRC in Africa and began to review its relations with South Africa, "neglected for so many years. Pretoria, feeling intensified pressure from Communist powers and militant Africans and realizing the impossibility of appeasing Peking, decided to improve its relations with Taipei."[43]

In 1973 the ROC opened a consulate in Cape Town, followed by the upgrading of diplomatic relations to ambassador level on April 26, 1976, which completed the pivot to Pretoria and the antagonism that followed from the liberation movements.

## *The Tan-Zam Railway*

As the worry grew, mostly from Tanzania' Julius Nyerere and Zambia's Kenneth Kaunda that a Portuguese and South African military retaliation on Tanzania, for sheltering liberation movements could not be discounted, building a railway line to connect the landlocked frontline state of Zambia with Tanzania became imperative. Making their countries more vulnerable was that these leaders had sought to preempt these "bad consequences of geography" by undertaking closer military cooperation with China and procuring more arms.[44]

In 1970 construction began on the Tanzania-Zambia (also known as TAZARA) railway, which was completed in 1975. The Agreement to build the Tan-Zam railway had been signed in Beijing between China, Zambia, and Tanzania. A 30-year $500 million interest-free loan was granted for what became a 1,160-mile railway. This initiative goes beyond socialist-capitalist duel of ideologies; it is China's attempt to defy what it came to see as the "new-imperialism" from the "two superpowers," the Soviet Union and the United States. Beyond this, American Afro-sinologist, Jamie Monson suggests, Beijing's investment in Africa "was part of a drive to be acknowledged as a world power."[45] As if to underscore the Sino-Soviet dispute going on at the time, some scholars have noted that China was reticent to highlight the economic benefits of TAZARA and often talked about the "need to combat imperialist forces" as the overarching reason for the project.[46]

For the other newly independent states throughout the continent, basking in the heady, enthusiasm of new independence, the "radical" tenor of China's anti-imperialism and continued revolutionary narrative became unpalatable. But for southern Africa, still embroiled in the liberation-independence struggle, the "racial line" could still find traction; therefore, TAZARA was a chance to showcase China's material "support for liberation through a 'just struggle' against white settler imperialism."[47] In addition to superpower duels and liberation struggle, Monson argues that another reason may have come to China during this project, one that would continue to this day: it is that China was coming to terms with the reality that "its lasting political influence in post-colonial Africa could come through development assistance, in particular from the positive example of China's own rural development experience."[48] China may have envisaged a time when it would need to harken to a material contribution to the liberation of this strategic region, and TAZARA offered such undeniable and tangible evidence that would serve as a monument to a primordial solidarity far beyond fleeting ideology

Interestingly, what Monson identifies as having formed the basis by which China engaged with southern Africa using TAZARA, the triplets of "development, ideology, and technological transfer," continue to be a clarion call for South African leaders today.[49] Although ideology has since dropped from the list—indeed the Chinese themselves often resist the African enthusiasm for replicating at home whatever they admire in China—these facets of China's interaction continue to elude southern African planners, as judged by the economic and industrial fate of the region in almost 50 years since the TAZARA's completion. Still, China's success, in mobilizing the rural poor, taking cognizance of agriculture as the production base, did become attractive further afield, even among Africans either still fighting for independence or newly independent states. It is easy to see how African countries, trying to re-acquaint themselves to their own socio-culture and effect a return to a semblance of "authenticity" for the sake of development, after years of colonial domination, became easily attracted to the Chinese position even as some were left with little hope for its actual realization.

By 1978, according to American Afro-sinologist, Deborah Brautigam, most of the *seventy-four* countries receiving aid from China were African.[50] Also, China surpassed the United States in the number of assistance programs it had in Africa.[51] Furthermore, the transition between Mao, who had died in 1976, to Hu Guofeng, and eventually to Deng Xiaopeng, precipitated a chain of events that led to economic "reform and opening up" that was the beginning point of the Chinese economic rise that saw it become second-largest economy decades later, in 2010.

## 1980–1998: TAIPEI AUTUMN, BEIJING SPRING

For Africa, the 1980s have been described as a "lost decade" where economies of many countries went from "bad to worse."[52] For China, Deng Xiaoping consolidated power and shifted the country's focus to economic development. The ideological polemics of the Mao era gave way to "pragmatism and the assertion of the economic over the political," making modernization the *"raison d'etre* of China's foreign policy, including in Africa."[53] Political stability as a prerequisite for development became "a, if not *the* major theme" of all policy advice to Africa.[54]

During a 1989 Beijing visit by Uganda leader, Yoweru Museveni, who had taken power three years earlier, Deng Xiaoping explained this essentialism by drawing parallels between African aspirations and Chinese ones in a global context:

> China was closed for a long time, which handicapped its economic develop-ment. . . . China has achieved status: people dare not look down upon us. Hegemonists and imperialists always bully the developing countries, including African countries, by interfering in their efforts to shake off control, develop their economies and obtain political independence. They do the same with China. . . . The biggest lesson we have learned is that we should not isolate our-selves from the rest of the world, lest we become ill-informed. While we were fast asleep, the worldwide technological revolution would be forging ahead.[55]

China remained mindful of the prospect, however overestimated at the time, of African countries expanding their capacity to determine the course of global events, even if this meant at the largely symbolic multilateral level such as the United Nations. But South Africa was still waging its libera-tion struggle, and any Chinese engagement, however ambitious, had for the entirety of the decade taken place within this constraining reality.

In 1982 Chinese premier, Zhao Zhiyang, while on a tour of Africa, met ANC leaders in Lusaka, resuming a long process of ANC-PRC reconciliation. A year later Oliver Tambo led an ANC delegation to Beijing where he sought and received pledges for arms. It had been eight years since a high-level ANC. Tambo left "convinced " that relations were deepening and "maximum support" was forthcoming, a hope buttressed by Chinese reassurances that aid would have come "sooner, if [he] had asked."[56] China was eager to lessen the strain of the Sino-Soviet split on its relations with a party which was by now the clear leader of the liberation movement.

A significant part of the role China played in South Africa's liberation struggle at this time was indirect. By 1970, Tanzania and Angola may have won their independent, but Namibia, Angola, Zimbabwe (then Rhodesia), and Mozambique were not free nations. The trickle-down benefits from these states for South Africa's ongoing liberation struggle cannot be overestimated. In Zambia, Chinese soft loans to the Kaunda government paid for hous-ing. In Mozambique, Chinese military advisors helped erstwhile ANC ally FRELIMO in its own war. The same was provided to Zimbabwe's ZANU fighters who like their South African counterparts varied their bases between Zambia, Mozambique and Tanzania. It is this era of fluid loyalties to which China, as the 1994 democratic dispensation beckoned, would harken in order to project a shared past of united struggle—its direct *and* indirect help therein—in order to deter incoming leaders from entertaining anticipated entreaties from Taipei. However, the results of this strategy were not soon forthcoming.

On March 10, 1980, a much-publicized visit by Taiwanese officials took place. Taiwanese leader Sun Yun-suan was greeted by apartheid Prime Minister P.W. Botha at the airport in Cape Town. During a visit which saw much cooperation, including in the nuclear energy sector, Sun was bestowed with the Order of Good Hope, apartheid South Africa's highest decoration for foreigners.[57] The two leaders spoke of a focus on the "communist threats to peace and security," singing the familiar tune of trying to "deter international communist threats," a rhetorical appeal to anti-Communist sensibilities of this Reagan era.[58]

However, the 1990s remained a mixed bag for Africa as far as Western attention was concerned. Whereas the Cold War had often dictated the extent to which the continent featured in the foreign policies of big powers, especially the United States, some changes had taken place. Together with the Berlin Wall, Soviet Communism fell and *perestroika* saw small states split from the Soviet Union, most of them joining NATO. On February 2, 1990, the last apartheid president of South Africa, FW de Klerk, announced the unbanning of all political parties and release of political prisoners, including Nelson Mandela. For its international rehabilitation to be complete, South Africa needed to act with the times and sort out its relations with the Soviet Union as well as China. In February 1992, two months after the dissolution of the Soviet Union, de Klerk and president of a reconstituted Russian Federation, Boris Yelstin, formalized relations between the two countries.

Some changes were beginning to take place with China too. Apartheid South Africa's foreign affairs minister, Pik Botha, paid a secret visit to Beijing in October 1991, with his counterpart, Qian Qichen, also paying a low-key visit to Pretoria on February 2, 1992.[59] If these events promised any rapprochement between Pretoria and Beijing, they failed to deliver and South Africa remained firmly in the Taiwan camp. Still, it did begin to dawn on Taipei that it had been on the wrong side of history, as evidenced by extensive efforts to court the ANC. The strategy was to use money. In August 1993, Nelson Mandela led an ANC delegation to Taiwan. Although Mandela refused the plea by Taiwan to set up ANC offices in Taipei, he requested— and later received—a total of $12 million toward the ANC's 1994 election campaign.[60]

On May 26, 1994, following a commanding ANC election victory, Taiwan's leader, Lee Teng-hui attended Mandela's inauguration. A raft of back-and-forth visits soon followed: foreign affairs minister, Alfred Nzo, visited Taipei in December 1994; deputy speaker of the parliament, Govan Mbeki, and defense minister, Joe Modise, in January 1995; public enterprises minister, Stella Sigcau, in February 1995; and arts and culture minister, Dr.

Ben Ngubane, in March 1995.[61] But try as South Africa did, it still could not ignore the feelings of its supporters at home and the expectations of its allies abroad who remained disappointed that a pro-Beijing switch had not taken place immediately upon the ANC's coming to power in 1994. In 1996 South Africa was one of only African countries that still formally recognized Taiwan.[62]

In the waltz of domestic give-and-take on which the country had embarked when it negotiated its transition toward democracy in 1994 and gained world-wide adulation as a result, South Africa had unwittingly danced itself into a corner in the realm of foreign policy regarding China. Mandela's government believed that its "almost unprecedented international prestige" would be enough to convince the PRC to "share" its relations with any country with what it considered its territory of Taiwan.[63] This optimism increasingly appeared to be misplaced, and nowhere was the divergence of views regarding the "two Chinas" more apparent than in the first democratic cabinet of the Government of National Unity (GNU) itself. Ministers of the same government openly voiced opposing views on the issue. Although by June 1996, the GNU had come to an end, it did not quiet former-apartheid cabinet members who continued to lobby for Taiwan from the opposition benches.

On March 24, 1996, foreign minister Alfred Nzo paid a visit to the PRC. He again argued for the "two China" policy.[64] The minister acknowledged that South Africa faced a dilemma between "enhancing [its] relations with the People's Republic of China while at the same time not jeopardizing existing friendly relations with the Republic of China on Taiwan."[65] Not only did South Africa still think it could successfully implement its "two Chinas" idea, its officials still spoke of a "Republic of China."

Also, this lack of cohesion was found within the ranks of the ANC's cabinet itself. Opposition politicians pointed out that the foreign affairs minister's efforts to establish relations with Beijing were contradicted by defense minister Joe Modise's assurances during a visit to Taiwan that Pretoria would "never sever ties."[66] Essentially, opponents of the switch cited four reasons for their opposition: first, Taiwan was still making a significant contribution to the development of the country; second, once Hong Kong returned to the PRC [in 1997] it was Taiwan that would become an "economic hub of the Far East;"[67] third, Taiwan's "isolation" was seen as a "remnant of the cold war era;"[68] and fourth, unlike the PRC, Taiwan had become a "full-fledged democracy."[69]

But proponents had their own reasons: first, the PRC was a permanent member of the UN Security Council; second, over 159 countries had already recognized the PRC; third, the PRC had already become the third-largest economy in the world in 1993; fourth, Hong Kong's impending to return to the PRC from Britain in 1997 made recognizing the PRC more necessary as it means a "less vulnerable" position for South Africa in its significant dealings with the island territory.[70]

Strikingly, whatever the reasons for recognizing the PRC, which ANC officials could ably articulate in parliament and on the media, a puzzling failure to translate these into a formal switch persisted. Indeed, South Africa and Taiwan had intensified their engagement. By 1994 South Africa-Taiwan trade stood at $1.4 billion, exceeding trade with Brazil, Russia, India, and the PRC combined, which stood at $1.3 billion. By 1996 Beijing's own trade with South Africa began a steady rise that would see it surpass Taiwan in 1999, while trade with Hong Kong began an almost identical decline.[71] Hong Kong hardly mattered in this regard, thanks to the inexorable reality that Beijing was to assume control over its territory in July 1997 anyway. More than any perception of China's growing stature in the world, Hong Kong therefore played a significant role in focusing the minds of the ANC government leaders.

If South Africa's intransigence seemed to defy the expectations of Beijing and some supporters, another event soon made matters worse, with China upping the ante by sending not-so-subtle messages. In April 1996, China's trade minister, while in South Africa for a United Nations Conference on Trade and Development summit, refused to participate unless a Taiwanese journalist was barred as per UN rules which do not formally accredit Taipei's "state" journalists at UN functions. Many saw this as a warning sign to South African policymakers themselves.[72] By August in 1996, the Chinese were still insisting on their position that what South Africa nonchalantly took as an issue of "two Chinas" was a critical matter on which there was "no room for maneuver . . . and no room for any compromise."[73] If South Africa had taken the hint, it barely showed.

On August 22, 1996, a beaming Mandela emerged from his official residence in Cape Town hand-in-hand with the Dalai Lama, much to the "ire" of the PRC.[74] To South Africans, this was not, on the face of it, a diplomatic problem. But to those well-versed in China's policy on Tibet, a platform as prominent as Mandela's being granted to someone who in the same meeting declared South Africa an encouragement for Tibet's "[own] non-violent freedom struggle," it was.[75] To "Beijingists," Mandela's bombastic naiveté did not constitute a self-determined stance but was an irresponsible move that would not put South Africa in good stead, and showed the old statesman was out of his depth on the issue.

The Taiwan-PRC debate had turned into an embarrassing international fiasco in which most in the West were participants but not decision-makers. Increasingly, South Africa was unwittingly entangling itself in a West-South global narrative concerning the PRC, and the longer Pretoria continued recognizing Taiwan, the longer the country was seen as a proxy in an anti-Beijing "resistance." However South Africa estimated things, any resistance was doomed considering the fact that every G7 member-country, indeed almost all Western economies had enjoyed more than two decades of formal relations with Beijing by 1996. While Western observers derided South Africa for leaning toward Beijing, and though some still maintained that a switch would not take place under Mandela's watch, there was an admission within the same circles that China "would win in the end."[76] Ultimately, South Africa sought an exemption other countries which had established formal relations with China had failed to receive: France in 1964; Japan in 1972; Kenya in 1963; Nigeria in 1971; Zimbabwe in 1980; and so forth. Riding high on a wave of the international admiration, South Africa sought to replicate on the global sphere the give-and-take "miracle" it had achieved at home, and fell short.

By September, China had announced a $18 billion investment in a "Dragon City" comprising more than 500 factories near the impoverished town of Potchefstroom.[77] This initiative, at the time "the biggest investment made by the Chinese anywhere in the world," would mean more than 500,000 much-needed jobs.[78] Coming less weeks after Taiwan Premier's visit and after Mandela declared his reticence to sever ties with Taiwan, not only did this further up the ante, but it also demonstrated a Chinese brand of diplomacy, one that is characterized by a shrewd willingness to help the other side save face and have a dignified albeit inevitable climb-down. Demonstrating centuries of experience in statecraft, China simply decreased South Africa's opportunity cost in switching from Taiwan.

In November 27, 1996, a visibly demur Mandela announced in a live television address that "a permanent continuation of diplomatic recognition of the Republic of China on Taiwan is inconsistent with South Africa's role in international affairs."[79] He spoke of his government's hope for a "smooth transition . . . within the next twelve months," although he still seemed to hold out hope for an outcome where South Africa would recognize the PRC "but continue to conduct constructive relations with Taiwan." At midnight on July 1, 1997, Hong Kong became a Special Administrative Region (SAR) of the PRC when the British returned its sovereignty. If South Africans pronouncements had thus far been ambiguous, when the PRC's foreign minister, Qian Qichen, met his South African counterpart, Alfred Nzo in Pretoria, six months later, the matter was put beyond doubt. On January 1, 1998, they signed a joint communiqué declaring that "the Government of the Republic of South Africa recognizes that there is but one China in the world, the Government of the People's Republic of China is the sole legal government representing the whole of China and recognizes China's position that Taiwan is an inalienable part of China."[80] Thus did South Africa formally establish diplomatic relations with the PRC.

## NOTES

1. R. G. Boyd, *Communist China's Foreign Policy* (New York: Praeger, 1962), 8.
2. Ibid., 9.
3. Brian Bunting, *Moses Kotane, South African Revolutionary* (London: Inkululeko Publishing, 1975), 278.
4. Nelson Mandela, *Long Walk to Freedom: The Autobiography of Nelson Mandela* (Boston: Little, Brown and Company, 1994), 160.
5. Elinor Sisulu, *Walter and Albertina Sisulu: In Our Lifetime* (Claremont, South Africa: David Phillip Publishers, 2002), 91.
6. Mandela, *Long Walk to Freedom*, 160.
7. "The Freedom Charter," *Wits Historical Papers*, accessed September 20, 2020, http://www.historicalpapers.wits.ac.za/inventories/inv_pdfo/AD1137/AD1137-Ea6-1-001-jpeg.pdf
8. Also present were representatives from Guinea, Uganda, Senegal, Northern Rhodesia (later Zambia), Jordan, and Kenya. The Africanist-communist schism culminated in the expulsion of Makiwane and other "Africanists" from the ANC in 1975 and, ultimately, his assassination in 1980.
9. Li Anshan, "African Studies in China: A Historiographical Survey," *African Studies Review* 48, no. 1 (April 2005): 62.
10. Ibid.
11. D. M. Moore, "The South African Air Force in Korea: An Assessment," *Military History Journal*, 6 no. 3 (June 1984): 88–94.
12. Ibid., 88.
13. Ibid., 92.
14. Thomas Bosrstelmann, *Apartheid's Reluctant Uncle: The United States and Southern Africa in the Early Cold War* (New York: Oxford University Press, 1993), 137, 185.
15. Alfred D. Low, *The Sino-Soviet Dispute: An Analysis of the Polemics* (Cranbury, NJ: Associated University Presses, 1976), 119.
16. Lulu Callinicos, *Oliver Tambo: Beyond the Engels Mountains* (Claremont, South Africa: David Phillip, 2004), 304.
17. Vladimir Shubin, *The Hot "Cold War."* (Scotsville, South Africa: University of Kwazulu-Natal Press, 2008), 243.
18. Ibid., 242.
19. Scott Thomas, *The Diplomacy of Liberation* (New York: Taurus Academic Studies, 1996), 161.
20. Ibid.
21. Ibid., 162.
22. Ibid.
23. Ronnie Kasrils, *Armed and Dangerous: My Undercover Struggle against Apartheid* (Oxford: Heinemann, 1993), 195.
24. Thomas, *The Diplomacy of Liberation*, 162.
25. Ibid., 164.
26. Ibid., 165–6.

27. Stephen Ellis and Tsepo Sechaba, *Comrades against Apartheid* (Bloomington, IN: Indiana University Press, 1992), 43.

28. George, T. Yu, *China and Tanzania: A Study in Cooperative Interaction* (Berkeley: Regents of the University of California, 1970), 86.

29. Editorial, "Africa Must Be Free!" *Renmin Ribao* (Beijing), April 15, 1961.

30. George T. Yu, *China's Africa Policy: A Study of Tanzania* (New York: Praeger Publishers, 1975), 152.

31. Ian Taylor, *The Forum on China-Africa Cooperation (FOCAC)* (New York: Routledge, 2011), 12–13.

32. Ellis and Sechaba, *Comrades against Apartheid*, 167.

33. Quoted in Shubin, *The Hot "Cold War,"* 128–29.

34. Ibid., 129.

35. Ibid.

36. Ibid., 60.

37. Ibid., 65.

38. Ellis and Sechaba, *Comrades against Apartheid*, 45.

39. Ibid.

40. Liang-Tsai Wei, *Peking versus Taipei in Africa: 1960–1978* (Taipei: Asia and World Institute, 1982), 385.

41. Quoted in Ibid., 383.

42. "African Countries' Support of China in History" *The Global Times*, April 14, 2020, https://www.globaltimes.cn/content/1185568.shtml

43. Ibid., 363.

44. Yu, *China and Tanzania*, 65.

45. Jamie Monson, *Africa's Freedom Railway* (Bloomington, IN: Indiana University Press, 2009), 3.

46. Ibid., 26.

47. Ibid., 27.

48. Ibid., 28.

49. Ibid., 149.

50. Deborah Brautigam, *The Dragon's Gift: The Real Story of China in Africa* (New York: Oxford University Press, 2009), 42.

51. Ibid.

52. Zhu Zhongui, "Political Changes in Africa," *Contemporary International Relations* 3, no. 2 (1993): 14.

53. Ian Taylor, *The Forum on China-Africa Cooperation (FOCAC)* (New York: Routledge, 2012), 17.

54. Ibid.

55. Deng Xiaoping, "Maintain the Tradition of Hard Struggle," excerpt from a talk with President Yoweri Museveni of the Republic of Uganda on March 23, 1989, accessed September 23, 2020, https://dengxiaopingworks.wordpress.com/2013/03/18/maintain-the-tradition-of-hard-struggle/

56. "Interview with Oliver Tambo," *Noticias* (Maputo), August 5, 1983.

57. Ironically, Nelson Mandela later awarded the same decoration PRC president, Jiang Zemin, when the former paid a state visit to Beijing in May 1999.

58. "Premier Sun Visits Four African Countries," *Taiwan Review*, May 1, 1980.

59. Roger Pfister, *Apartheid South Africa and African States: From Pariah to Middle Power, 1961–1994* (New York: Tauris Academic Studies, 2005), 139.

60. "Nelson Mandela in My Eyes," *Beijing Review*, December 19, 2013; Hansard of the National Assembly of the Republic of South Africa, vol. 11 (1996), col. 3196.

61. Ministry of Foreign Affairs, *The Republic of China Yearbook* (Taipei: Government Information Office, 1996), 136.

62. Ibid., 176.

63. Hansard of the National Assembly of the Republic of South Africa, vol. 11 (1996), col. 3181.

64. Hansard of the National Assembly of the Republic of South Africa, vol. 11 (1996), col. 3163.

65. Ibid., 752.

66. Ibid., 3178.

67. Ibid., 3179.

68. Ibid. 3179.

69. Ibid. 3179.

70. Hansard of the National Assembly of the Republic of South Africa, vol. 11 (1996), col. 391.

71. Department of Trade and Industry of the Republic of South Africa, "Trade Reports," http://tradestats.thedti.gov.za/ReportFolders/reportFolders.aspx?sCS_referer=&sCS_ChosenLang=en (accessed September 4, 2020).

72. "Outcry Over Foreign Reporter's Treatment," *Mail and Guardian*, May 1, 1996.

73. Tan Tarn How, "Taiwan Under Attack for Muscling in on the World Scene," *The Strait Times* (Singapore), August 28, 1996.

74. "Dalai Lama Visits Tutu and Mandela," *Hobart Mercury* (Australia), August 23, 1996.

75. "Hello Dalai Lama," *San Jose Mercury*, August 20, 1996.

76. "Hallo, China—or is it Taiwan?" *The Economist*, September 14, 1996.

77. R. W. Johnson, "China Offers £11bn Investment," *The Times*, September 3, 1996.

78. Ibid.

79. Office of the President of the Republic of South Africa, "Statement by President Nelson Mandela on South Africa's Relations with the Greater China Region," South African Government Information, http://goo.gl/zlfx3S (accessed August 21, 2020).

80. Ministry of Foreign Affairs of the People's Republic of China, "Joint Communiqué Between the Government of the People's Republic of China and the Government of the Republic of South Africa on the Establishment of Diplomatic Relations," http://www.fmprc.gov.cn/mfa_eng/wjdt_665385/2649_665393/t15813.shtml (accessed August 21, 2015).

# Chapter 3

# South Africa, China, and the African "De-naissance"

For over a decade since African economies waded the storm of the 2007–2008 financial crisis, certain assumptions concerning the state's role in the economy have continued to come under serious debate, as has the role played by countries of the global South in the governance of the international systems which determines many economic—hence developmental—outcomes. At the center of this debate are prominent developing economies, including China and South Africa. This chapter looks at South Africa-China relations on this multilateral front in order to explore the role they have played in raising the profile of "South-South" platforms such as the Forum for China-Africa Cooperation (FOCAC) and factors that have transformed them to be the go-to platform at the expense of others like the New Partnership for Africa's Development (NEPAD).

## CHINA IN THE GLOBAL AND AFRICAN POLITICAL-ECONOMIC SPACE

Between December 13, 1963, and February 5, 1964, Chinese Premier Chou En-Lai, in the first trip to Africa by a high-ranking Chinese official, began a tour that took him to Egypt, Algeria, Morocco, Tunisia, Ghana, Mali, Guinea, Sudan, Ethiopia and Somalia. At the time, a Ghanaian law student in London represented a significant body of opinion in some African quarters when he wrote:

We in Africa want rapid advancement in order to catch up with the developed countries, preserve our dignity and prove to the outside world that Africa is rich and capable of doing what Europe or America has done. But as our development must be rapid, it would be sheer folly to follow a country which itself is not half-way through the advancement on which we have always set our eyes; so whether we like it or not, we have more to learn from our past masters, especially industrially, for in this field China has very little to offer.[1]

The comment was about a qualitatively different China than that of the twenty-first century, which by 2020 had already made notable achievements like the following: surpassed the United States to become the world's largest goods trader;[2] surpassed the United States as the largest trading partner for Africa and the EU;[3] taken the place of Japan as the second-largest economy in the world;[4] exceeded $10,000 in its per capita GDP;[5] and overtook most of the developed countries as the third-largest food donor, over half of which went to sub-Saharan Africa.[6]

The Ghanaian student's sentiments, however, demonstrate a debate that continues to rage more than 50 years later. It is about China's utility as a partner in the achievement of a development that has largely eluded much of post-independence Africa, including a vast segment of post-apartheid South Africa. It also symbolizes the West-East divide when it comes to developmental modus operandi and policies that continue to contend for Africa's attention.

On the Chinese side, this changing dynamic may be traced back to the "reform and opening up" of Deng Xiaoping in 1979. Regarding China's developmental direction for the proceeding decades, he noted that "of course we do not want capitalism, but neither do we want to be poor under socialism."[7] Having set itself upon a path to development through increased growth and expanded industrialization, almost two decades since China's economic reforms began, China's economy began to change dramatically, and it had become a matter of time before its political standing began to correspond to its economic standing. This reality was not lost on post-apartheid South African leaders and played a decisive role in the latter's foreign policy decisions, beginning with the issue of Taiwan. Beyond bilateral issue, China's rise has culminated in the country becoming another player in the globally contested space of development ideas.

When South Africa established formal relations with the PRC on January 1, 1998, recognizing "but one China in the world," a shift was taking place.[8] The ideas space regarding global economic governance and development, and South Africa's place therein, had decidedly been transformed from the Washington-Moscow dichotomy that had dominated the second half of the twentieth century and ended with the dissolution of the Soviet Union in 1989. Turning first into a "Washington Consensus," it would, however, at the turn of the second millennium, begin another transformation. Owing to what was by then a development success story coming out of China, where millions of people were being lifted out of poverty with rapid speed, the contested ideas space transformed into what some have seen as a Washington-Beijing rivalry for developmental consensus.[9] Others, however, have located this beyond one country, argue that a "new Asian hemisphere" has emerged, that is a period that heralds a diminution of the "Western domination of world history," accompanied by an "enormous renaissance of Asian societies" in general.[10] One area worth considering as an illustration of this changing dynamic is education.

> From 1983 to 2003, students from Asian countries (China, Taiwan, India, and South Korea) earned more than 50 percent of the US Science Engineering doctoral degrees awarded to foreign students—89,700 of 176,000, almost four times more than the students from Europe. Chinese students received more than 35,300 Science and Engineering degrees from US universities. . . . India students earned more than 17,500.[11]

The change in the global situation, while not exclusively in favor of China, was however manifested through China more than other countries, more so because of Beijing's heavy involvement on the African continent by the turn of the second millennium. If this dynamic of China's developmental change and growth had been slow to manifest itself in South Africa, China's forays in the rest of the continent had made it clear, at least, that it was impending. In the year formal relations between China and South Africa were established, the Chinese economy grew by 7 percent, while the South African economy shrank at −1.1 percent.[12] By 2019, South Africa's economy had shrunk by the same percentage (−1.1 percent) while China had achieved 5.6 percent growth. Since relations began between the two, 4.3 percent is the most South Africa's economy has grown, in 2006, while China reached 13.6 percent in 2009.[13]

This rapid growth in the Chinese economy, which never fell below 5.5 percent between 1998 and 2019, is more significant when viewed in contrast to not only South Africa but the Southern African Development Community (SADC) region (from −0.8 in 1998 to −1.6 in 2019); the rest of the African continent (from 0.5 in 1998 to 0.6 in 2019); middle-income economies comparable to South Africa (from 0 in 1998 to 0.4 in 2019), as well as the world average (from 1.5 in 1998 to 1.4 in 2019).[14] In this period, notably, not only did South Africa's economic growth pale to that of China but Pretoria' economy shrank more in a manner consistent with the southern African region—not its "peer" middle-income economies. Indeed middle-income developing economies grew by 3 percent in 2019, further demonstrating how South Africa's lack of growth is a departure from what is expected of the country as a middle-income developing economy.[15]

So it was against this backdrop of South African stagnation against pressing developmental imperatives at home that the country and China established relations at a time when the economic outcomes of Deng's reforms were beginning not only to be apparent but also to have a measurable impact internationally. In 1998 the Chinese economy was still ranked seventh in size (behind the United States, Japan, Germany, France, Italy, and the United Kingdom) at just over $1 trillion;[16] the Chinese economy was smaller than that of the state of California.[17]

As South Africa-China relations grew they had to contend with narrative that saw China's relations with African countries, including South Africa, purely as a function of China's competition for natural resources and Beijing's search for political status. This quest, enabled by Africa's desperation for sustainable development, was seen as driven by the latter's alienation from what is perceived as Western indifference. Many observers—particularly in the West, some in Africa itself—have wondered if China would be a responsible state, given the amount of market access and increasing political clout it began to acquire on the continent. But this emphasis on practicality, Chinese scholars have argued, negates an "important element in Sino-African relations: that the development of the relationship over the past 50 years has been based on equal treatment, respect for sovereignty and common development."[18] Africans have also put forward a similar view, influenced by the fact that Africa's economic lot—at the hands of mainly Western principals—has not improved since independence, notwithstanding her enormous natural resource endowment.

Although China's relations with South Africa's relations are much newer than with most other African countries, they have not only accelerated at a faster pace but, owing to the country's advanced infrastructure and economic standing, but also become central to China's African relations as a whole.[19] Therefore, China's engagement with South Africa from the earliest period may be viewed as directly linked to the changing dynamics of China's raison d'etre, in its search for a status commensurate to its economic growth and rise, and the African search for dignified development, something which Thabo Mbeki's South Africa sought to champion.

## Mbeki and the Quest for an African Renaissance

By the time Thabo Mbeki was inaugurated president on June 14, 1999, the reality of a unipolar world had also set in, as had its comprehensive effects on policy at a multilateral and national level. An environment was formed which was characterized by what economist Wilfred David calls "global development antinomy," where "hierarchically structured and vertically integrated" global systems congealed to produce a paradoxical "systemic conflict at the global, national, and local levels."[20] This affected not only South Africa but also the rest of the continent. Instead of an envisaged increase in investment in South Africa, foreign direct investment (FDI) saw a decline, in what seemed to have been a collective Western disengagement from Africa.

In 1997 FDI into South Africa stood at $3.8 billion, more than double that of Nigeria, which was $1.6 billion.[21] However, by the following year, South Africa's FDI had dropped to $561 million, and Nigeria's to $1.2 billion.[22] For the rest of sub-Saharan Africa, FDI decreased from $2.8 to $5.2 billion in the same period.[23] When put in a global context, a more accurate picture emerges of the extent of the decline in investment in Africa which, according to some African scholars, "exacerbated" the region's "marginalization."[24] In 1998 the FDI into Brazil alone stood at $28 billion, more than quadruple the combined FDI into entire sub-Saharan Africa ($5 billion), South Africa ($561 million) and Nigeria ($1.2 billion),[25] and Nigeria ($1.2 billion) put together. Notably, in 1998, FDI into China stood at $44 billion, putting the country second only to the United States as a recipient of foreign direct investment.[26] As China's economic standing in the world was improving, Africa's prospects for economic development were weakening.

In this context, Mbeki declared a need for an African renaissance to "depart from a centuries-old past which sought to perpetuate the notion of an Africa condemned to remain a curiosity slowly grinding to a halt on the periphery of the world."[27] According to this perspective, a constraining structural condition existed in the global systems of economic governance and cooperation, which deprived "smaller countries" of the world "a proper place in the decision-making processes of these institutions which take decisions which have a universal impact."[28]

This prescription was followed by a South African commitment to assuming a central role in building structural mechanisms that would contribute to the continent assuming a global role commensurate with its central geographic standing. As he puts it in a speech at the prestigious Tshingua University on December 11, 2001, Mbeki saw this as possible only through united cooperation with China.

> [T]he countries of the North are mainly rich, developed and prosperous while those of the South are poor and underdeveloped. . . . Together with China, we are commonly defined by our situation as belonging to the South. This very circumstance suggests that we have every reason to act together to change our conditions for the better.[29]

This South African view is consistent with neostructuralist perspective, which holds that challenges to countries' developmental progress are "not to be found primarily in policy-induced distortions in relative prices" but are "rooted in endogenous structural factors."[30] The assumption is that decision-making elites are able to effect structural change or attempt an improvement in undesirable conditions. But the extent to which they will be able to do so given that they are willing depends upon the amount of agency space sufficient to make decisions of that nature.

For its own strategic ends, then, South Africa sought to be placed at the center of crafting a narrative for African engagement with the global structures of governance under a collective identity and objectives. This perspective was buttressed by the notion of South Africa not being immune to the deleterious effects of bad governance on the continent—"if something goes wrong in South Africa, people further afield do not say; 'Something has gone wrong in South Africa;' they say, 'Something has gone wrong in Africa.'"[31] A need existed for South Africa to assume leadership in crafting a progressive position for Africa's own relations with itself and the world. In the face of changes since the 1990s, where the West had been seen to turn away from Africa, yet still managed to exert significant and constraining influence on African countries through conditionalities and structural adjustment programs, China seemed poised to fill a void and play an enabling role in this objective of finding alternatives for (South) African development partners and models.

## SOUTH AFRICA IN FOCAC: A RETICENT PARTICIPANT

From May 8 to 22, 1996, Chinese president Jiang Zemin undertook a tour of Africa which included stops in Kenya, Egypt, Ethiopia, Mali, Namibia and Zimbabwe. Notably, Jiang excluded South Africa because the latter still recognized Taiwan, which made relations with the PRC impossible.[32] Giving a keynote speech at the Organization for African Unity (OAU) headquarters in Addis Ababa, Jiang outlined China's policy on Africa. It included the following: (1) sincere friendship, (2) equality and sovereignty, (3) common development on the basis of mutual benefit, (4) increased consultation and cooperation in international affairs, and (5) cooperation in the establishment of a new international political and economic order.[33] Although this was China's policy for its relations with the entire continent, it remains "moot" regarding South Africa, as formal relations still did not exist between the two.

Four years later, however, on April 25, 2000, President Jiang Zemin visited South Africa, two years after formal relations. The times were not only different but global dynamics had also changed, necessitating, Jiang and Mbeki believed, closer cooperation on a multilateral level. To that end, China and South Africa signed the Pretoria Declaration and formalized their relations as a "Partnership." The declaration referred to a "new order," among other outcomes a united approach would bring about. The two countries pledged to

> support each other in efforts to create a new international political and economic order. The two sides maintain that in this future New Order, the diversity of the world should be respected; the principles of sovereign equality and non-inter-ference in the internal affairs of other countries should be upheld; no country should dominate others; the negative effects of globalization—especially on developing nations—should be reduced and restricted.[34]

The signing of the Pretoria Declaration was important for two reasons. First, it demonstrated a shared perspective between Mbeki and Jiang, of a need for structural reform at the international level, making the cooperation with South Africa more than bilateral but multilateral as well. Secondly, it completed a process of close cooperation, which China by this time enjoyed with a major-ity of African countries, but not with South Africa. Absent this cooperation, at a comprehensive and advanced level, China's continued cooperation with the rest of the African continent at an advanced level as well as South Africa's dream of an African renaissance to integrate Africa into the global structures of governance remained mutually exclusive.

South Africa also established a Bi-National Commission with China, mak-ing it one of the very few countries to do so.[35] This meant that frequent, high-level exchanges and visits could take place—and they did. Within one year, reciprocal visits by speakers of respective assemblies, Secretary-generals of the ruling parties, among others, had taken place. More than visits, the Pretoria Declaration opened the way for the formation of a structural organ of cooperation between China and the whole continent, which had hitherto remained in limbo, held up by the slow evolution of China's relations with Africa's most economically important country that South Africa was seen by the Chinese to be.[36] This organ is the FOCAC.

## Origins of FOCAC

On November 4, 2006, when President Hu Jintao welcomed over 40 African heads-of-state to the Beijing Summit of FOCAC, it was the first time that this organ of China-Africa cooperation gained widespread international attention. Some saw this, the "the largest ever such meeting in China," as part of a grand Chinese strategy "designed to add more political ballast to the growing economic partnership" with African countries.[37] More saw it as having two more purposes: an official one, to "expand trade, to allow China to secure the oil and ore it needs for its booming economy, and to offer aid to help African nations improve roads, railways and schools;" and an unofficial one, to "redraw the world's strategic map, forming tighter political ties between China . . . and a continent whose leaders often complain of being neglected by the United States and Europe."[38] Thus the narrative of a "grand Chinese design" for Africa took shape.

However, Chinese scholars dispute this. First, they point to the fact that the Beijing Summit was not the beginning but the culmination of a multilateral initiative that had which already existed. Indeed, FOCAC's first ministerial meeting was on October 12–14, 2000. Some Africans pointed out that FOCAC simply followed the example of other high-level engagements other countries had by this time undertaken with African countries: the 3rd Tokyo International Conference on African Development (TICAD) in 2003; and the 22nd France-Africa Summit in 2003; the 1st Africa-EU Summit in 2000; among others.

What is evident is that following the Beijing Summit, a flurry of summits involving other countries and regions soon followed. Within two years of the Beijing Summit, France, the EU, India, Japan, and Turkey also held high-level summits with African heads-of-state. Most of these were either held the first time or had not held a heads-of-state summit with Africa for a number of years. The EU had last held such a summit in 2000.[40] FOCAC, therefore, may be seen as pivotal not only in establishing a multilateral structure where Africa's relations with China may be pursued with an approach but it is an indirect catalyst to an unprecedented global "turn" toward Africa and the resulting cooperation on other direct multilateral structures. The Beijing summit would not have been as significant, if at all possible, without the improvement of South Africa-China relations first, as well as the "Partnership" in the Pretoria Declaration. The successful outcomes from this epochal summit and others that followed, put paid to the declaration's claims of seeking to create a "new order."

## Is FOCAC a Chinese or African Idea?

However divergent the views have been on Chinese intentions regarding FOCAC, Chinese scholars point out that contrary to the narrative of a Chinese-initiated body, FOCAC was the brainchild of African countries themselves. These were countries that wanted to formalize relations with China from "one to multi-partnership."[41] In March 1996, a Zimbabwean official who had been ambassador to China returned home and was promoted to head the Department of African Affairs of his nation's Ministry of Foreign Affairs. After a visit to Guinea, Togo, Benin, and Côte d'Ivoire, he "realized the importance of Africa on the international political and economic stage and the urgency of reinforcing" relations between Africa and China.[42]

**Table 3.1  High-level FOCAC Summits Compared to Those Convened by Other Countries, 2000–2020**

| Date | Summit | Convener | Venue |
|---|---|---|---|
| October 12–14, 2000 | *1st Ministerial Conference of FOCAC* | *China* | *Beijing, China* |
| December 15–16, 2003 | *2nd Ministerial Conference of FOCAC* | *China* | *Addis Ababa* |
| December 3–4, 2005 | 23rd Africa-France Summit | France | Bamako, Mali |
| November 4–5, 2006 | *1st FOCAC Summit & 3rd Ministerial Conference* | *China* | *Beijing, China* |
| February 15–16, 2007 | 24th Africa-France Summit | France | Cannes, France |
| December 8–9, 2007 | 2nd Africa-EU Summit | EU | Lisbon, Portugal |
| April 8–9, 2008 | 1st India-Africa Forum Summit | India | New Delhi, India |
| May 28–30, 2008 | 4th Tokyo International Conference on African Development | Japan | Yokohama, Japan |
| August 18–20, 2008 | 1st Turkey-Africa Cooperation Summit | Turkey | Istanbul, Turkey |
| November 8–9, 2009 | 4th Ministerial Conference of FOCAC | China | Sharm el-Sheikh, Egypt |
| September 14–15, 2010 | Iran-Africa Summit | Iran | Tehran |
| November 29–30, 2010 | 3rd Africa-EU summit | EU | Tripoli, Libya |
| May 24–25, 2011 | 2nd India-Africa Forum Summit | India | Addis Ababa, Ethiopia |
| May 31–June 1, 2010 | 25th Africa-France Summit | France | Nice, France |
| *July 19–20, 2012* | *5th Ministerial Conference of FOCAC* | *China* | *Beijing, China* |
| June, 1–3, 2013 | 5th Tokyo International Conference on African Development | Japan | Yokohama, Japan |
| April 2–3, 2014 | 4th EU-Africa Summit | EU | Brussels, Belgium |
| August 4–6, 2014 | US-Africa Leaders' Summit | United States | Washington, United States |
| November 19–21, 2014 | 2nd Turkey-Africa Partnership Summit | Turkey | Malabo, Equatorial Guinea |
| October 26–29, 2015 | 3rd India-Africa Forum Summit | India | New Delhi, India |
| *December 4–5, 2015* | *2nd FOCAC Summit & 6th Ministerial Conference* | *China* | *Johannesburg, South Africa* |
| November 29–30, 2017 | 5th EU-Africa Summit | EU | Abidjan, Côte d'Ivoire |

*(Continued)*

**Table 3.1  High-level FOCAC Summits Compared to Those Convened by Other Countries, 2000–2020** (*Continued*)

| Date | Summit | Convener | Venue |
|---|---|---|---|
| *September 3–4, 2018* | *3rd FOCAC Summit & 7th Ministerial Conference* | *China* | *Beijing, China* |
| October 23–24, 2019 | 1st Russia-Africa Summit | Russia | Sochi, Russia |
| January 20, 2020 | 1st UK-Africa Investment Summit | United Kingdom | London, United Kingdom |

*Note*: FOCAC Summits are italicized.
*Source*: FOCAC, BBC, African Union, Ministry of Foreign Affairs of Japan Ministry of Foreign Affairs of Turkey, Middle East Institute, and the Foreign Office of the United Kingdom.[39]

It was not until 1999, however, that the idea received a favorable Chinese hearing. In that year, Malagasy minister of Foreign Affairs, Lila Ratsifandrihama, visited China where she pressed the Chinese officials for a broader organ of cooperation with the continent.[43] She stated that "since the bilateral relations between China and African countries are strong and considered to be in such good condition as both sides continue to cooperate in many areas, why not consider establishing a multilateral forum?"[44] The following year, seven months after China and South Africa signed the Pretoria Declaration upgrading their relations from simple diplomatic relations to a "Partnership," the first Ministerial Conference of FOCAC, comprising 44 African countries and 17 organizations, met in Beijing and produced the Beijing Declaration of FOCAC that formally established the body.[45]

## NEPAD and FOCAC—Competing or Complimentary Approaches?

On the eve of Thabo Mbeki's attendance at the FOCAC Summit in Beijing, the South African government declared that it viewed China as being among

> countries in the Southern Hemisphere [which] share many of the same social and developmental challenges, including those induced by globalization and historic inequity. The interdependent global order with a multipolar dimension means that like-minded countries have to form alliances on common issues. . . . In this regard, China represents an enormous opportunity for South Africa and Africa, but at the same time poses certain challenges.[46]

The South African government was, however, unable at this time to articulate the exact nature and manifestation of any challenges it saw coming from its accelerated rate of engagement with China. This South African ambiguity, unwittingly perhaps, left room for the explanatory gap to be filled by a more skeptical segment of the China-Africa debate.

Mbeki participated in the Beijing FOCAC summit. Although relations between the two countries were initially "privileged around trade," South Africa's participation in the Summit, in addition to the Pretoria Declaration showed that they had also taken a comprehensive outlook, which encompassed other forms of structural change that itself would make trade easier.[47] However, Mbeki's African renaissance dream still meant that the material and intellectual wherewithal for the renewal of Africa was expected to take place from within Africa, using African ideas. Ultimately, this meant that FOCAC would have to compete with Africa's own nascent plan: the NEPAD.

Whether Mbeki perceived that in order for NEPAD to succeed, FOCAC had to take a back sit, or was voicing a popular descent on China's accelerated engagement with the continent, together with the increased trade deficit relations were causing, is not clear. Mbeki's generally lukewarm take on closer China-Africa cooperation not only continued in speeches but it also was noticed by Beijing. In December 2006, less than a month after the Beijing Summit, Mbeki addressing a group of South African students, warned that

> the potential danger in the relationship between Africa and China is that it is possible to build . . . an unequal relationship, the kind that has developed between African countries as colonies—including this one—and the colonial powers. . . . In terms of this the African continent exported more material and imported goods, condemning it to underdevelopment, being only a supplier of raw materials . . . I'm saying this is a potential danger in terms of the relationship that could be constructed between China and the African continent.[48]

What was clear also was that the Chinese felt stung by this sentiment, hitherto attributed to opposition figure within the continent as well as Western governments considered rivals of Beijing in for Africa's attention.

In February, Chinese president Hu Jintao visited South Africa and made a speech seen as an attempt to allay South African, and by extension greater African fears regarding China.

> For more than one hundred years in China's modern history, the Chinese people were subjected to colonial aggression and oppression by foreign powers and went through similar suffering and agony that the majority of African countries endured. . . . Because of the sufferings they experienced . . . the Chinese people are most strongly opposed to colonialism, oppression, and slavery of all manifestations. . . . China has never imposed its will or unequal practices on other

countries and will never do so in the future. It will certainly not do anything harmful to the interests of Africa and its people. China respects the political systems and paths to development independently adopted and pursued by the African people that suit their national conditions.[49]

The Chinese reaction was markedly specific and categorical. Hu sought tried a tactic which Beijing had also used during Cold War schisms in Africa—to place the country squarely at the center of a global South that has suffered from outside domination and as a result would not itself effect it on others, and, most importantly, seeks to join with the developing world for a united strategic partnership.

If anything, Mbeki may have sought to tactically project a reticence to engage too deeply with China in a manner that compromises South Africa's own agency. By so doing, perhaps he sought to demonstrate a feeling that South Africa was being "crowded" by yet another power at a time seen as opportune for South Africa's own outward forays into the continent. Therefore, a multilateral cooperation body, which seemed to favor South Africa's intentions, and Pretoria's own strategic designs for the continent, rather than one that was China-based.

NEPAD was founded by South Africa, Nigeria, Algeria, Egypt, and Senegal in 2001, as an amalgamation of two already-existing regional frameworks: the Mbeki-led Millennium Africa Recovery Plan unveiled at the World Economic Forum in Davos in January 2001, and the Omega Plan unveiled at the Summit for Francophone African Leaders in Cameroon led by Senegalese President Abdoulaye Wade, also in January 2001. The plan was ratified by the OAU in 2002, promising to provide "unique opportunities for African countries to take full control of their development agenda, to work more closely together, and to cooperate more effectively with international partners."[50] Under the auspices of NEPAD, Mbeki spearheaded what he hoped would be an African economic and developmental revival endogenously driven.

However ambitious NEPAD was, its criticism within the continent followed three tracks. The first was consensus. Beyond platitudes of support, African countries were loathe to participate in what seemed like a déjà vu scenario of "charity-led, or borrowing-led" development initiatives which NEPAD was seen as ultimately constituting.[51] Secondly, NEPAD was criticized as being based on Western outlooks on economic development that was premised on targeting growth and aid. While its claim to be "recognized as Africa's development plan by all the governments of the North, and the international financial institutions, and by many international governance institutions," may have seemed like a compliment for the body, it also became a source of criticism in an epoch where financial institutions dominated by the North had come under heavy criticism.[52]

Some cited as problematic the very fact that primary frameworks that would come to make up the structure of NEPAD were first introduced in Western-dominated forums such as at the World Economic Forum at Davos and that NEPAD leaders were eager to "partner" with leaders of the North, such as attending G8 meeting as "guests." Such moves had weakened continental confidence in the program's autonomy and agency. To the consternation of African critics, Mbeki and Wade's eagerness to discuss NEPAD with the West "before African governments had had a chance to discuss it among themselves with their own people," accelerated this line of criticism, which became public at times.[53]

In 2003, Gambian leader, Yahya Jammeh, averred "people are sick and tired of African beggars. Nobody will ever develop your country for you. I am not criticizing NEPAD but the way it was conceived to be dependent on begging."[54] While the time seemed ripe, then, for a program as NEPAD, in the estimation of South Africa and its allies, its feasibility remained challenged within Africa itself. Thus did a narrative emerge of NEPAD as essentially being a neoliberal project under the guise of a continental partnership, driven by South Africa. In a continent where memories of South Africa's apartheid-era infractions on general goodwill still existed, these accusations, demonstrating a weariness toward "big country" domination, were difficult to deflect or ignore.

In the lead-up to the Beijing Summit the Chinese government released its "Policy Paper on Africa" in January 2006. If NEPAD was seen as being short on details, Western-centric, and too reliant on Western partnerships, FOCAC not only filled a gap in these areas but it also promised the opposite. The policy paper was specific about cooperation on the basis of mutual enhancement of global profiles between China and African countries through seven specific areas; the policy placed emphasis on Africans finding their own solutions to their problems, and these solutions would not only be through aid but through trade and multisector exchanges including people-to-people exchanges.[55]

The success of FOCAC, the Beijing Summit of 2006, as well as the specifics of the Chinese Policy Paper on Africa, put alternative programs, including FOCAC, on the defensive. South Africa, as a leader of the initiative, seemingly had a choice to make. The critique of China associated with the Mbeki period was seen as continuing the vein of misplaced and disingenuous fears of China. Critiques charged that Western countries themselves had expanded their dealings, particularly trade, with China in as unprecedented a fashion as the Africans.

With China's stated policy as the foreground, and the specificity of FOCAC initiatives, a sentiment arose that saw any opposition to FOCAC as an attempt to keep African countries beholden to Western trade agreements which had benefited African countries less. Contrasted with what Africans see as a respectful, humble, unassuming, and culturally relativist attitude of the Chinese, it is easy to see how the Africans found engagement with China mutually beneficial.

When the FOCAC Beijing Summit took place, therefore, on November 5, 2006, according to Nigerian scholar Olayiwola Abegunrin, it served as a "pointer of several Sino-African dynamics": aid to Africa was doubled; a "strategic partnership" for international cooperation was established; the China-Africa Development Fund was established with $5 billion in starting cash; African exports to China were opened up by increase from 190 to 400 of the number of goods receiving preferential treatment; and "pledges were made for 30 hospitals, 30 malaria treatment centers, and 100 rural schools in African countries," among other things.[56] This summit may be seen as the climax of a newer, up-to-date Chinese foray into Africa manifesting itself, one which NEPAD could not conceivably have been expected to pip.

By continuing its indifference to China, therefore, it became increasingly clear to South Africa that the country risked alienating the rest of the region, which had long embraced the idea of China as a partner in development, not an alternate. Also, South Africa risked putting at risk its own developmental aspirations, which a better partnership with China would assist. The benefits of closer relations with China, however, soon became clear following the 2007/2008 recession, and by then there would be a new leader in Pretoria. The next chapter looks at how a confluence of events made closer relations almost inevitable between the two countries, and how the extent to which these constituted a further change in the global dynamic.

## NOTES

1. William Anti-Taylor, "China through African Eyes," *Race & Class* 5, no. 4 (1964): 51.

2. Jamil Anderlini and Lucy Hornby, "China Overtakes US as World's Largest Goods Trader," *Financial Times*, January 10, 2014.

3. "Africa's New Number One," *The Economist*, April 12, 2014; "China is Now EU's Biggest Trading Partner; Overtakes US," *The Star*, accessed October 6, 2020, https://www.thestar.com.my/aseanplus/aseanplus-news/2020/10/05/china-is-now-eu039s-biggest-trading-partner-overtakes-us.

4. R. A., "Second in Line," *The Economist*, August 11, 2010.

5. Frank Tang, "China Set to Break Key Economic Barrier Despite Trade War," *South China Morning Post*, January 1, 2020.

6. World Food Program, "China Emerges as World's Third Largest Food Aid Donor," July 20, 2006, accessed September 16, 2020, http://www.wfp.org/node/534.

7. Deng Xiaoping, "We Can Develop Market Economy under Socialism," *The Selected Works of Deng Xiaoping*, accessed September 16, 2020, https://goo.gl /4TXjSC.

8. Ministry of Foreign Affairs of the People's Republic of China, "Joint Communiqué Between the Government of the People's Republic of China and the Government of the Republic of South Africa on the Establishment of Diplomatic Relations," accessed September 16, 2020, http://www.fmprc.gov.cn/mfa_eng/wjdt _665385/2649_665393/t15813.shtml.

9. Meine Peiter van Dijk, "Introduction: Objectives of and Instruments for China's New Presence in Africa," in *New Presence of China in Africa*, ed. Meine Peiter van Dijk (Amsterdam: University Press, 2010).

10. Kishore Mahbubani, *The New Asian Hemisphere: The Irresistible Shift of Global Power to the East* (New York: Public Affairs Book, 2008), 9.

11. Ibid., 65.

12. UNCTAD, "Output and Income," accessed June 2, 2020, https://unctadstat.u nctad.org/wds/ReportFolders/reportFolders.aspx?sCS_ChosenLang=en.

13. Ibid.

14. Ibid.

15. Ibid.

16. Office of the Legislative Analyst of the State of California, "California's Economy," accessed September 16, 2015, http://goo.gl/NJEXnh.

17. Ibid.

18. Li Anshan, "China and Africa: Policy and Challenges," *China Security* 3, no. 3 (Summer 2007): 69.

19. Chinese scholar, interview by author, Jinhua, September 16, 2014.

20. Wilfred David, *The Humanitarian Development Paradigm: A Search for Global Justice* (Lenham, MD: The University Press of America), 100.

21. UNCTAD, "Foreign Direct Investment," accessed June 2, 2020, https://un ctadstat.unctad.org/wds/ReportFolders/reportFolders.aspx?sCS_ChosenLang=en.

22. Ibid.

23. Ibid.

24. Felix M. Edoho, "Globalization and the Marginalization of Africa: Contextualization of Africa-China Relations," *Africa Today* 58, no. 1 (2004): 104.

25. Op. cit., UNCTAD.

26. Ibid.

27. Thabo Mbeki, "The African Renaissance, South Africa and the World," *United Nations Archive*, accessed September 16, 2020, http://archive.unu.edu/unupress/mbe ki.html.

28. Ibid.

29. Thabo Mbeki, "Address at Tsinghua University," Speech in Beijing, China, December11, 2001, accessed September 21, 2020, http://www.dirco.gov.za/docs/s peeches/2001/mbek1211.htm.

30. Joseph Ramos and Osvaldo Sunkel, "Towards a Neostructuralist Synthesis," in *Development from Within: Towards a Neostructuralist Approach for Latin America*, ed. Osvaldo Sunkel (Boulder, CO: Lynne Rienner, 1993), 6.

31. Mbeki, "The African Renaissance."

32. For further reading on South Africa's China policy at the time see Appendix 3.

33. Ministry of Foreign Affairs of the PRC, "President Jiang Zemin's Visit to Six African Countries," accessed June 21, 2020, https://www.fmprc.gov.cn/mfa_eng/zi liao_665539/3602_665543/3604_665547/t18035.shtml.

34. Appendix 3.

35. Ian Taylor, *China and Africa: Engagement and Compromise* (New York: Routledge, 2006), 149.

36. Liu Hongwu, interview with author September 16, 2014.

37. Richard McGregor, "Sino-African Summit Ends With Swipe at Critics," *Financial Times*, November 6, 2006.

38. Joseph Kahn, "China Opens Summit for African Leaders," *The New York Times*, November 2, 2006.

39. FOCAC, accessed August 21, 2020, http://www.focac.org/eng/ljhy_1/dyjbzjhy _1/CI12009/; "25th Africa-France Summit," *BBC*, accessed August 21, 2020, https ://www.bbc.co.uk/worldservice/africa/2010/06/100601_afriquefrancesummit.shtml; Africa-EU Partnership, accessed August 21, 2020, https://africa-eu-partnership.org/e n/our-events/1st-africa-eu-summit; African Union, accessed August 21, 2020, https:// au.int/ar/summit/2ndafricaindia Ministry of Foreign Affairs of Japan, "TICAD," accessed August 21, 2020, https://www.mofa.go.jp/region/africa/ticad/index.html; Ministry of Foreign Affairs of Turkey, "Turkey-Africa Partnership Summit," accessed August 21, 2020, http://africa.mfa.gov.tr/default.en.mfa; Middle east Institute, "Iran Invests Time and Energy in Africa," accessed August 21, 2020, https ://www.mei.edu/publications/iran-invests-time-and-energy-africa; Foreign Office of the United Kingdom, "UK-Africa Summit 2020," accessed August 21, 2020, https:// www.gov.uk/government/topical-events/uk-africa-investment-summit-2020.

40. "The Africa-EU Partnership," accessed September 16, 2015, http://www.africa -eu-partnership.org/en/3rd-africa-eu-summit.

41. Li Anshan, et al., *FOCAC: Twelve Years Later: Achievements, Challenges, and the Way Forward* (Beijing: Peking University, 2012), 16.

42. Ibid., 16–17.

43. Li Anshan, interview with Author, September 29, 2014.

44. Anshan, et al., *FOCAC: Twelve Years Later*, 17.

45. Ibid.

46. Ministry of Foreign Affairs of South Africa, "President Mbeki to lead South African Delegation to China-Africa Co-operation Summit," October 29, 2006, accessed September 16, 2015, http://www.dfa.gov.za/docs/2006/chin1030.htm.

47. Ian Taylor, "The Ambiguous Commitment: The People's Republic of China and the Anti-Apartheid Struggle in South Africa," *Journal of Contemporary African Studies* 18, no. 1 (2000): 104, 91–106.

48. "Mbeki Warns Africa on Relationship with China," *Mail and Guardian*, December 13, 2006.

49. Hu Jintao, "Enhance China—Africa Unity and Cooperation to Build a Harmonious World," Speech at University of Pretoria, South Africa, accessed August 21, 2020, http://www.dirco.gov.za/docs/speeches/2007/jintao0207.htm.

50. New Partnership for Africa's Development (NEPAD), "History," accessed on September 16, 2015, http://www.nepad.org/history.

51. Ama Mazama, *Africa in the 21st Century: Toward a New Future* (New York: Routledge, 2007), 243.

52. New Partnership for Africa's Development (NEPAD), "History."

53. Mazama, *Africa in the 21st Century*, 200.

54. "NEPAD and Its Relevance to Zimbabwe," *Financial Gazette (Harare),* October 23, 2003.

55. Ministry of Foreign Affairs of the PRC, "China's Africa Policy," accessed June 23, 2020, https://www.fmprc.gov.cn/zflt/eng/zgdfzzc/t481748.htm.

56. Olayiwola Abegunrin, *Africa in Global Politics in the Twenty-First Century: A Pan-African Perspective* (New York: Palgrave Macmillan, 2009), 120.

*Chapter 4*

# A Farewell to Alms?

## *Pretoria Looks East*

On September 25, 2008, the ruling African National Congress (ANC) recalled Thabo Mbeki as the president of South Africa, leading to his resignation. Kgalema Motlanthe became the "caretaker" president until May 9, 2009, whereupon Jacob Zuma assumed the presidency after an ANC victory in the April elections. Many changes would soon take place in what was fast becoming a symbiotic nexus of China's pre-eminence in the world and South Africa's relations with Beijing. These changes happened in three areas: South Africa and China's participation in the G20, South Africa's participation in the Forum for China-Africa Cooperation (FOCAC), and South Africa's participation in the G8 before and after joining BRICS. A major characteristic of this era was the marked cessation of tendencies associated with the Mbeki era, where Pretoria publicly contradicted China or expressed reluctance toward the latter's initiatives. This chapter looks at the strategic outcomes associated with these times and how they evolved over time, and the extent to which China-South Africa coordination in international affairs was exclusively between the two or a general trend with other developing economies as well. Also, the chapter interrogates the role of China in raising South Africa's profile, including acceptance into BRICS.

In 2007 the world was thrust into a global recession. The collapse of American investment banks such as Lehman Brothers, Bear Stearns, and Meryl Lynch threatened the collapse of more financial institutions. Although this was prevented by an American bailout of selected financial institutions, the value of stocks was eviscerated in a contagion that spread throughout the global economy, causing a severe downturn. In the wake of the global recovery efforts from the recession, which began to take shape in 2009, commentators noted how developing economies had weathered the effects of the downturn better than developed ones and generally came out "stronger than anyone had expected."[1] China was among these economies. In 2009, Beijing still managed to overtake the United States as the largest market for automobiles.[2]

The data on economic growth of various economies over time concurs with this view of a general softer landing by China. Between 2008 and 2009, all economies saw a contraction as per capita GDP dropped across the board. But the extent to which this drop in growth took place is instructive of what commentators, even in the West, saw as a prelude to the "re-shaping" of the global economic space.[3] In 2008, as the recession began, the Chinese economy still managed to grow by 9.6 percent. On the other, data on developed economies shows markedly low levels of growth: the G8 economies achieved only 0.1 percent, the OECD 0.2, the EU 0.2, while the world average stood at 1.5 percent.[4] For its part, South Africa achieved a 3.2 percent per capita growth, well above the abovementioned. Also notable was that African economies as a whole grew by 6.1 percent.[5]

A year later, at the zenith of the global recession, the developed economies had done even worse. The G8 economies had achieved a per capita GDP growth of -4 percent, the OECD -3.5, the EU -4.4, while the world averaged -0.2 percent growth. Most consequentially, China had only managed to drop to 9.2 percent.[6] India, another ascendant Asian economy, had actually grown from 3.9 the previous year to 8.5 percent in 2009.[7] For its part, South Africa followed the international trend of contraction and stood at -1.5 percent.[8] However, by 2010, South Africa's per capita growth rate had recovered and stood at 3 percent.[9]

What had changed for South Africa's economy that would cause it, first, to contract at a relatively less sharper rate than other economies, and second, recover quicker when developed economies had only recovered to 2.9 percent by 2010?[10] The accelerated South Africa-China trade may have something to do with it. By 2009, China had become South Africa's largest trading partner on the African continent. The fact that China's economy did not contract as much meant that Chinese demand remained steady enough to sustain a supply of South African exports sufficient enough for the latter to weather the recession storm.[11] This singular moment in South Africa-China relations played a decisive role not only in solidifying strategic relations between the two countries but in laying the foundation for a South African pivot. South Africa under Zuma, from the very beginning of his era onward, began seeing its developmental fate as intractably linked to that of China. It is a change that in the years to come would be demonstrated in every sphere of South Africa's international engagements, including its participation in multilateral bodies.

## SOUTH AFRICA AND THE EMBRACE OF FOCAC

The first multilateral sphere in which Zuma-era South Africa demonstrated a marked change in its approach toward its relations with China is FOCAC. When the body was founded in 2006, Mbeki's grand plans for Africa's participation in NEPAD seemed to be in competition with those promised by FOCAC. But by 2009, a change had taken place where countries simply sought to weather the storm of the recession, which South Africa had done thanks to China's cooperation and its vast market's demand for exports.[12] Whereas China's hunger for South Africa's primary products had hitherto been a demerit in the debate over China-South Africa relations, it was now considered an unmitigated boon. This dramatic change was also demonstrated in the high-level exchanges which took place. In September 2009, President Zuma met with his Chinese counterpart on the sidelines of the United Nations; on August 24, 2010, Zuma undertook a state visit to the PRC; and on November 16 Hu Jintao made a state visit to South Africa.

South Africa's participation in FOCAC demonstrated a new urgency and importance to which South Africa was attaching its relations with China. Data of all FOCAC summits shows how at the early stages in the existence of the body, while South Africa still perfunctorily attended the requisite meetings, the country did not go out of its way, as demonstrated by the times it sent high-level delegations to attend. There are two types of high-level meetings in FOCAC, the summits for head-of-state, of which only three have taken place, in 2006, 2015, and 2018. Secondly, are the ministerial conferences, which, while not requiring the presence of heads-of-state or government, have still seen some African heads-of-state attend anyway. Attending has often been an anecdotal indication of the level of importance a particular attaches to its relations with not just FOCAC but the convener, China. Also, typically, the heads-of-state of regional economic powers have typically attended.

The data shows that for the first two ministerial conferences, out of a total of 11 African heads-of-state, South Africa's president Thabo Mbeki did not attend. Notably, Zuma attended the second ministerial conference in 2003 while he was still South Africa's deputy president. It may be that taking South Africa-China relations more seriously, and upgrading them to a strategic level, was an abiding foreign policy goal of Zuma long before he ascended into the presidency, even while Mbeki, his principal, was still reticent and outwardly non-committal on a strategic pivot favoring Beijing. From 2009 to 2018, four ministerial conferences took place. Although typically not required by convention, Zuma attended all of them, with the exception of 2018, which was attended by his successor.

This South African participation in FOCAC, therefore, including in its ministerial meetings, was so entrenched into South Africa's foreign policy

**Table 4.1   South Africa's Participation in FOCAC, 2000–2018**

| Date | Summit | Venue | Attending African heads-of-states | Did South African president attend? |
|---|---|---|---|---|
| October 10–12, 2000 | 1st Ministerial Conference of FOCAC | Beijing, China | 5 | No |
| December 15–16, 2003 | 2nd Ministerial Conference of FOCAC | Addis Ababa | 6 | No[a] |
| November 3–5, 2006 | 1st FOCAC Summit & 3rd Ministerial Conference | Beijing, China | 35 | Yes |
| November 8–10, 2009 | 4th Ministerial Conference of FOCAC | Sharm el-Sheikh, Egypt | 9 | Yes |
| July 19–20, 2012 | 5th Ministerial Conference of FOCAC | Beijing, China | 6 | Yes |
| December 4–5, 2015 | 2nd FOCAC Summit & 6th Ministerial Conference | Johannesburg, South Africa | 48 | Yes |
| September 3–4, 2018 | 3rd FOCAC Summit & 7th Ministerial Conference | Beijing, China | 53 | Yes |

Source: FOCAC;[13] [a]Then-deputy president Jacob Zuma attended.

that when Cyril Ramaphosa took over Zuma on February 15, 2018, after the latter, like Mbeki, was recalled by the ANC and resigned; his successor continued the perfect attendance of all FOCAC meeting in the year. This data shows a qualitative increase in the importance South Africa, beyond an individual leader, has demonstrably attached to FOCAC, one that is starker when data of South Africa's participation in another forum, the G8, is analyzed.

## FROM G8 "INVITED GUEST" TO G20 MEMBER

The 2008 recession had taken place and was followed by a cascade of multilateral responses to stem the tide of its effects. Summits took place which, unlike before, were more inclusive in the number of participants. In the immediate aftermath of the global financial crisis, the G8 (consisting of the United States, Canada, United Kingdom, France, Italy, Germany, Japan, and

Russia), which had dominated global economic governance and narrative since the 1990s, gradually saw itself supplanted by the G20. The G20 came into being as a "consensus-oriented club" of countries "with a mission to prevent financial, economic, and related crises, and to institute the social protections that would make globalization work for all."[14] By virtue of its size, the G20 is more inclusive of various regions of the world and their leading economies. It is the body for the world's twenty largest economies—Argentina, Australia, Brazil, Canada, China, France, Germany, India, Indonesia, Italy, Japan, South Korea, Mexico, Russia, Saudi Arabia, South Africa, Turkey, the United Kingdom, the United States, and the European Union.

The first G20 summit convened in Washington in November 2008. This crisis meeting to craft a solution out of the recession was seen as a progressive step as well as a departure from the "the closed, rich club" of the G8, and an acknowledgment that "the rest of the world has become too important to bar from the room."[15] After the first summit in Washington, the G20 would meet twice in the span of five months, in April and September 2009.

But as far as South Africa was concerned, the G8 had not entirely taken a back seat. South Africa, under the aegis of NEPAD leadership, had since 2002 been a regular attendee at G8 summits as an invited "guest," part of a controversial "outreach" program where a handful of leaders from global South economies would have meeting on the sideline of the G8 and join on the last day for photos, among a list of other limited activities. South Africa continued to attend every G8 summit until 2011. At the 33rd G8 summit in Heiligendamm, Germany, the G8 leaders instituted the Heiligendamm Process, which regularized the participation of Mexico, China, Brazil, India, and South Africa. Known as the "Outreach 5," this gave limited participation in certain meetings of G8 summits, and was seen as a culmination of a "G8 + 5" idea of British prime minister Tony Blair.[16] This demonstrated a Western attempt early in the 2000s to set South Africa apart as an exemplary economic ally, albeit a junior one, together with other developing countries. For its part, China was also invited as early as 2003 as part of Outreach 5. However, the 35th G8 in 2009 was China's last and the country abruptly stopped attending thereafter. Notably, so did India and Brazil.

This cessation of participation by these major developing economies, immediately following the recession in 2009, correlates with the rise in profile and activity of the more inclusive G20, whose summits, as the data demonstrates, would thereafter continue taking place with relative frequency. In 2010 the G20 again met twice, in June and November. But as the data demonstrates, the proceeding summits of the G20 became less frequent—meeting only once a year.

There are two explanations for this change: firstly, as the global economic recovery began to take root, there was a diminution of incentive for the

Table 4.2  South Africa and China Participation in G8 versus G20, 2002–2019

| G8 Summits | | | | G20 Summits | |
|---|---|---|---|---|---|
| Summit | Date, Location | Invited African nonmembers | Other invited nonmembers | Summit | Date, Location |
| 28th | June 26–27, 2002 Kananaskis, Canada | Algeria, Nigeria, Senegal, South Africa | | | |
| 29th | June 1–3, 2003 Évian-les-Bains, France | Algeria, Egypt, Nigeria, Senegal, South Africa | Brazil, China, Greece, India, Malaysia, Mexico, Saudi Arabia, | | |
| 30th | June 8–10, 2004 Sea Island, United States | Algeria, Ghana, Nigeria, Senegal, South Africa, Uganda, | Afghanistan, Bahrain, Iraq, Jordan, Turkey, Yemen | | |
| 31st | July 6–8, 2005 Gleneagles, Scotland | Ethiopia, South Africa | Brazil, China, India, Mexico, | | |
| 32nd | July 15–17, 2006 St. Petersburg, Russia | South Africa | Brazil, China, India, Mexico | | |
| 33rd | June 6–7, 2007 Heiligendamm, Germany | South Africa | Brazil, China, Ethiopia, India, Mexico | | |
| 34th | July 7–9, 2008 Hokkaido, Japan | Algeria, Ethiopia, Ghana, Nigeria, Senegal, South Africa, Tanzania | Australia, Brazil, China, India, Indonesia, Mexico, South Korea, | 1st | November 14-15, 2008 Washington, United States |
| 35th | July 8–10, 2009 L'Aquila, Italy | Algeria, Angola, Egypt, Libya, Nigeria, Senegal, South Africa | Australia, Brazil, China, Denmark, India, Indonesia, Mexico, South Korea, Spain, Turkey | 2nd | April 2, 2009 London, United Kingdom |
| | | | | 3rd | September 24-25, 2009 Pittsburgh, United States |
| 36th | July 25–26, 2010 Ontario, Canada | Algeria, Egypt, Ethiopia, Malawi, Nigeria, Senegal, South Africa | Colombia, Haiti, Jamaica | 4th | June 26-27, 2010 Toronto, Canada |
| | | | | 5th | November 11-12, 2010 Seoul, South Korea |

| No. | G8 Date & Location | Invited | No. | G20 Date & Location | Invited |
|---|---|---|---|---|---|
| 37th | May 26–27, 2011 Deauville, France | Algeria, Egypt, Ethiopia, Equatorial Guinea, Senegal, *South Africa* | 6th | November 3-4, 2011 Cannes, France | x |
| 38th | May 18–19, 2012 Camp David, United States | x | 7th | June 18-19, 2012 San José del Cabo, Mexico | x |
| 39th | June 17–18, 2013 Lough Erne, United Kingdom | x | 8th | September 5-6, 2013 St. Petersburg, Russia | Ireland |
| 40th[17] | June 4–5, 2014 Brussels, Belgium | x | 9th | November 15-16, 2014 Brisbane, Australia | x |
| 41st | June 7–8, 2015 Schloss Elmau, Germany | Ethiopia, Liberia, Nigeria, Senegal, Tunisia | 10th | November 15-16, 2015 Antalya, Turkey | Iraq |
| 42nd | May 26–27, 2016 Kishiko Island, Japan | Chad | 11th | September 4-5, 2016 Hangzhou, China | Bangladesh, Indonesia, Laos, Papua New Guinea, Sri Lanka, Vietnam |
| 43rd | May 26–27, 2017 Taormina, Italy | Ethiopia, Guinea, Niger, Nigeria, Tunisia | 12th | July 7-8, 2017 Hamburg, Germany | X |
| 44th | Quebec, Canada June 8–9, 2018 | Kenya, Rwanda, *South Africa*, Seychelles, Senegal | 13th | November 30-December 1, 2018 Buenos Aires | Argentina, Bangladesh, Haiti, Jamaica, Marshall Islands, Norway, Vietnam |
| 45th | August 24–26, 2019 | Burkina Faso, Egypt, Rwanda, Senegal, *South Africa* | 14th | June 28-29, 2019 Osaka, Japan | Australia, Chile, India, Spain |

*Source:* G8;[18] G20.[19]

multilateral inclusivity the financial crisis had engendered. Western economies reverted to their comfort or default space as the G8 re-took center stage. A second explanation originates from the quest for structural responses by developing economies, responding to being excluded in multilateral economic governance bodies *before* the financial recession of 2008. The existence of the G20, although a significant shift, did not eliminate the sources for developing countries' complaint. Therefore, a response had to go beyond the structural architecture of the G20 itself, whose profile seemed to ebb and flow according to crisis and how much developed economies were invested in it; it had to be a completely new structure. For Zuma's South Africa, that structure was BRICS, whose foundations for establishment were laid in 2009—the same year that China, India and Brazil attended G8 summits as "guests" for the last time.

## FROM G8 "INVITED GUEST" TO BRICS MEMBER

When FOCAC was established in 2006, numerous other bodies already existed. The G8, the most high-profile among these, is the grouping of what has been known as the "most powerful industrialized countries" (United States, Canada, United Kingdom, Italy, France, Japan, and Russia). Except for its first meeting when it excluded Canada, as early as its second summit, in France in 1975, the grouping has been the G7. In latter summits, however, starting with the 23rd Summit in the United States in 1997, Russia's inclusion made the grouping a G8. But an analysis of the data regarding South Africa's participation in G8 *versus* its participation later in BRICS, shows that starting in 2010, when three of the "Outreach 5" counterparts (China, India, and Brazil) stopped attending G8 summits, a structural change in the dynamics of global economic governance and diplomacy took place.

The dissatisfaction had not only been with the insistence of developed economies on the exclusionary G8 summit but also with the failings of the G20. Although the latter was a bigger, more inclusive grouping, its utility only came into being during the time of the 2008/2009 financial crisis and the global effort to find broad-based solutions. However, criticism of the G20 still persisted. Although the G20 had put forth "principles for tougher rules, and governments pledged to develop 'internationally agreed' regulations by the end of 2010," there was no agreement, for instance, on the "specific numbers on how high capital reserves should be."[20] Although G20 was a step toward a more equitable representation on the global stage for emerging economies, including China and South Africa, it was not enough.

For China, disagreements within the G20 and especially the G8 had also emanated from Beijing's rival, Japan. The latter remained a full member of the G8 and throughout the G8's "outreach" initiatives in the 2000s demonstrated a contrarian position; loathe to "favor its rival China."[21] By 2009, the emerging economies had been "thoroughly discontented with their treatment. Even at best, they were not admitted on equal terms. The G8 set the rules and the agenda for the outreach meetings, and the emerging powers had to take what they were offered."[22] On June 16, 2009, in Yekaterinburg, Russia, leaders of Brazil, India, and China joined their Russian counterpart in stressing the centrality of the G20 in dealing with the financial crisis. They also made a declaration calling for structural reform in multilateral financial bodies, arguing that "the emerging and developing economies must have greater voice and representation in international financial institutions, whose heads and executives should be appointed through an open, transparent, and merit-based selection process."[23]

This signified the first summit and the formation of BRIC (Brazil, Russia, India, and China). By the second BRIC summit in Brasilia, Brazil, China's president Hu Jintao lobbied the other countries for South Africa, which had attended the meeting as a "guest," to be admitted into the grouping. When China hosted the third summit, in 2011, in Sanya, Hainan, China, South Africa became a fifth member, transforming the body from BRIC to BRICS. This signified a further consolidation by major developing countries toward a strategic partnership and influence. The events preceding the formation of BRICS, therefore, may be seen as somewhat "push" factors that were either a cause or catalyst to the change in the global dynamics that necessitated this new alliance. This is an important context that scholars argue is indispensable to understanding "how these global changes interacted with specific economic and political contexts at the national level."[24]

For South Africa, membership in BRICS would have been improbable without China's lobbying and support. South Africa's full membership into BRICS had a direct effect on the country's participation in G8, as it had with other members. As the data shows, after becoming a BRICS member in 2011, South Africa stopped participating in the G8 summits it had dutifully attended for over 10 years. By 2014, the last remaining BRICS member in G8, Russia, had also stopped attending G8 summits. Thus did G8 return to being G7. In 2015, South Africa-China relations were upgraded to the highest possible level, the Strategic Comprehensive Partnership. The events of 2008 and 2009 following the financial crisis accelerated a South-South convergence. Although this had long been the clarion call of South African leaders, including Mbeki, it was during Zuma's era that a constellation of global dynamics combined, if not fortuitously, for the country to integrate into a body upon which it would pin its developmental plans. In 2014, the sixth BRICS summit agreed to form a BRICS bank, named the New Development Bank, as well as set up a $100 billion Contingency Reserve to shield member countries against exposure to economic crises akin to the 2008/2009 meltdown. China announced it would put forward $41 billion toward the fund, dubbed the "mini IMF;" South Africa would put in $5 billion; and the rest of the members $18 billion each.[25] By the end of the same year, all BRICS countries decreased their holdings of US government bonds; China, which is the largest foreign holder of US government bonds, by 2.3 billion to 1.25 trillion, South Africa to $10.3 billion.[26]

In this chapter we have sought the highlight the elements of which data suggests characterize the changing dynamics of China-South Africa relations since their establishment in 1998. The return of Western countries into Africa after a 1990s reticence was not accompanied by a qualitative transformation in the multilateral structures of global economic governance. While South Africa shared Africa's disenchantment with the Western prescriptions for development, under Mbeki, the country did not always share the continent's confidence in China as a serious developmental partner. This is South Africa's lackluster enthusiasm for FOCAC at its founding in 2000.

But by the Beijing Summit in 2006, while Mbeki's caution toward closer relations with China had not abated, owing to what he may have seen as a competition of FOCAC with NEPAD, the global environment was changing. This would make it a pragmatic decision, not an ideological one, to form a closer partnership with China, which the country formed when relations were upgraded to strategic partnership in 2004. This upgrade of relations helped China's own relations with the continents through FOCAC.

The global financial crisis of 2008/2009 was pivotal in shaking the confidence of developing countries' leaders on Western monopoly over financial institutional governance. Also, it exposed as inadequate the "outreach" programs of the G8, which seemed unsuited to a changed global situation of developing countries being responsible for the majority of global economic growth. Even after the rise in profile of the G20, disagreements continued around the extent of structural reform, if any, which developing economies saw as an effective reneging just as the global economy began to recover. The retreat into an elitist corner, the decades' long grievances surrounding inclusion in the structural mechanism of global economic governance, together with a mutual awareness of each other's strategic and developmental imperatives, form the combination of circumstances in Zuma's era which have had a pivotal and decisive role in accelerating relations between these two countries and increased the hope for developmental outcomes for South Africa. That this strategic pivot did not show any signs of abating during Ramaphosa's first two years in office is a strong indication of the long-term, structural commitment of the entire ANC and the government it runs, beyond individual proclivities.

**Table 4.3** South Africa, China, Brazil and India Participation in G8 before and after BRICS, 2002–2019

| G8 Summits | | | | BRICS Summits | |
|---|---|---|---|---|---|
| Summit | Date, Location | Invited African nonmembers | Other invited nonmembers | Summit | Date, Location |
| 28th | June 26–27, 2002 Kananaskis, Canada | Algeria, Nigeria, Senegal, **South Africa** | x | | |
| 29th | June 1–3, 2003 Évian-les-Bains, France | Algeria, Egypt, Nigeria, Senegal, **South Africa** | **Brazil**, **China**, Greece, **India**, Malaysia, Mexico, Saudi Arabia, | | |
| 30th | June 8–10, 2004 Sea Island, United States | Algeria, Ghana, Nigeria, Senegal, **South Africa**, Uganda, | Afghanistan, Bahrain, Iraq, Jordan, Turkey, Yemen | | |
| 31st | July 6–8, 2005 Gleneagles, Scotland | Ethiopia, **South Africa** | **Brazil**, **China**, **India**, Mexico, | | |
| 32nd | July 15–17, 2006 St. Petersburg, Russia | **South Africa** | **Brazil**, **China**, **India**, Mexico | | |
| 33rd | June 6–7, 2007 Heiligendamm, Germany | **South Africa** | **Brazil**, **China**, Ethiopia, **India**, Mexico | | |
| 34th | July 7–9, 2008 Hokkaido, Japan | Algeria, Ethiopia, Ghana, Nigeria, Senegal, **South Africa**, Tanzania | Australia, **Brazil**, **China**, **India**, Indonesia, Mexico, South Korea, | | |
| 35th | July 8–10, 2009 L'Aquila, Italy | Algeria, Angola, Egypt, Libya, Nigeria, Senegal, **South Africa**, | Australia, **Brazil**, **China**, Denmark, **India**, Indonesia, Mexico, South Korea, Spain, Turkey | 1st | June 16, 2009, Yekaterinburg, Russia |
| 36th | July 25–26, 2010 Ontario, Canada | Algeria, Egypt, Ethiopia, Malawi, Nigeria, Senegal, **South Africa** | Colombia, Haiti, Jamaica | 2nd | April 16, 2010 Brasilia, Brazil |

*(Continued)*

**Table 4.3   South Africa, China, Brazil and India Participation in G8 before and after BRICS, 2002–2019** (Continued)

| G8 Summits | | | | BRICS Summits | |
|---|---|---|---|---|---|
| Summit | Date, Location | Invited African nonmembers | Other invited nonmembers | Summit | Date, Location |
| 37th | May 26–27, 2011 Deauville, France | Algeria, Egypt, Ethiopia, Malawi, Nigeria, Senegal, **South Africa** | x | 3rd | April 14, 2011 Sanya, China |
| 38th | May 18–19, 2012 Camp David, United States | x | x | 4th | March 29, 2012 New Delhi, India |
| 39th | June 17–18, 2013 Lough Erne, United Kingdom | x | Ireland | 5th | March 26-27, 2013 Durban, South Africa |
| 40th | June 4–5, 2014 Brussels, Belgium | x | x | 6th | July 14-16, 2014 Fortaleza, Brazil |
| 41st | June 7–8, 2015 Schloss Elmau, Germany | Ethiopia, Liberia, Nigeria, Senegal, Tunisia | x | 7th | July 8-9, 2015 Ufa, Russia |
| 42nd | May 26–27, 2016 Kishiko Island, Japan | Chad | Bangladesh, Indonesia, Laos, Papua New Guinea, Sri Lanka, Vietnam | 8th | October, 15-16, 2016 Benaulim, India |
| 43rd | May 26–27, 2017 Taormina, Italy | Ethiopia, Guinea, Niger, Nigeria, Tunisia | X | 9th | September 3-5, 2017 Xiamen, China |
| 44th | Quebec, Canada June 8–9, 2018 | Kenya, Rwanda, **South Africa,** Seychelles, Senegal | Argentina, Bangladesh, Haiti, Jamaica, Marshall Islands, Norway, Vietnam | 10th | July 25-27, 2018 Johannesburg, South Africa |
| 45th | August 24–26, 2019 | Burkina Faso, Egypt, Rwanda, Senegal, **South Africa** | Australia, Chile, **India**, Spain | 11th | November 13-14, 2019 Brasilia, Brazil |

Source: G8; BRICS.[27]

## NOTES

1. "Counting their Blessings," *The Economist*, December 30, 2009.

2. David Pilling, "Asia Emerges from Global Crisis with Growth Intact," *Financial Times*, September 9, 2010.

3. Edmund Andrews, "Leaders of G-20 Vow to Reshape Global Economy," *The New York Times*, September 25, 2009.

4. UNCTAD, "Output and Income," accessed June 2, 2020, https://unctadstat.unctad.org/wds/ReportFolders/reportFolders.aspx?sCS_ChosenLang=en.

5. Ibid.

6. Ibid.

7. Ibid.

8. Ibid.

9. Ibid.

10. Ibid.

11. Interview with South Africa diplomat, Beijing, September 25, 2014.

12. David Lipton, "South Africa: Facing the Challenges of the Global Economy," Speech at the International Monetary Fund, May 8, 2013, accessed September 16, 2015 https://www.imf.org/external/np/speeches/2013/050813.htm.

13. FOCAC, accessed August 21, 2020, http://www.focac.org/eng/ljhy_1/dyjbzjhy_1/CI12009/.

14. John Kirton, "From G8 2003 to G13 2010? The Heiligendamm Process's Past, Present, and Future," in *Emerging Powers in Global Governance: Lessons from the Heiligendamm Process*, ed. Andrew F. Cooper and Agata Antkiewicz (Ontario: Wilfrid Laurier University Press, 2010), 79.

15. "After the Fall," *The Economist*, November 13, 2008.

16. Gordon S. Smith, "G7 to G8 to G20: Evolution in Global Governance," *CIGi G20 Papers*, accessed September 16, 2015 https://www.ciaonet.org/attachments/18458/uploads.

17. Summit originally scheduled to take place in Sochi, Russia but venue changed after other G8 member countries decide to exclude Russia from participating. Henceforth held as a G7 Summit.

18. Karen Mingst, "Group of Eight," *Encyclopedia Britannica*, accessed August 21, 2020, https://www.britannica.com/topic/Group-of-Eight.

19. G20 Information Center, "G20 Summits," accessed April 19, 2020, http://www.g20.utoronto.ca/summits/index.html.

20. Andrews, "Leaders of G-20 Vow to Reshape Global Economy."

21. Nicholas Bayne, "The Decline of the G8 and Lessons for the G20," in *The New Economic Diplomacy: Decision-Making and Negotiation in International Economic Relations*, ed. Nicholas Bayne, Stephen Woolcockeds (Farnham, UK: Ashgate, 2011), 251.

22. Ibid.

23. Office of the President of Russian Federation, "Joint Statement of the BRIC Countries' Leaders," June 16, 2009, accessed September 16, 2015 http://archive.kremlin.ru/eng/text/docs/2009/06/217963.shtml.

24. Matthias Vom Hau, James Scott and David Hulme, "Beyond the BRICs: Alternative Strategies of Influence in the Global Politics of Development," *European Journal of Development Research* 24, no. 2 (2012): 194.

25. "BRICS Create Development Bank, 'Mini-IMF,'" *The Times of India*, June 16, 2014.

26. "India Cuts Exposure to US Government Securities at $77.5 Billion in October," *The Times of India*, December 21, 2014.; Jack Freifedler, "For Third Straight Month, China Cuts US Debt Holdings," *China Daily,* June 17, 2014.

27. Mingst, "Group of Eight." Encyclopedia Britannica, accessed August 21, 2020, https://www.britannica.com/topic/Group-of-Eight; BRICS, "Summits," accessed April 19, 2020, https://infobrics.org/news/summits/

*Chapter 5*

# China's Economic Growth and South Africa's Unemployment

Since China's success in lifting millions of its people out of poverty began to gain worldwide attention in the last couple of decades, a global discussion has continued to take place where certain assumptions concerning the state's role in the economy have come under serious review. Some of these assumptions, some scholars aver, have contributed to making developing economies, including South Africa, more "fragile," regardless of which country—from the global south or north—they are dealing with.[1] This vulnerability has existed because scholars have often failed to approach economic development, indeed the economic relations of nations, from "a multidisciplinary standpoint;" scholars also failed to understand a states' developmental imperatives in the context of "failure" elsewhere in the market; failed to see "dynamic synergetic" phenomena in developmental relations among states; and failed to "observe, and classify qualitative differences between economic activities."[2] In an attempt to avoid these failures this chapter analyzes the intersection of the Chinese imperative of economic growth through, among other things, production and merchandize exports, with the South African imperative of fighting unemployment. We are concerned mainly with what time series data as well as field interviews reveal about on-the-ground intersection of these imperatives and what, ultimately, this indicates about prospects for making a dent in South Africa's unemployment.

## CHINA AND SOUTH AFRICA COMPARED

In many ways, South Africa and China are markedly different countries, with equally different economic means. Although the fifth-most populous country on the continent, South Africa's population of 59 million is roughly equivalent to only one of China's 34 provinces and territories—Hubei, while China has 1.4 billion people.[3] Although South Africa is the ninth largest country in Africa, its total area of 470, 900 square miles is only equivalent to Tibet; China, with an area of 3.7 million square miles, is the third largest country in the world.[4] Politically, South Africa, while older as an oppressive apartheid republic (of 1948), and even older as a British-protected Union (of 1910), is a young democracy only in its second decade as a multiparty system of governance. China, although still widely—if not contestably—considered an "authoritarian" one-party state, is over 66 years old as a singular communist "People's Republic," older as a contested nationalist "Republic" (declared in 1912), and even older as a civilization.[5]

Socially, South Africans are generally free to move about the country in pursuit of whatever economic opportunity their means may afford and still access certain state benefits. Until late 2015, when plans to reform it began, China strictly enforced a *hukou* policy of population registration that restricts the movement of people around the country by tying access to entitlements such as education and healthcare to the place of citizens' original domicile.[6] South Africa's birth rate stood at 2.4 per woman in 2009 and citizens are free to have as many children as they want; China had a strict one-child policy, which was changed to two in 2014, albeit still contingent on certain conditions.[7]

There is a divergence of perspectives between Chinese and some South African scholars on the roles these differences play in contemporary South Africa-China relations. One Chinese scholar posits that since the future of China's relations with South Africa is "closely related to the future of China's relations with Africa," attention must be paid by scholars to redeeming features of these South Africa-China relations, in order for redeeming features of China's relations with the continent to also emerge.[8] This follows a generally positive outlook on relations with South Africa. But for some South African scholars, "formidable" differences remain.[9] Democracy and certain government decision-making processes associated with what South Africans may see as "good governance" are flagged as flagged by the Chinese perspective as areas of concern, if not obstacles to relations. Furthermore, Chinese scholars respond to this critique by pointing to what they see as a "disorganized," "disorderly," and often economically unstable environment which multiparty democracy has not precluded a vast number of African countries from experiencing.[10]

## SOUTH AFRICA'S DEVELOPMENTAL DIALECTIC

If there remain marked differences between South Africa and China in the sociopolitical spheres it is in the socio-economic sphere where similarities emerge. Both South Africa and China have liberal economies at markedly varied degrees. Until 2014, South Africa was the largest economy in Africa; China is the second largest economy in the world.[11] Since the two countries established relations in 1998, not only have they seen a sharp increase in levels of partnership, which currently stand at "Comprehensive Strategic Partnership," but there was a demonstrably high South African regard for Beijing as a trade partner.

In 1998, half of the imports into South Africa were from the EU and the United States alone, at 39 and 11.6 percent, respectively. Imports from China were only 1.8 percent.[12] From 2006 through 2019, however, a different trade picture began to emerge. EU imports decreased from 33.7 in 2006 to 27 percent in 2019, the United States 8.5 to 6.7 percent, and Japan 8.7 to 4 percent.[13] China's imports doubled, from 6.7 to 14.5 percent.[14] Notably, this was accompanied by an increase in imports from other developing economies too. In 1998 BRI (Brazil, Russia, and India) imports stood at just 2.1 percent, but they increased from 3.8 in 2006 to 6.1 in 2019.[15] The same is true for African imports, which made up only 7.8 percent in 1998, but increased from 10.7 to 19 percent in the same period.[16] Beginning in 2019, China (at 10.3 percent) was the only country with a double-digit percentage share of imports into South Africa.[17]

But the quantitative switch to China's advantage, itself a function of rising strategic relations, has not, however, led to an amelioration of the developmental condition of a vast number of South Africans, which is characterized by poverty and inequality, coupled with continued unemployment of a vast segment of the population. A look at the variable of population growth, urban population, as well as inequality is instructive.

## Population

It is difficult to dismiss the growth of South Africa's population as a contributing factor in the nominal manifestation poverty. It is important to look at these in contrast to not only China but also other developing economies of comparable standing, so as to ascertain the dramatic rise in proper context. While South Africa's population is small compared to other countries, including China and Brazil, the rate at which the population has grown, however, holds certain ramifications for developmental outcomes. In 2000 South Africa's population was only 45 million, but by 2019, it was 59 million.[18] This is a 24 percent, which, although smaller than that of sub-Saharan Africa (at 40 percent), is much larger than China's 10 and Brazil's 17 percent growth.[19] For South Africa, this highlight a consistent pattern dissonance between how the country perceives itself—a middle income developing economy—as opposed to a more modest developmental reality that coheres more to the sub-Saharan condition kind of rather a "semi-developing" economy. This chasm between aspiration and reality also manifests itself in other variables.

## *Urban Population*

Population growth makes the problem of seeking a developmental way forward more complex when looked at in conjunction with the growth of the urban population. If unemployment is already bad in South Africa's cities, any growth in the urban population can be said to merely make it worse. In 2000, only 57 percent of South Africa's population was urban.[20] By 2020, it was projected to be 65 percent, a 12 percent growth. It was further projected to grow to 69 percent by 2030.[21] By contrast, in 2020, only 34 percent of the population of India and 58 of China was urban.[22] Not only is South Africa's urban population above the average for Africa (at 41 percent), but it is also above the world (at 56 percent) as well as G20 economies (at 60 percent).[23] Only Russia and Brazil had a higher percentage of urban populations, although both have far less growth than South Africa between 2020 and 2030.[24] The high percentage of South Africa's urban population is another facet of the seriousness of the development condition in the country. It is in the urban space where most frustrations surrounding issue of non-delivery of services, themselves emanating from the people's disappointments with developmental outcomes, where the likelihood for instability is most at risk of occurring.

## **Inequality**

According to United Nations Gini coefficient[25] data, South Africa is the most unequal society in the world, and has been for over two decades.[26] Also, unlike other developing economy counterparts like Brazil, India, and China, there have demonstrably been little prospects for improvements. In 2000, South Africa, at the time the largest economy in Africa, had a Gini coefficient of 67, the highest in the world. Brazil's coefficient, at 57.5 in 2001, was the second, although markedly lower than South Africa's.[27] By 2015, South Africa's inequality stood at 65.4.[28] During the same 15-year period, Brazil's Gini coefficient had decreased to 50.8; China's stood at 40.1; and India at 39.3.[29] Strikingly, it is not only middle income but also lower income developing economies within Africa that have tended to reflect better outcomes in fighting inequality.

From this data emerges a picture of South Africa's recent developmental lot: a country whose rise in population and urban population has not been accompanied by a qualitative decrease in inequality. This inequality is characterized by the following two features: first it is distinctive, that is higher than most economies in the region and the world; second, it is long-standing, and successive governments have failed to arrest it. It is demonstrated in various fields including how individual outcomes of any economic growth are—income—shared among the populace.

Beyond the Gini coefficient, other measurements also illustrate a developmental condition that remains significantly challenging. South Africa is at the bottom in the share of income held by the lowest 20 percent of the population.[30] In 2008 only 2.6 percent of the South Africa's income was held by the lowest 20 percent of the population; in 2014 it was worse, at 2.4 percent.[31] Also, South Africa's inequality as not only worse when compared to China (6.5 percent in 2016), but also other African countries (Nigeria was 7.1 percent in 2018; Mozambique 4.2 percent in 2014).[32] Like the Gini coefficient, the measurement of the lowest 20 percent's share of income reveals the unique way in which inequality blights South Africa: it is long-lasting and entrenched.

## The Imperative of Employment

The sum developmental domain where the three variables of population growth, urban population growth, and inequality find expression in the lives of South Africans is unemployment. Employment determines more than the practical needs. It addresses a humanitarian aspiration whereby individual worth in society, their dignity, social relations, indeed general perception of their life prospects hinge on whether or not they have a job. For a young graduate, employment is not only a culmination of a difficult effort as a student, but it also symbolizes an initiation into the "real world" of men and woman with practical purpose in society. Unemployment, therefore, especially one that is prolonged as South Africa's has been, is harmful not just at the temporal level, but it harms the very humanity of the unemployed. The extent to which China-South Africa's strategic relations solve this singular problem for Pretoria, is perhaps the most important developmental question of our time.

In 2009, the unemployment rate stood at 32.4 percent; it was 35.5 in 2015; and 38.4 in 2019.[33] In ten years, the employment rate seems to have gone against and frustrated the efforts of policymakers.[34] It is easy to conclude that unemployment figures look bad because of the "expanded definition" of unemployment used by South Africa, which, unlike the strict (international) one, also counts discouraged job-seekers (those who have given up on looking for employment). However, even the strict unemployment data still paints a picture of a country that is still unsuccessfully grappling with a problem that has continued to rise. In 2009, "strict" unemployment was still at 23.7 percent, 25.3 in 2012, and 28.7 in 2019, demonstrating a problem that seems to only worsen with time.[35]

South Africa's unemployment, which has constantly been on the rise, is also made worse by its entrenchment over time. In 2009, 60.3 percent of the unemployed had been without work for more than a year. In 2015, it increased to 65.9 percent, and to 71.2 percent by 2019.[36] This "problem-within-a-problem" of long-term unemployment has given rise to other problems that have continued to characterize South Africa's unique developmental imperative. This is better illustrated by in the category of those considered "not economically active," the people who are not considered part of the workforce. Although students, home-makers, retired, persons are among these, it also includes "discouraged work seekers." Unlike students and retired people, whose economic inactivity may be easily qualified, this group comprises those who have essentially given up.

On a humanitarian level, where human aspirations extend beyond the realm of daily economic activity but to the psychological well-being of people, this category of South Africans is perhaps the most tragic, made more so by its growth over time with seemingly no end in sight. In 2009, only 11.2 South Africans of working age were considered discouraged work seekers; but in 2015 it was 6.2 percent were, and 18.3 in 2019.[37]

Another manifestation of the humanitarian toll of unemployment is when the data is analyzed by how unemployed people became unemployed—whether they were job loser, job leavers, re-entrants (those who had been unemployed before and were becoming unemployed again), or new entrants (those who had never been unemployed before). Year after year, the largest category was for new entrants. In 2009 this category was 39.8 percent of all unemployed; 37.7 in 2015; and 38.8 percent in 2019.[38] This illustrates exposing a fluctuation that for 10 years barely moved more than two percentage points, hence the difficulty embedded in any effort to change the situation for the better.

Furthermore, "new entrants," there is also a growing category of those who simply graduated from high school or college and went straight into the realm of unemployment. Constituting close more than a third of the unemployed in 2019, more than job losers, the new entrants are victims to the most glaring of South Africa's developmental lag through no fault of their own. The second-largest category is those who became unemployed because of job loss. Unlike new entrants, job loser saw an increase from constituting 34.2 percent in 2009 to 32.9 in 2015, and 30.7 percent in 2019. This may either illustrate the shrinking of the economy which eliminated jobs or most likely a growth in the number of people needing work. Also more tragic yet heartening to observe is the small and decreasing number of those who became unemployed because they left a job. They were only 6 percent in 2015, and only 4.7 in 2019.[39] This may show either a commitment to work among South Africans when opportunity has been granted, or people sticking it out due to lack of opportunities, the latter constituting an "arrested" aspiration.

## The Three Manifestations of Unemployment

In attempting to describe in detail South Africa's unemployment imperative, more salient characteristics emerge by which unemployment has embedded itself into the South Africa's politico-socio-economic nexus. If unemployment has a gender, it is female; a face, it is black; and an age group, it is young. To this end, this section goes into relevant detail on how unemployment varies by these categories because they have a developmental bearing on the country's stated objectives of being nonsexist, nonracial, and paying attention to youth and their aspirations. If we are to consider the intersection of imperatives, we must consider the intercourse of these categories with the economy over time and how South Africa-China relations affect them.

### Gender

In almost all indices found in the data, women were worse affected by unemployment, including those who participate in the activities of the formal economy. In 2009, only 58.8 percent of working-age women—compared to 65.2 percent of men—were participating in the labor force, that is to say, had the opportunity to be employed or unemployed.[40] In 2015, this number increased to 62.1 percent and to 63.9 percent in 2019.[41] This may seem like a notable improvement in women at least joining the labor force. However, caution must be exercised because men's participation also generally increased over time. Also, men's participation rate was above the national average most of the time, while women's participation was below the national average every year.

Gender disparity was also apparent in the unemployment rate itself where women consistently suffered much higher unemployment than men. In 2009 women's unemployment rate was 7.9 percent higher than that of men; in 2015, it had not changed, although the difference dropped to 6.7 percent in 2019.[42] Women were also over-represented as discouraged work seekers, that is, those who can work but have given up looking for work. In 2012, only 44.1 percent of men were discouraged workers, compared to 55.9 of women.[43] In 2015, 56 percent of women were discouraged workers; men saw a decrease, to 44 percent.[44] Although there was a decrease to 53.6 for women, there was, interestingly, an increase (to 46.4 percent) for men.[45] What is notable about the qualitative difference not only in employment but also in the level of despondency is that it may suggest a status quo of the "casualization of" of women's labor, which often either leaves them "trapped in low-productivity jobs that are oftentimes physically onerous," or relegates them to being economic "*persona non grata*," where their labor's value is diminished if at all accounted for.[46]

*Race*

The years of economically displacing the black population in South Africa during apartheid has had a lasting effect, which is well-documented in unemployment rates. It was this status quo which former president Thabo Mbeki referred when he spoke of South Africa as a "country of two nations. One of these nations is white, relatively prosperous, regardless of gender or geographic dispersal. . . . The second and larger nation of South Africa is black and poor. . . . This nation lives under conditions of a grossly underdeveloped econom[y]."[47] In 2008, black African unemployment stood at 37.8 percent; by 2015 it was 39.8 percent; by 2019 it had grown to 42.9.[48] White unemployment during the same period also saw an increase, but from the relatively slight (indeed the lowest) figure of 6.1 to 9.1, and to 9.6 percent.[49] Every year, black African unemployment was exclusively above the national average by at least 3 percentage points.[50] The skewing of unemployment by race not only adds another dimension to SA's developmental challenges and what any remedy for it from strategic China-Africa relations should mean but also has long-lasting, potentially negative ramifications for the country's cohesion and ultimately sociopolitical stability.

Interestingly, Chinese scholars and experts interviewed in this research, while acknowledging the long, painful history of South Africa, and the racialized economy apartheid produced, were reticent to engage with this imperative as an imperative with which not only China should concern itself but also South Africa. Some scholars saw it as "backward" to discuss economic matters around issues of redress and universal justice.[51] They point to China's own experience as a possible inspiration, but not as an example to follow. However, a distinction has to be made between manifestations of economic stratification in China, which may not have occurred along racial line, and those manifestations in South Africa that stubbornly have. That this is not China's imperative on its domestic front means it is less likely to be China's prerogative in South Africa-China relations. However, as it is an ongoing South African imperative to effect a transformation of its society, there is a need for leaders and scholars on both sides to begin to articulate the ramifications of South Africa's unique racial history, more especially since it still features so dominantly in the present-day economy and how it shapes unemployment. And this expression must be found in South Africa-China engagements.

## Youth Unemployment

In the same way that unemployment has entrenched itself along gender and racial lines, it has continued to disproportionately affect the youth. Of those that were unemployed in 2012, up to 68.5 percent of them were youth (15–34 years).[52] This proportion remained steady over time, and stood at 63.4 in 2019.[53] But what makes the gravity of youth unemployment better to understand is when the percentage of the population itself that makes up youth is considered, as well as which youth are in school and which are not, combined with the variable of race. In 2012, black youth made up 78.6 percent of the population. Neither of those that were neither unemployed nor in school, the black youth made up 79 percent.[54]

In 2018, the number had grown significantly, to 84 percent.[55] This data dispels the facile explanation of youth unemployment as meaning youth being in school. From it a picture emerges of a youth that is dislocated from the mechanisms that often give meaning to life at their age—having a job or going to school. Considering the large numbers of new entrants into unemployment (discussed earlier), young, black African women are the worst affected by what amounts to South Africa's underdevelopment vis-à-vis unemployment. Any developmental wherewithal forthcoming from the comprehensive partnership South Africa has sought to forge with China will have as an abiding priority, solution for addressing unemployment. Seeing that there is a perspective between Chinese and South African scholars and practitioners on the importance of these outlined imperatives concerning unemployment, South Africa ought to take the initiative in the multilateral quest for a breakthrough.

## Unemployment and (Chinese) Migration: Correlation or Causation?

In 2014, South Africa-China relations were at their highest level, and this has continued to be seen in the increase in trade. Trade between the two countries accounted for 12.6 percent of South Africa's total trade, the largest with a single country. A major characteristic of South Africa-China's advanced-level relations, and as a corollary, of the increase in trade, has demonstrably been the increase in movement of people from China into South Africa.

### Why Migration?

While migration is an important factor in various interactions between people and nations, it nevertheless remains a sensitive subject for discussion by scholars. British economist Paul Collier sees this sensitivity around discussing migration issues as an unintended consequence of an otherwise understandable reaction of commentators, practitioners, and scholars alike. In the face of "xenophobes and racists" who oppose immigration on the wholesale notion that it is bad for indigenous populations, and "desperate not to give succor to these groups, social scientists have strained every muscle to show

how immigration is good for everyone."[56] For South Africa, the tragic incidents of violence against mainly southern African migrants, in May 2008 and 2015, and intermittently since, which have often resulted in the deployment of the military and loss of many life, make this reticence even more understandable in the country's context.

However, migration, especially from China, has grown dramatically in the past five years. Its effects, if any, must be engaged with, if not to identify or distinguish between correlation or causation vis-à-vis South Africa's imperative of unemployment and finding a developmental breakthrough. That is also the sole intention of our looking at migration in this section, and it must be emphasized. Collier avers that in this instance, instead of shying away from a sensitive topic, a question that perhaps should be avoided because it is not necessary is, "Is migration bad or good?" Likening this question "Is eating bread bad or good?" Collier argues that just as overeating can cause obesity, so can migration "be excessive."[57]

The manner and emerging trends from the data regarding Chinese migration, therefore, are this section's only concern. In keeping with Collier's perspective that "left to itself, migration will keep accelerating so that it is liable to be excessive," certain features may be identified to see if they pre-empt an excessiveness that may be prevented regarding Chinese migration effects on the imperative of unemployment in South Africa.[58] For a country as large as China, with a population of 1.4 billion, the extent to which migration from its shores can be "excessive" as far as South Africa is concerned is, perhaps, not difficult to imagine.

### Net Migration

The net migration rate (the mathematical difference between immigrants and emigrants and in given country) is instructive of the patterns of migration for South Africa, in contrast to China and a host of other countries. The net migration index is important here because some—interestingly, Asian scholars—have been forthright in stating that "high levels of migration can cause problems such as increasing unemployment and potential ethnic strife (if people are coming in)," thus the need here to be informed of what the data says about South Africa's patterns.[59] To be fair, some South African scholars argue that far from being reticent on this matter, the South African government has been "sensitive to the developmental dimensions of migration" since the early 2000s.[60]

In 1997, South Africa's net migration rate was 159, and China's was -500, a significant net emigration for the latter (outflow), a sizeable net immigration (influx) for the former.[61] In 2007, South Africa's net migration was 1,403, while China's had deepened to -2,206. Notably the rest of the world's and sub-Saharan Africa's net migration rate have remained, significantly, below 0, signifying that while the rest of the developing world, including China, was shedding its population, South Africa was gaining significantly.[62] It is not far-fetched, therefore, to expect that further investigation into migration patterns holds explanatory potential concerning a lot of South Africa's own developmental imperatives. In simple terms, the data illustrates that together with the British, South African emigrate least while receiving the most immigrants.

*Immigration*

In 2012, of the total of 1,283 permanent residency permits granted by South Africa, 88 went to Chinese immigrants. After Zimbabwe and the United Kingdom, Chinese immigrants ranked third. A year later, the number had quadrupled to 366 permanent residency permits offered to Chinese immigrants. For non-African recipients, China was rivaled only by India (at 500). In 2015, after India, Chinese immigrants were the second-largest recipients of permanent residency permits. While this dramatic change speaks to an increase in Chinese immigration that corresponded with the further consolidation of relations, further indicators may suggest another potential variable.

The second indicator is that of the type of reasons for the temporary and permanent residency permits. In 2012 of those 141,550 immigrants who received temporary residency permits, 61.4 percent received them for work; by 2014, this had grown to 62.9 percent. This trend is similar to India but, notably, it differs when it comes to European immigrants who came in for less work. This is what requires further study on the possible displacement effect from China.

The third indicator concerns the median age of immigrants granted temporary or permanent residencies in South Africa (Figure 40). Of those granted temporary residency, together with Pakistan (31 years), China (31 years) was second, after India (30 years), in having the youngest median age of non-African immigrants granted a permit. As for those granted permanent residency permits, China (34 years) was third, after Pakistan (29) and India (32 years), in having the youngest median age of immigrants.

## DISCUSSION OF DATA

Among South Africa's three major developmental imperatives, overcoming inequality, poverty, and unemployment, this study decided to focus on the latter. Through the data above, this study has sought to not only expose the extent to which unemployment has entrenched itself in the South Africa

**Table 5.1   South African Residency Permits Granted**

|  | 2012 | | 2013 | | 2014 | |
|---|---|---|---|---|---|---|
|  | *Temporary* | *Permanent* | *Temporary* | *Permanent* | *Temporary* | *Permanent* |
| Total | 141,550 | 1,283 | 101,910 | 6,801 | 69,216 | 4,136 |
| All African countries | 76,947 | 682 | 55,951 | 4,555 | 36,390 | 2,638 |
| Zimbabwe | 24,370 | 251 | 18,899 | 1,939 | 12,521 | 1,497 |
| UK | 5,893 | 141 | 3,839 | 258 | 2,391 | 163 |
| China | 9,548 | 88 | 6,857 | 366 | 5,739 | 336 |
| India | 10,934 | 76 | 7,829 | 500 | 6,195 | 399 |
| Germany | 3,613 | 65 | 2,362 | 188 | 1,466 | 74 |
| Nigeria | 14,089 | 60 | 10,265 | 470 | 6,087 | 173 |
| DRC | 3,922 | 44 | 2,798 | 587 | 1,614 | 276 |
| Pakistan | 7,501 | 41 | 5,721 | 197 | 4,551 | 88 |

*Note:* Ranked by top permanent residency recipients in 2012
*Source:* Statistics South Africa. "Documented Immigrants into South Africa," Statistics South Africa, accessed December 23, 2019, http://www.statssa.gov.za/?s=documented&sitem=publications.

**Table 5.2 Percentage of Type of Permanent and Temporary Residency Permits Granted**

*Permanent Residency Permits*

| | 2012 | | | | | 2013 | | | | | 2014 | | | | |
|---|---|---|---|---|---|---|---|---|---|---|---|---|---|---|---|
| | Relative | Work | Business | Refugee | Other | Relative | Work | Business | Refugee | Other | Relative | Work | Business | Refugee | Other |
| All | 49.9 | 34.4 | 7.3 | 3.9 | 4.5 | 58.3 | 31.6 | 2.6 | 5.5 | 2 | 63.1 | 29.7 | 2.2 | 4 | 1 |
| UK | 63.1 | 7.8 | 7.8 | 0 | 21.3 | 72.5 | 14 | 3.1 | 0 | 10.4 | 70.6 | 12.9 | 1.8 | 0 | 14.7 |
| **China** | **36.4** | **40.9** | **19.3** | **0** | **3.4** | **44.3** | **46.2** | **8.5** | **0** | **1** | **58.6** | **36.9** | **3** | **0** | **1.5** |
| India | 50 | 40.8 | 9.2 | 0 | 0 | 59.8 | 38.4 | 1.4 | 0.2 | 0.2 | 68.2 | 31.3 | 0.5 | 0 | 0 |
| Germany | 49.2 | 15.4 | 18.5 | 0 | 16.9 | 50.5 | 20.2 | 7.4 | 0 | 21.9 | 41.9 | 35.1 | 2.7 | 0 | 20.3 |
| Africa | 42.8 | 45.7 | 3.7 | 7.3 | 0.5 | 57.2 | 33 | 1.5 | 8.1 | 0.2 | 61.7 | 31.6 | 0.3 | 6.2 | 0.2 |
| Zimbabwe | 49.4 | 49.8 | 0.8 | 0 | 0 | 55.4 | 44.4 | 0.1 | 0.1 | 0 | 60.1 | 39.9 | 0 | 0 | 0 |
| Nigeria | 40 | 55 | 3.3 | 0 | 1.7 | 62.3 | 34.9 | 2.3 | 0.4 | 0.1 | 61.3 | 38.2 | 0.6 | 0 | 0 |

*Temporary Residency Permits*

| | 2012 | | | | | | 2013 | | | | | | 2014 | | | | | |
|---|---|---|---|---|---|---|---|---|---|---|---|---|---|---|---|---|---|---|
| | Business | Work | Relatives | Study | Visitor | Other | Business | Work | Relatives | Study | Visitor | Other | Business | Work | Relatives | Study | Visitor | Other |
| All | 1.1 | 23.5 | 26.6 | 14.2 | 31.7 | 2.9 | 1.9 | 23.6 | 23.4 | 15.1 | 32.5 | 3.5 | 2.9 | 26.3 | 21.6 | 16.2 | 30.8 | 2.2 |
| UK | 1 | 12.5 | 20.3 | 8.5 | 49 | 8.7 | 1.2 | 12.1 | 18.2 | 9.1 | 51.5 | 7.9 | 1.3 | 14 | 19.7 | 8.1 | 48.2 | 8.7 |
| **China** | **1.8** | **61.4** | **13.9** | **3.3** | **18.4** | **1.2** | **4.1** | **60.3** | **12.2** | **3.9** | **17.7** | **1.8** | **3.7** | **62.9** | **9.8** | **1.8** | **20.9** | **0.9** |
| India | 0.7 | 38.1 | 23.7 | 4.4 | 33.5 | 0 | 0 | 41.2 | 21 | 4.1 | 29.4 | 4.3 | 1.7 | 42 | 19.7 | 4.3 | 29.3 | 3 |
| Germany | 0.8 | 16.9 | 10.6 | 8.1 | 56.7 | 6.9 | 0.7 | 16.9 | 9 | 7.6 | 57.2 | 8.6 | 1.8 | 16.5 | 10.4 | 9 | 52.5 | 9.8 |
| Africa | 0.8 | 20 | 28.4 | 20.1 | 28.1 | 2.6 | 1 | 20 | 22.4 | 22 | 31.7 | 2.9 | 2.6 | 20 | 21.1 | 24.7 | 30.8 | 0.8 |
| Zimbabwe | 0.1 | 35.3 | 18 | 21.8 | 23.7 | 1.1 | 0.2 | 30.8 | 16.9 | 21.9 | 28.9 | 1.3 | 0.3 | 26.3 | 13 | 27 | 32.8 | 0.6 |
| Nigeria | 1.1 | 10.5 | 40.6 | 12.9 | 33.4 | 1.5 | 3.1 | 11.6 | 29.7 | 16.3 | 37.7 | 1.6 | 6.4 | 17.4 | 30.6 | 13.8 | 31.5 | 0.3 |

*Note:* Ranked by country with most recipients

*Source:* Statistics South Africa. "Documented Immigrants into South Africa," Statistics South Africa, accessed December 23, 2019, http://www.statssa.gov.za/?s=documented&sitem=publications.

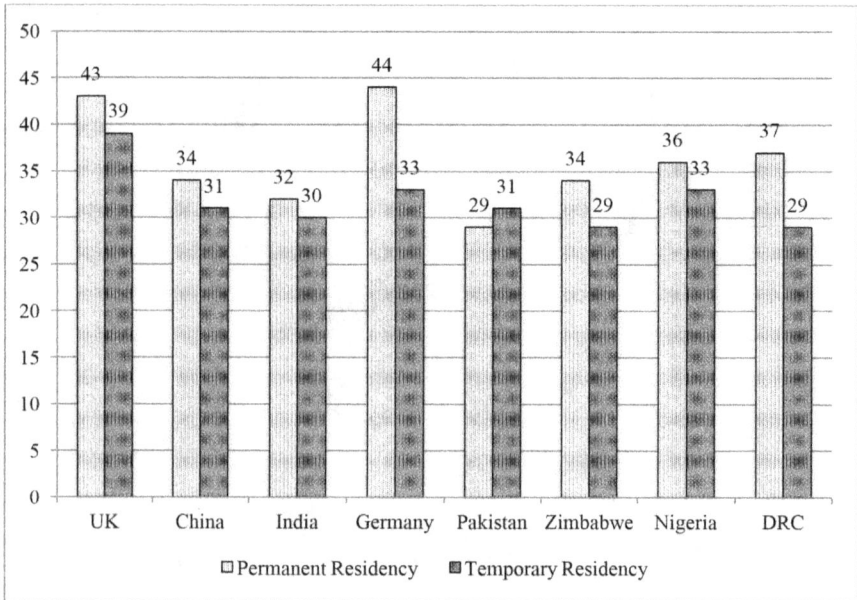

**Figure 5.1   Median Age of Immigrants from Five Top Countries.** *Source*: "Documented Immigrants into South Africa," Statistics South Africa, accessed December 23, 2019, http://www.statssa.gov.za/publications/P03514/P035142015.pdf.

political economy and increased over time but also find out if a link exists between unemployment and Chinese immigration.

Firstly, of the 4,136 granted permanent residency permits in 2014, China ranked third (granting 336), after Zimbabwe (1,497) and India (399). Virtually, for every Chinese granted permanent residency, four Zimbabweans were granted it as well. Secondly, of the 336 Chinese immigrants granted permanent residency in 2014, the largest proportion received it under the "work" category (37 percent), followed by "relatives" (59 percent) "business" (3 percent), and the refugee (0 percent) categories. The "relative" category is where a relative, already a citizen or co-applicant, applies on behalf of the incoming person to join them in the country.

Thirdly, of the 69,216 temporary residency permits granted in 2014, China ranked fourth (granting 5,739), after Zimbabwe (12,521), India (6,195), and Nigeria (6, 087). Virtually, for every Chinese granted temporary residency, two Zimbabweans were granted as well. Fourthly, of the 5,739 Chinese granted temporary residency in 2014, the largest proportion received it under the "work" category (63 percent), followed by "visitor" (21 percent), "relatives" (10 percent) "business" (4 percent), and student (1.8 percent) categories. The "relative" category is where a relative, already a citizen or co-applicant, applies on behalf of the incoming person to join them in the country.

Data suggests that not only China has a high net emigration but India as well. India, together with Pakistan and China, has the youngest number of migrants coming into South Africa. South Africa's unemployment is highest among the same age group as emigrating into South Africa from these countries (as well as Zimbabwe and Nigeria). It is therefore difficult to isolate China as possibly contributing to the high rates of unemployment. When Chinese immigration was low, South Africa's stubborn and long-term unemployment rate was still high. Also difficult is to distinguish if the replacement of locals by immigrants takes place at all. Do Chinese immigrants go into economic activities that would otherwise be done by South Africans? There is no answer given by the data in this regard. Further fieldwork would most likely have revealed this, but this is beyond the limited scope of this study. The types of professions of those granted permanent residency permit would be the most important information to ascertain.

But correlation still exists, especially regarding the most unemployed age group—those under 35—and the biggest proportion of incoming permanent residents, which is also around 35. But this occurrence of young immigration is confined to Chinese immigrants but is a characteristic of almost all the top five immigrating countries as well, such as India, Pakistan, Zimbabwe, Nigeria and Congo. Further analysis of data regarding the general impact of all these countries put together may yet reveal a link, but any such link is, again, confronted by the persistently high unemployment before and after these countries began to make up the majority of immigrants. Therefore, any link between immigration of Chinese (or any of the said countries) and unemployment must be relegated to the realm of correlation. But whether there is causation or correlation, the imperative of unemployment remains, which is the reason in the next chapter we continue to address this with the specific case of Yiwu and the prospects therein.

## NOTES

1. Erik S. Reinert, Yves Ekoue Amaizo, and Rainer Kattel, "The Economics of Failed, Failing, and Fragile States," in *Towards New Developmentalism*, ed. Shahrukh Raki Khan and Jens Christiansen (New York: Routledge, 2011), 59.

2. Ibid., 65.

3. "The CIA World Facebook," accessed November 11, 2020, https://www.cia .gov/the-world-factbook/countries/china/.

4. Ibid.

5. Gavin Lewis, "China's Success is Limited," *Financial Mail*, December, 10, 2010.

6. "Residents Without *Hukou* Pin Hopes on New Policy," *China Daily*, December 3, 2015.

7. "Lifting One-child Policy Echoes People's Will," *Global Times*, October 30, 2014.

8. Interview with a Chinese academic, Jinhua, September 16, 2014.

9. Interview with South African academic, November 12, 2014.

10. Interview with a Chinese academic, September 17, 2014.

11. "Nigeria's Success Due, in Part, to SA's Success," *Financial Mail*, April 10, 2014.

12. "Trade Reports," *Department of Trade and Industry of the Republic of South Africa*, accessed November 11, 2020 http://tradestats.thedti.gov.za/ReportFolders/reportFolders.aspx?sCS_referer=&sCS_ChosenLang=en.

13. Ibid.

14. Ibid.

15. Ibid.

16. Ibid.

17. Ibid.

18. "Indicators," *World Bank*, accessed December 23, 2019, https://data.world-bank.org/indicator.

19. Ibid.

20. Ibid.

21. Ibid.

22. Ibid.

23. Ibid.

24. Ibid.

25. A measure which calculates a country's inequality and expresses it by a value between 0 and 100. The closer a country's Gini coefficient is to 100 the more unequal it is.

26. "World Income Inequality Database," *UN-Wider*, accessed December 23, 2019, https://www.wider.unu.edu/project/wiid---world-income-inequality-database.

27. Ibid.

28. Ibid.

29. Ibid.

30. "Indicators," *World Bank*, accessed December 23, 2019, https://data.world-bank.org/indicator.

31. Ibid.

32. Ibid.

33. "Quarterly Labor Force Survey," *Statistics South Africa*, accessed November 11, 2019, http://www.statssa.gov.za/?page_id=1866&PPN=P0211&SCH=7891.

34. For more unemployment figures, see Appendix 5 and Appendix 6.

35. "Quarterly Labor Force Survey," *Statistics South Africa*, accessed November 11, 2019, http://www.statssa.gov.za/?page_id=1866&PPN=P0211&SCH=7891.

36. Ibid.

37. Ibid.

38. Ibid.

39. Ibid.

40. Ibid.

41. Ibid.

42. Ibid.

43. Ibid.

44. Ibid.

45. Ibid.

46. Wilfred L. David, *The Humanitarian Development Paradigm: Search for Global Justice* (Lanham, MD: University Press of America, 2004), 73.

47. Thabo Mbeki, "Reconciliation and Nation Building: Statement of Deputy President Thabo Mbeki at the Opening of the Debate in the National Assembly," *Cape Town*, May 29, 1998, http://www.dfa.gov.za/docs/speeches/1998/mbek0529.htm (accessed October 8, 2015).

48. "Quarterly Labor Force Survey," *Statistics South Africa*, accessed November 11, 2019, http://www.statssa.gov.za/?page_id=1866&PPN=P0211&SCH=7891.

49. Ibid.

50. Ibid.

51. Interview with Chinese scholar, September 17, 2014.

52. "Quarterly Labor Force Survey," *Statistics South Africa*, accessed November 11, 2019, http://www.statssa.gov.za/?page_id=1866&PPN=P0211&SCH=7891.

53. Ibid.

54. Ibid.

55. Ibid.

56. Paul Collier, *Exodus: How Migration is Changing the World* (New York: Oxford University Press, 2013), 25–26.

57. Ibid.

58. Ibid.

59. Joyashree Roy et al., "Developing Pathway," in *Global Environmental Changes in South Asia: A Regional Perspective*, ed. A. P. Mitra and C. Sharma (Berlin: Springer, 2012), 44.

60. Aurelia Segatti, *Contemporary Migration to South Africa: A Regional Development Issue* (Washington, DC: World Bank Publishing, 2011), 54.

61. "World Population Prospects," United Nations Population Division, World Bank Open Data, accessed December 23, 2019, https://data.worldbank.org/indicator/SM.POP.NETM.

62. Ibid.

## Chapter 6

# Yiwu

## Can It Make a Dent on South Africa's Unemployment?

The imperative of providing employment for millions of long term, discouraged, mostly black, young, and female South Africans, as expounded in the preceding chapter, is an urgent one. As such, it requires innovative and practical solutions, which take advantage of the prevailing conditions in the South Africa-China trade nexus even while seeking to change fundamental aspects embedded in it. The following are two major characteristics of this reality: first, China is the largest trading partner not just for South Africa but most developing and developed economies as well; second, as discussed in earlier chapters, a global dynamic exists which has seen China become the largest trader of finished goods or commodities in the world. This chapter, then, discusses findings from fieldwork conducted in the commodities trade hub-city of Yiwu in the Zhejiang province of China.

China has garnered highly efficient production mechanisms and as such ranks at the top in small commodities production, which, thanks to dedicated and sustained state support, has made it a dominant exporter. Given this reality, there are no easy solutions to South Africa's imperative of tackling intractable unemployment, itself linked to other imperatives of ending poverty and inequality. Practical solutions have to be put forward, however, which prima facie may not signal an immediate departure from the status quo of importing finished commodities from China. Solving this problem, through export-substitution initiatives, for instance, while most desirable to some, would be a longer-term strategy that is perhaps beyond the scope of this study, nor will it produce quick results against unemployment.

Instead, an easier, more practical solution is within the grasp of South African policy makers. After a discussion of the context around merchandise trade into South Africa and putting it in a global context, this chapter proposes solutions around a general two-pronged approach: first, a solution that

113

is immediate and is likely to make an immediate impact on unemployment; and second, another that is longer-term and requires aggressive skills transfer from Yiwu and other parts of China to South Africa. For both approaches, an emphasis is put on a strategy that emerged from China's efforts dealing with these imperatives itself: experimentation. China undertook pilot projects and experimented using one small area or cohort, with the intention of concurrently evaluating and amending the projects over a relatively short period of time, and then scaling them to a bigger area or cohort. Indeed, this was one of the first and most salient points made by former Chinese government officials and scholar alike with practical experience in Africa when asked for recommendations for South Africa.[1] Preliminary data related to South Africa's trade patterns and their interaction with unemployment, and China's link therein, is presented as an empirical motivation for these approaches.

## THE ANATOMY OF SOUTH AFRICA-CHINA TRADE

It is important to put into perspective the role trade has played as a contributor to employment and unemployment. An analysis of employment data for the important and disproportionately affected demographic, women, is analyzed. In 2008 the trade sector was responsible for the majority of jobs for women in South Africa, at 25.9 percent.[2] A year later, the biggest source of employment for women was no longer trade but the community and social services sector, at 26.6 percent.[3] By 2019, only 21.6 percent of women were employed in trade and 38.6 percent in the community and social services sector.[4] For an entire decade, women's participation in trade declined without pause. Notably, women's participation also declined in manufacturing (from 10.3 in 2009 to 8.5 percent in 2019) as well as agriculture (from 4.2 to 3.8 percent).[5] Together with trade, these two sectors may be expected to benefit the most from a deepening of South Africa-China cooperation.

Interestingly, although the community and social services industry surpassed trade as an employer of women, unemployment still rose within this sector itself, again demonstrating the extent of the unemployment problem. The data of those that became unemployed between 2016 and 2019 reveals trade as the largest industry to shed jobs. In 2018, up to 23.1 percent of those that became unemployed had worked in the trade sector.[6] The construction sector was second, at 17.2 percent, showing a failure in South Africa's economy provide construction jobs for the long term.[7]

### Is South Africa-China Trade Unbalanced?

This section looks at the role played by trade as an economic activity between South Africa and China in order to address questions that have pervaded the narrative of economic relations between China and not only South Africa but also Africa as a whole. These questions have centered on the make-up and balance of trade.

In the new dynamic that prevails, where South Africa has seen a marked shift in trade partners and a diversification of its trade, the growth of China-South Africa trade over time cannot be observed without a comparison to some of these partners, old and new. In 1998, when South Africa established its formal relations with China, the United States was its top trade partner nation, at $6.4 billion, followed by Germany at $6 billion.[8] By 2009, when China surpassed both the United States and Germany as South Africa's second largest trade partner, questions began to be raised about the exact nature of the South Africa-China trade.

The first manner by which these questions manifested themselves was regarding the balance of trade, which, so went the narrative, favored China. An evaluation of the data, however, suggests a more widespread problem for South Africa that is not isolated to trade with China alone. Indeed, since 1998, South Africa's imports from China have consistently surpassed exports, leading to a trade deficit every year except in 2003. But at same time as a deficit with China persisted, South Africa also ran a trade deficit with Germany and the EU every year except, like China, 2003. In 1998, the $2.8 billion deficit South Africa had with Germany was quadruple that with China (at $692 million). As relations with China grew, so did the trade deficit, which was until 2010 always surpassed by Germany's (with the exception of 2003). But from 2014 onwards, deficit with Germany began to decrease as China's began to increase. By 2018, trade deficit with China was quadruple that with Germany and EU.

The issue of South Africa's balance of trade, therefore, is complex and bigger than two countries. Its source, perhaps, is in South Africa's own production patterns and capacity before and after relations with China was established. From the data, an economy that has joined the top cluster of trade partners with South Africa has also almost invariably enjoyed a trade surplus relationship with Pretoria. It is telling that South Africa had never in the period shown suffered a trade deficit in its trade with the rest of the African continent (except in 2003).

## Is South Africa-China Trade Too Concentrated?

The second manner in which practitioners and scholars alike have raised questions on China-South Africa trade is around the issue of the concentration of trade, where a narrative of China's import of finished goods into and export of raw material from South Africa and Africa as a whole has unfolded.[9] The concentration index measures exports and imports by how diverse they are,

Table 6.1    **South Africa's Trade Balance, 1998–2019 (Dollars)**

|        | China          | Germany        | EU (excl. Germany) | Africa         |
|--------|----------------|----------------|--------------------|----------------|
| 1998   | -692,834,846   | -2,763,434,151 | -2,678,230,406     | 2,544,163,795  |
| 1999   | -614,836,641   | -2,366,970,230 | -1,006,402,616     | 2,537,969,163  |
| 2000   | -738,363,682   | -2,133,489,419 | -978,421,043       | 2,848,280,155  |
| 2001   | -720,870,335   | -2,664,695,107 | -340,961,622       | 2,426,514,151  |
| 2002   | -1,133,641,440 | -3,681,099,037 | -2,709,285,601     | 2,061,731,912  |
| 2003   | 0              | 138,918        | 1,177,560          | -1,232,465     |
| 2004   | -2,701,046,003 | -5,195,366,800 | -2,397,676,640     | 2,620,589,321  |
| 2005   | -3,721,431,598 | -6,277,867,940 | -1,549,308,957     | 2,278,380,269  |
| 2006   | -5,011,263,308 | -6,591,332,553 | -2,587,940,843     | 257,792,965    |
| 2007   | -5,438,727,085 | -6,071,999,338 | -3,574,950,953     | 260,564,207    |
| 2008   | -6,359,058,030 | -6,715,144,739 | -3,653,700,032     | 1,083,601,072  |
| 2009   | -2,819,627,557 | -3,858,538,260 | -2,711,705,038     | 13,247,726,677 |
| 2010   | -3,399,145,076 | -3,266,545,609 | -3,743,836,045     | 15,368,829,987 |
| 2011   | -1,722,530,308 | -4,841,256,149 | -5,052,429,893     | 17,400,712,250 |
| 2012   | -4,300,991,294 | -5,700,737,292 | -5,868,182,598     | 15,706,163,085 |
| 2013   | -3,959,952,473 | -6,440,002,692 | -5,572,091,389     | 15,577,726,147 |
| 2014   | -6,681,665,313 | -5,457,520,896 | -4,055,878,996     | 14,634,823,726 |
| 2015   | -8,272,165,600 | -4,304,159,032 | -4,036,067,858     | 14,711,562,709 |
| 2016   | -6,671,041,594 | -3,250,734,856 | -2,782,466,327     | 13,808,628,120 |
| 2017   | -6,818,338,494 | -3,530,961,237 | -2,599,562,399     | 16,374,643,140 |
| 2018   | -8,592,613,171 | -2,138,390,840 | -2,070,443,760     | 13,875,508,943 |
| 2019   | -6,656,567,527 | -1,227,427,038 | -2,565,759,173     | 13,958,478,571 |

*Source*: Department of Trade and Industry of South Africa. "Trade Reports," Department of Trade and Industry of the Republic of South Africa, accessed February, 15, 2020, http://tradestats.thedti.gov.za/ReportFolders/reportFolders.aspx?sCS_referer=&sCS_ChosenLang=en

giving each country, either as an exports destination or an imports source, a score from 0 to 1 (the closer to 1 the more concentrated or less diverse). The data on some of South Africa's top export destination countries reveals that South Africa's exports to China in 2006 were the third-most concentrated at 0.285, after Japan (0.469) and the United States (at 0.347).[10] In 2012, exports to China became the most concentrated, at 0.442; and by 2014 they were 0.471.[11] Exports to Germany, South Africa's second-largest trade partner, were relatively diverse, at 0.251 in 2014.[12]

What is notable, as far as implications for South Africa's future trajectory of trade are concerned, is that exports to African countries, and BRIC countries as a whole, were the most diverse. These export destinations hold the biggest potential, it seems, for an industrialized, value-adding South African economy and bode well not only for South-South relations but for regional economic integration driven by a South African industrial revolution.

According to the data, South Africa's imports from China, at 0.115, together with those from the United States (0.104) and the EU (0.117), have in 2014 and subsequent years been the least concentrated.[13] Nigeria (0.996) and South Arabia (0.857) are understandably high as sources of South Africa's oil imports.[14] Imports from the rest of the African continent as a whole have remained the third-highest concentrated. In 2014, they stood at 0.612, an increase from 0.539 in 2012.[15] The data suggests that these imports from the rest of Africa are more concentrated more than any of South Africa's exports to China or Japan have ever been. The implication is that, as far as what it exports to an economy, South Africa is to the African economy what China is to South Africa's own economy. Chinese exports to South Africa are highly diverse, but Chinese imports from South Africa are highly concentrated. Accordingly, South Africa's exports to the rest of the continent are highly diverse, but South Africa's imports from the continent are highly concentrated. While not excluding South Africa from the dynamic of an African country exporting a concentrated amount of goods to China for the latter's diverse, value-added imports, this picture still puts South Africa in a different "middle-of-the-line" category because the country also exports diverse, value-added goods to the rest of the continent.

## "FINISHED GOODS" NARRATIVE: WHAT THE TRADE MATRIX REVEALS

The concentration index does not offer any clarity on the specific type of exports and imports. This section fills this gap using the trade matrix (i.e., the grouping of exported and imported goods using the UN categories and classification system) data to address what is a third manner in which questions on China-South Africa trade have been raised, which is around the issue of specific goods. Although South Africa exports to China appear highly concentrated, a more nuanced perspective emerges when attention is paid to the specific group of these exports using their formal categories.

In tables 6.1 and 6.2 data from South Africa's Department of Trade and Industry is presented. The top eight products exported by South Africa to China, Africa and the World were selected, as well as the top eight products imported from China, Africa, and the World. For exports, the products were coded (table 6.2) according to whether or not they were only a top export to China by either South Africa, Africa or the world by themselves; a top export to China by South Africa, Africa, and the World; a top export to China by only South Africa and Africa; a top export to China by only Africa and the World; a top export to China by only South Africa and the World; and whether it was both a top export by one of the three into China *and* a top export by China to one of the three at the same time. The same coding was done for imports from China into South Africa, Africa, and the World. The products were ranked by the largest export or import value in 2019.

**Table 6.2    Coding Key and Results for Tables 7.3 and 7.4**

| Coding | | | Results | |
|---|---|---|---|---|
| Color | Meaning | | Imports | Exports |
| | Among top imports/exports of <u>only one</u> country or territory to/from China | | 2(0) | 11 (4) |
| | Among top imports/exports of <u>SA</u>, <u>Africa</u> & <u>World</u> into/from China | | 6 | 2 |
| | Among top imports/exports of only <u>SA</u> & <u>Africa</u> into/from China | | 0 | 1 |
| | Among top imports/exports of only <u>Africa</u> and <u>World</u> into/from China | | 0 | 1 |
| | Among top imports/exports of <u>SA</u> & <u>World</u> into/from China | | 2 | 2 |
| | Among top exports <u>into China</u> *and* top imports <u>from China</u> too | | 1 | 1 |

*Note*: ()—Imports/exports into/from South Africa only.
*Source*: Author; Department of Trade and Industry of South Africa[16]

## Exports

Firstly, according to the data, between the top 8 exported products from South Africa, Africa, and the World, totaling 24, South Africa only had 1 product category in common with Africa, 2 in common with the world. Africa also had four product categories exclusive to itself. This may suggest that a majority of South Africa's top exports to China, although shown to be highly concentrated in the concentration index, the specific products exported, upon closer analysis of their classification, were different from Africa.

This adds a nuanced perspective on making a judgment of China-South Africa trade based on the narrative of a "typical" African export of raw materials to China. Most importantly, it demonstrated a growth area upon which, with the appropriate attention of South African policymakers, the country's quest to reduce its trade deficit with China, grow its economy, as well as provide employment, may be promulgated. But this requires attention at a bi-lateral level, using the mechanism of the Bi-national Commission, as well as at the national level where planning and economic incentives may be made available to expand productive capacity in these exclusive top exports to China. South African top exports such as products in categories of "non-metallic mineral manufactures," "pulp and waste paper," and "vegetables and fruits" have an enormous potential for South African industrial expansion focused on adding value to them and reducing unemployment.

Secondly, South Africa only shared two top export categories with both Africa and the World ("metalliferous ores and metal scrap" and "non-ferrous metals") and only shared one exclusively with Africa ("textile fibers and their waste"). On the one hand, this suggests that the export of primary products or raw material to China is not exclusive to South Africa, but, on the other hand, South Africa has more commonality with the world than Africa in this regard. Ultimately, China has a large demand for these products, which cannot be satisfied by Africa or South Africa alone; the supply for at least some of them is an international phenomenon which is often, if not unfairly, pinned on Africa alone, including South Africa. Indeed, Africa shared one export products exclusively with the World ("petroleum, petroleum products and related materials").

Thirdly, as it did with Africa, South Africa shared only one top category export with the World. This is another emphasis on the relatively uniqueness of the categories exported by the country to China, which is a significant opportunity for comparative advantage yet to be identified by South Africa. Lastly, products classified as "office machines and automatic data processing machines" were both among the World's to exports *to* China as well as among top imports by the World and South Africa *from* China. It will be important for future studies to determine the intra-class variances in the category of these products—to make a distinction on which specific items within the category were exported to, and which were exported from, China. This, perhaps, has a potential to inform further studies in this area on the mode and scope of Chinese value addition on products in the same category the exports.

## Imports

Firstly, South Africa shared two top import categories exclusively with the World ("miscellaneous manufactured articles, n.e.s." and "office machines and automatic data processing machines"). This may signify a convergence of South Africa's import and consumption patterns with those of the World. In other words, what is mostly imported by the world has tended to be mostly imported by South Africa as well. Secondly, of its eight top categories of imports, South Africa shared six with both Africa and the World. It shared the remaining two categories exclusively with the World, and it did not share any category of imports exclusively with Africa.

Thirdly, the convergence of import and consumption patterns is also demonstrated by the data on the World, South Africa, as well as Africa together. Products in the categories classified as "telecommunication equipment" (such as cellular phones and so forth) "footwear," and "electrical machinery" are the top exports found among all three importing markets. This and the above point are significant for highlighting a point which may depart from widely held perceptions on the world's import patterns vis-a-vis China: that (South) Africa overwhelmingly and exclusively imports finished products from China.

This correspondence of South Africa's patterns of import and consumption with those of the world is the reason why I am seeking a way forward to address its unemployment imperatives, South Africa must be cognizant of and take advantage of patterns as they obtain. In other words, South Africa's developmental outcomes, at least as far as this imperative is concerned, may well find some realization from prevailing patterns of importing from China, which are hardly going to change significantly in the foreseeable future, together with seeking an expansion of its production and export capacity. This is what made the Yiwu International Trade City a compelling case to study in this regard.

## YIWU: NOT A "MIRACLE" BUT A PLAN

The trade in merchandise historically constituted a significant part of South Africa's economic activity. In 1998 it was 40 percent of South Africa's GDP.[17] While this was higher than the world average (35 percent), it was closer to sub-Saharan Africa's figure of 42 percent.[18] By contrast, China was closer though slightly lower than the world average, at 31 percent.[19] In 2003 however, China surpassed South Africa at 52 percent of its GDP was made up of trade in merchandise.[20] In 2014, however, trade as percentage of South Africa's GDP stood at 61 percent, China was at 41 percent, sub-Saharan Africa, 46, and the world, 48.[21] This demonstrates trade not only as a potential but as an existential reality of South Africa's economic activity, one which holds, perhaps, more unexplored prospects in addressing the unemployment imperative. The extent to which this high level of trade activity is able to have a measurable effect on the lives of ordinary South Africans, especially black women who are disproportionately affected by unemployment, has a determining potential for the country's developmental progress. But keeping in mind the high rate of trade between South Africa and China, it is difficult to imagine a realization of this potential trade potential—and its short- to medium-term benefits—that does not engage China. To that end, the Yiwu International Trade City, in Yiwu, Zhejiang province, China was studied for what it may or may not hold for South Africa's developmental imperative of addressing unemployment.

### Origins of Yiwu

The fortunes of Yiwu and its place in the export economy of China, and by extension the world economy are first gleaned by a foreigner far away from Zhejiang province where town is located. About 600 miles away, at the international terminal of Hong Kong airport, large banners proclaim to the traveler: "Come to Yiwu for your shopping. The largest small commodities

Table 6.3 Trade Matrix of Top Eight Products Exported by South Africa, Africa, and World to China, Thousands of Dollars, 2011–2019 (Listed by Largest Value of Exports for Each of the Three Exporters in 2019)

| Exporter | 2011 | 2013 | 2015 | 2017 | 2019 |
|---|---|---|---|---|---|
| **South Africa Total** | 32,095,190 | 48,388,425 | 30,151,410 | 24,388,596 | 27,764,936 |
| Gold, non-monetary | n/a | n/a | 14,881,830 | 7,074,666 | 8,740,712 |
| Metalliferous ores and metal scrap | 8,991,297 | 8,721,803 | 5,429,202 | 8,102,767 | 8,708,089 |
| Non metallic mineral manufactures, n.e.s. | 1,300,442 | 2,461,367 | 3,851,087 | 4,041,554 | 4,506,003 |
| Non-ferrous metals | 2,255,066 | 3,174,113 | 2,713,316 | 1,729,104 | 2,194,595 |
| Iron and steel | 1,379,103 | 1,022,893 | 1,699,234 | 1,601,864 | 1,678,317 |
| Pulp and waste paper | 194,006 | 178,908 | 344,296 | 308,691 | 333,622 |
| Vegetables and fruits | 51,605 | 107,889 | 200,141 | 263,683 | 289,138 |
| Textiles fibers and their wastes | 145,829 | 207,480 | 205,188 | 237,048 | 286,492 |
| **Africa Total** | 45,358,923 | 60,202,692 | 36,036,074 | 46,945,279 | 64,884,213 |
| Petroleum, petroleum products and related materials | 32,816,298 | 44,416,235 | 23,885,858 | 30,343,365 | 41,209,990 |
| Non-ferrous metals | 4,545,006 | 4,570,346 | 3,878,464 | 5,865,067 | 7,642,802 |
| Metalliferous ores and metal scrap | 3,806,790 | 5,280,910 | 2,737,241 | 4,727,809 | 7,160,066 |
| Cork and wood | 1,146,476 | 1,532,859 | 1,975,407 | 2,209,512 | 3,031,934 |
| Gas, natural and manufactured | 642,634 | 928,537 | 624,480 | 1,158,139 | 1,928,251 |
| Oil seeds and oleaginous fruits | 411,146 | 634,488 | 974,897 | 638,400 | 1,082,599 |
| Tobacco and tobacco manufactures | 333,240 | 609,863 | 712,989 | 670,788 | 773,484 |
| Textiles fibers and their wastes | 735,988 | 823,573 | 195,294 | 184,536 | 326,026 |
| **World Total** | 1,743,394,866 | 1,949,992,315 | 1,679,564,325 | 1,843,792,939 | 2,076,352,734 |
| Petroleum, petroleum products and related materials | 238,055,917 | 260,948,364 | 161,214,907 | 193,586,384 | 285,563,441 |
| Metalliferous ores and metal scrap | 177,739,162 | 171,493,462 | 108,789,920 | 142,130,126 | 194,614,011 |
| Road vehicles | 65,179,543 | 73,989,140 | 69,496,113 | 79,099,539 | 85,403,726 |
| Professional and scientific instruments, n.e.s. | 82,391,886 | 87,853,883 | 80,241,634 | 76,601,283 | 77,148,393 |
| Organic chemicals | 62,927,109 | 65,544,367 | 47,757,784 | 55,446,593 | 67,309,981 |
| Office machines and automatic data processing machines | 57,822,160 | 57,177,048 | 50,598,231 | 101,042,400 | 60,917,338 |
| Non-ferrous metals | 56,214,493 | 51,026,801 | 43,211,018 | 46,535,697 | 55,310,404 |
| Gold, non-monetary | n/a | n/a | 78,977,995 | 51,392,352 | 55,202,334 |

*Source:* Department of Trade and Industry of South Africa. "Trade Reports," Department of Trade and Industry of the Republic of South Africa, accessed February, 15, 2020, http://tradestats.thedti.gov.za/ReportFolders/reportFolders.aspx?sCS_referer=&sCS_ChosenLang=en

Table 6.4  Trade Matrix of Top Eight Products Imported by South Africa, Africa, and World from China, Thousands of Dollars, 2011–2019 (Largest Value of Imports for Each of the Three Exporters in 2019).

| Importer | 2011 | 2013 | 2015 | 2017 | 2019 |
|---|---|---|---|---|---|
| **South Africa Total** | **13,362,300** | **16,830,776** | **15,857,922** | **14,808,767** | **16,570,937** |
| Articles of apparel & clothing accessories | 1,875,034 | 1,926,151 | 1,681,070 | 1,407,614 | 1,597,224 |
| Telecommunication and sound recording apparatus | 1,131,532 | 1,164,499 | 1,540,488 | 1,449,228 | 1,558,847 |
| Electrical machinery, apparatus and appliances, n.e.s. | 976,192 | 1,595,793 | 1,316,684 | 1,216,481 | 1,359,545 |
| Textile yarn and related products | 908,912 | 982,500 | 948,330 | 920,536 | 1,057,892 |
| Miscellaneous manufactured articles, n.e.s. | 629,750 | 961,010 | 976,401 | 918,116 | 1,021,920 |
| Other industrial machinery and parts | 685,769 | 909,111 | 813,308 | 793,451 | 959,919 |
| Manufactures of metal, n.e.s. | 649,073 | 825,879 | 749,887 | 678,941 | 798,630 |
| Office machines and automatic data processing machines | 765,934 | 779,191 | 760,772 | 744,353 | 760,682 |
| **Africa Total** | **59,558,899** | **75,745,070** | **92,458,588** | **79,699,126** | **96,557,208** |
| Textile yarn and related products | 7,839,144 | 8,888,837 | 9,585,414 | 8,989,814 | 10,616,368 |
| Electrical machinery, apparatus and appliances, n.e.s. | 3,969,715 | 5,210,126 | 7,054,305 | 6,021,243 | 7,449,877 |
| Articles of apparel & clothing accessories | 2,965,981 | 4,694,915 | 7,901,804 | 6,310,961 | 7,135,957 |
| Manufactures of metal, n.e.s. | 3,343,881 | 4,372,042 | 6,178,464 | 5,174,153 | 6,590,888 |
| Road vehicles | 4,783,532 | 6,022,954 | 5,412,792 | 4,660,936 | 5,533,925 |
| Other industrial machinery and parts | 2,897,317 | 4,173,423 | 4,431,361 | 4,351,449 | 5,530,792 |
| Iron and steel | 2,479,482 | 3,504,689 | 4,788,435 | 3,670,582 | 4,945,873 |
| Telecommunication and sound recording apparatus | 3,376,278 | 3,112,681 | 5,819,744 | 4,047,668 | 4,771,980 |

| | | | | | |
|---|---|---|---|---|---|
| **World Total** | **1,898,388,435** | **2,209,007,280** | **2,273,468,224** | **2,263,370,504** | **2,506,601,469** |
| Electrical machinery, apparatus and appliances, n.e.s. | 218,682,958 | 293,403,080 | 288,353,433 | 287,296,477 | 344,740,990 |
| Telecommunication and sound recording apparatus | 208,735,105 | 252,816,969 | 292,588,392 | 237,855,734 | 257,917,681 |
| Office machines and automatic data processing machines | 218,460,453 | 223,797,771 | 192,966,176 | 260,855,633 | 238,313,533 |
| Articles of apparel & clothing accessories | 153,773,608 | 177,434,934 | 174,572,923 | 157,463,892 | 172,388,369 |
| Miscellaneous manufactured articles, n.e.s. | 114,804,757 | 155,549,089 | 146,912,810 | 143,999,970 | 155,813,016 |
| Textile yarn and related products | 94,410,734 | 106,577,951 | 108,934,059 | 109,595,045 | 128,254,390 |
| Other industrial machinery and parts | 79,847,419 | 93,953,048 | 101,087,429 | 107,688,839 | 125,832,744 |
| Manufactures of metal, n.e.s. | 66,216,840 | 78,334,415 | 89,130,844 | 85,832,073 | 103,778,974 |

*Source:* "Trade Reports," Department of Trade and Industry of the Republic of South Africa, accessed February 15, 2020.

trade market in the world." Two-hour flights departing every hour connect the world to what has until recently been an unknown hinterland to non-Chinese. The world is more familiar with Guangdong in Guangzhou province instead.

In 1982, as a result of the "reform and opening up" Deng Xiaoping began in 1978, various provinces, prefectures, and towns began to develop their own plans to follow in order to participate in the ensuing economic growth. Yiwu, a prefecture-level city, was one of them. Following the leader's directive for people to use a method of production under the slogan *yizhen yipin* ("one town, one product") or *yicun yipin* ("one village, one product"), many towns and villages throughout Zhejiang and the surrounding provinces began to specialize in one product with the sole intention of increasing efficiency, productivity, and scale export.[22]

Because of its location, Yiwu became the central convergence point producers in isolated locations to bring their products to a central location where they would be sold at wholesale prices, thereby granting them access to a worldwide market.

The culture of mass specialization is demonstrated in the streets of Yiwu where similar types of products are clustered on the same street throughout the city: Changchun for ornaments; Zhaozhai for picture frames; Zhaozhai for lighters; Yidong for printing and package material; Dongjiang for small daily use household appliances; and Chouzhou for Christmas items and crafts.

Over the years, the large influx of traders from all over the world who came to Yiwu for business created a sub-cluster of foreign stores and restaurants in the city in what is perhaps unique in China away from metropolis of Guangdong. This area of town, known as "Exotic Street," an approximately three-square-mile cluster, is populated mainly by people from Africa and the Middle East, replete with a mosque. After undertaking field research in Yiwu, Hong Kong-based African scholar Adam Bodomo argued that it is this "efficient and civil treatment" with which Africans have been treated in Yiwu than has typically been seen in Guangzhou where instances of mistreatment and racial profiling of Africans have been widely reported, that makes Yiwu "a model international multicultural trade city."[23]

While I did not visit Guangzhou and was not able to compare treatment of Africans myself, I however can concur with Bodomo's assertion about Yiwu. Although I frequently walked about the city, sometimes late at night, with a camera in hand, frequently taking pictures and notes, I was never stopped by any police or not did I experience mistreatment of any kind by locals. Not once did I experience any harassment or feel cheated. This easy environment extended to simple services I observed the Chinese in Yiwu render to foreigners, including myself. At the hotel, the language barrier was not an uncomfortable experience because a visitor is given a step-by-step check-in guide in English. At the laundry services across the street, with no linguistic communication between myself and the proprietor, she received my clothes and simply punched the modest price on a calculator to show me. And upon my return at dusk she returned the clothes clean, pressed, neatly folded and individually packaged into a bag as if new from the store. At restaurants, the menus include pictures of the food so the nonspeaker of Chinese can order simply by pointing.

From the time one sets foot off the train at Yiwu station, there is a feeling that this town, far from the gleaming metropole of China most in the world have come to know, with simple, humble people, many of whom not long ago farmed rice for their subsistence, has more to teach big Chinese cities about hospitality in trade. A foreigner feels comfortable in Yiwu. There seems to be a pervasive reverence for foreigners among the people who are acutely aware, perhaps, that but for the congregation of foreigners over the past couple of decades, Yiwu's fortunes would be very different.

## Yiwu International Trade City

There are hundreds of markets scattered around Yiwu, but the focus was on Yiwu International Trade City. It is easy to be overwhelmed by the sheer size of the Yiwu International Trade City. It is an indoor facility, with five buildings, known as "districts," which are connected by covered bridges. The markets, which cover an area of 8.5 million square feet, consist of more than 400,000 products sold in over 500,000 "stands."[24] Although the stands differ, most are modest—approximately 40 square foot stores packed with goods. Except in designated areas or floors, these are samples which, upon order, are deliverable to the buyer almost instantly or by other arrangement. Services for translation, shipping, and others are available.

In 2011, Yiwu International Trade City alone had a turnover of over RMB5.1 billion ($768 million). As the "largest and most modern commodity distribution center and export hub" in China, Yiwu is intimately tied not only to the economy of the province but also to the other ones.[25] Fujian is to the south, Jiangxi to the southwest, Anhui to the northwest, and Jiangsu and the province-level city of Shanghai are to the north. Most of the products sold there come from the hinterlands in provinces farther afield from the ones contingent to Zhejiang, but have found a benefit in their export trading in Yiwu.

## The Africans and Yiwu

Firstly, there were no South Africans encountered throughout this research at Yiwu International Trade City, although this does not discount their presence.

There was a 6 to 4 ratio in favor of males among Africans encountered in all five of the districts. Africans were found throughout the five districts. They have secured business visas in order to travel there and most were repeat travelers. Some had been to other trading parts of China such as Guangdong, Guangzhou. Overwhelmingly, they found traveling throughout China easier than traveling in Africa.

Secondly, of the African women traders, a majority were Kenyan and Zimbabwean. They traveled with a female companion, mostly a member of their family, and the duration of their stay was typically strictly for the duration of their shopping. Thirdly, while almost all Africans I encountered were not coming to China for the first time, having heard about Yiwu from friends or fellow African shopping associates in Guangzhou, and having been convinced to come because of lower prices, and hence the promise of a bigger turnover, a few had not traveled to any other African country before. This, in no insignificant way, shows the extent to which China as a trading partner to certain African countries more often than not supplants the trade between African countries themselves. It is here that the point made earlier about there being enormous untapped potential in intra-Africa trade must be re-emphasized.

Fourthly, most of the Africans were not wholesalers back home but pro-prietors of small to medium enterprises, though some were store-owners simply buying to replenish their inventories. One trader from Ghana com-plained about how "impossible" it seemed to her to start a business operation at home.[26] The regulation was almost insurmountable. Instead of spending meager capital on securing licenses for her enterprise, she opted to direct the capital in investing on a trip, a hotel, and her inventory. This brings into sharp focus the prohibitive nature of certain regulations for budding entrepreneurs in African economies. If South Africa is to make a dent in its unemployment imperative, the issue of entry barriers into the lucrative sector of trade will have to take center stage in a policy.

Fifthly, almost all did not have enormous capital. They used capital from their own savings, those of family members, close friends, neighbors, fellow church members, and so forth. What this did demonstrate was an organic intuition that is sometimes lost when developmental solutions are sought about intractable developmental problems in (South) Africa. These Africans were not lobbied by anyone to come to a part of China where many of them are still "regarded strangely but treated respectfully,"[27] not to speak of the fact that they did not speak the Chinese language. But the returns, although comparatively less than could be expected in a wholesale industry, granted they had more capacity, were still enough of an enticement for the venture. As a Zimbabwean trader puts it, "all this is for my children," thus exposing a profound seriousness and personal aspect of the traders' motivations.[28] It is this humanitarian aspect of African traders in Yiwu which most translates to the South African situation. In simple, organic, aspirations like these lie opportunity for the expansion of the program by the South African government among South African women.

Lastly, and most importantly, almost all the traders interviewed employed an average of six people back home. This does not take into consideration the "downstream" effects of their trade where all have families as well as extended families who rely on them as well. The immediate, tangible, and far-reaching humanitarian development effects of this cannot be over-emphasized.

## PROPOSALS IN THE SHORT TERM: SPEED, EXPERIMENTATION, AND EVALUATING

Recognizing the urgency that solving the unemployment problem within the framework of South Africa-China relations, this study has separated its proposals between those that may be realized in the long term and those that must be implemented immediately. As for the latter, South African policymakers and scholars alike have to acknowledge that a certain level of experimentation must go side-by-side with any innovative strategy. Like China's own period of dealing with its developmental imperative, especially in the 1970s/1980s reform, responsive, rapid results-based approaches, some through trial-and-error, must not be precluded. The issue of traders' participation in trade through Yiwu, therefore, by South Africans, especially women, is one such proposal. While it may be counterintuitive, given the existing trade deficit, to encourage participation in an endeavor that could make the deficit worse, the rapid, developmental results of making a dent on stubborn unemployment may justify this approach—but only if coupled with a long-term export-oriented strategy.

### Toward a Dual Export-Import Strategy

The first proposal is regarding the flow of trade between China in general and Yiwu in particular. To their credit, the Chinese have sought to also encourage imports from Africa that will be tradable in Yiwu, to Chinese traders for onward sales throughout the country. Scholars in China concur that this is something that has received much attention from Chinese in officials in Zhejiang.[29]

To that end, the Yiwu Trade City has an entire floor in District 5 where African art is sold. On the face of it, this is a progressive idea. The "African Products Exhibition and Goods Center" has individual stands corresponding to each African country. At the "South Africa" pavilion, for instance, are found various items of South African art. A lion rug, for instance, sells for RMB50,000 ($7,600). Questions may be raised about the sustainability of selling wholesale animal products to a big Chinese market over time. However, this legal sale of animals which are not endangered is within the rights of the traders under both South African and Chinese law. Also, most of the products sold are smaller art products, many of which are made by artisans who reaped economic benefit as a result.

What may warrant attention, however, as far as the imperative we are attempting to address here is concerned is first the extent to which South Africa's unemployed, especially women, have been incorporated into the value chain of these products and have reaped the same economies of scale as perhaps their Chinese counterparts in Yiwu and beyond, those who are producers of products traded in the opposite direction.

The second consideration that may warrant attention and is connected to the first one is that while on the face of it, most pavilions represent an "African" trade import into China, the field research done on sight in almost all of them may suggest otherwise. Firstly, only two Africans were observed working in the pavilions—an Ethiopian at the "Ethiopia" pavilion and another African at the Senegal pavilion. Secondly, there was dubiously strong overlap or similarity in the art products in one pavilion and another supposed different country's pavilion. The "Cameroon" pavilion had almost identical art products to the Gambia, and Namibia pavilions, all relatively distant countries with very distinctive artistic traditions, whose diversity did not correspond to the products displayed under their name.

This point requires attention because it has serious implications not only for business practices and ethics but for the developmental imperative which it is hoped will be addressed by onward trade into China from Africa. It may well be that this similarity in products is a because a number of pavilions were, first, owned by Chinese businesspeople themselves and not Africans, and two, that some business people may operate more than one "country" pavilion, hence the liberal "sharing" of art products with little regard for there being a Chinese customer keen enough to notice or care about incorrect attribution of a product's country-of-origin.

Although pavilion proprietors may mean well in exposing China to African art, these glaring mistakes at some pavilions, though not all, puts a damper on a serious initiative by Chinese officials to decrease the deficit in trade. If both these issues are not addressed by Chinese authorities, they will make a serious dent in the credibility of what is a progressive step and may well have a deleterious effect on the goodwill of Chinese customers of products, who when they find out the true provenance of a product, may wrongfully project it on the image of the African country whose name it was associated with. Notably, the "Zimbabwe" pavilion was empty and deserted, an unusual occurrence given the closeness of relations between Beijing and Harare. The

"South Africa" pavilion, however, appeared the most-stocked, and with genuinely South African goods, as did the Ethiopian one.

The proposal here is that South African trade officials take Yiwu seriously, not only its potential for providing finished goods to South Africa but also for its prospects for South African exports via the hub. It is a ready-made center for trade into the large Chinese market. It is not practical to put the onus on reducing the deficit of trade patterns on Chinese officials who seriously and dutifully address their unemployment imperative through Yiwu. For South Africa, Yiwu is a good opportunity for experimental pilot programs, of which the "African Products Exhibition and Goods Center" is only a start.

### Utilizing the Ministry of Small Business Development to Create Empowerment and Agency for Women

In 2014, the South African government established a new cabinet department, the Ministry of Small-Medium Enterprises. The government drew a lesson from other countries with similar ministries. India has its own Ministry of Micro, Small and Medium Enterprises and Zimbabwe also has a Ministry of Small and Medium Enterprises and Cooperative Development.

The new ministry's stated mandate revolves around four areas: economic growth, partnerships, and radical transformation. The ministry's documents are vague, however, on the practical meanings of these lofty if not general goals. On radical transformation, for instance, the documents simply state the ministry aims to "facilitate radical economic transformation through increased participation of small businesses and cooperatives in the mainstream economy."[30] The ministry has come up with a number of schemes meant to support small businesses. These schemes include the following programs:

i. BBSDP—Black Business Supplier Development Program. A program aimed at fast-tracking the entry of Small, Medium and Micro Enterprises (SMMEs) into the mainstream economy by subsidizing tool and equipment acquisition.
ii. CIS—Co-Operative Incentive Scheme. A program to give incentives to co-ops by through needs-based grants.
iii. SEIF—Shared Economic Infrastructure Facility. A cost-sharing program between the Department of Trade and Industry and businesses involving the sharing of facilities and other business infrastructure.
iv. ITUP—Informal Traders Upliftment Project. A program to train informal traders on basic business "soft skills" such as customer service and "attitudinal" skills.[31]

While these programs are good signs and have clear plans and indeed the potential to lead to solutions similar to the ones proposed here regarding Yiwu and women participation, they fall short in three ways. First, there are no time-based targets and numbers of participants the government hopes to incorporate in the schemes. For the short-term goals of addressing the imperative of unemployment, lofty plans, however well constructed and hopeful, do not constitute a solution. Instead, they join a long list of what has been a familiar optimism when plans are launched, but they fall short of time-specific targets to keep policy makers and government officials accountable. The optimism has far too often been replaced by a reality of unfulfilled plans.

Secondly, the schemes have requirements that may constitute barriers to entry at least for the intended target, black unemployed women. Among the requirements of the BBSDP is that a business must not only already be in existence but that it also must have at least a turnover of R250 000 ($16,000) to R35 million ($2.3 million). These steep barriers to entry, taken together with what may otherwise be a positive 50 percent black ownership requirement, may have the unintended consequence of encouraging "fronting," where powerful non-black business interests collude with blacks and provide capital in order to benefit from such initiatives and thus defeat the empowerment aspect of them. The CIS is a positive initiative aiming to encourage women to form cooperatives, which may fit well into the Yiwu strategy that women farther afield in African countries are already doing in Yiwu with little government intervention. However, one of the requirements is that a cooperative be incorporated as well as have working capital. Ostensibly, this is achievable, but unlike the much more prohibitive BBSDP, the CIS offers no specifics on the amount of financial aid to be forthcoming to recipients.

A way forward may be to combine certain aspects of these programs. The government must immediately support the formation of women's co-ops, most of whom already exist through civic groups, churches, and other community formations. Each co-op, after obtaining seed capital from the Ministry of Small Business Development, must then choose two representative shoppers and use the co-op's own money—not the government's—for transportation to and from Yiwu and accommodation there. Then, the co-op must choose one to four products in which to specialize. The buyers without deviation will then buy these products and return and divide them among themselves for sale. First, there must be a pilot or "pioneer" group from exemplary co-ops. Ten co-ops from ten various townships, split between two specific metropolitan areas like Johannesburg or Durban, could be the first to go. Upon evaluation of the program in three months, then improvements can be made. The scheme could also be incorporated into the South Africa-China Bi-national Commission for oversight and additional assistance from appointed co-op ambassadors in Yiwu.

## PROPOSALS IN THE LONG TERM:
## THE INDISPENSABLE ROLE OF
## GOVERNMENT AND LEGISLATION

Building a "South African Yiwu" through Merit-based Scholarships to Zhejiang Normal University's China-Africa International Business School

A long-term strategy for addressing the unemployment imperative must include studying education in China. Near Yiwu is the Zhejiang Normal University in Jinhua, Zhejiang which has a Center for African Studies, dedicated to studying all aspects of Africa, including economic aspects. At an advanced level, South Africa needs to foster more collaborative projects where South African researchers in political economy and related fields may learn from Yiwu from an advanced, academic level and take advantage of the proximity to Yiwu (40 minutes by road) for field research.

In 2007, Zhejiang Normal University established the China-Africa International Business School (CAIBS), which offers Bachelors, Masters, and PhD-level qualifications in trade and other economically related subjects in Africa. This is the first university in China to do so. At a tertiary level, then, South African students may be supported, under a specific program, to study at CAIBS. Out of the 400 African students studying at Zhejiang Normal University, I encountered only 1 South African student. There were no reliable numbers on how many South Africans are studying there.

The ultimate long-term objective is to build a knowledge base which would be at the core of a "South African Yiwu" for goods in which South Africa has a comparative advantage. When asked about Chinese models, Chinese scholars are often quick to caution that any modeling must be "translated" to correspond to the local characteristics in a specific country. Having a critical core of young people trained in Zhejiang will help South Africa build intellectual mechanisms to "translate" the experience of Yiwu based not on fanciful and enthusiastic emulation, however admirable the Yiwu model may seem, but on an empirical foundation only sustained, on-the-ground research can provide.

South African scholar, Yazini April, in her study of Yiwu and the prospects for South Africa to follow its example, cautions that South Africa must first fix its governance problems and achieve horizontal and vertical "synergy" in government because the primary reason which made Yiwu and similar initiatives successful in China is the extent to which the Chinese state is "highly capable."[32] Education and training would go a long way in boosting state capabilities, especially "targeted" education, such as the educational opportunities proposed here would be.

## Protecting African Women in "Infant" Trade Sectors

The South African government may need to look at legislation that sets aside certain industries, especially for black women. Industries such as fruit vending and small electronic items sales may be perfect candidates for such a program. It would be a strategy not unlike South Korea's protection of infant industries during the time of its own take-off, as well as Malaysia's efforts to incorporate the Malays into the economy. To deal with their own country-specific imperatives, these countries had to apply unique, country-specific initiatives. The South African government may set aside special permits, which only women can get, in order to participate in certain businesses.

Perhaps owing to the country's past, there is understandably a marked unwillingness and sensitivity around issues of limiting access to any sector, especially the economy. However, there exists an equally onerous rationale for such an approach. If done humanely, legally, and sensitively, it would protect the most vulnerable segment of the population, which also happens to be the group that is most economically burdened by costs such as childcare, school fees, and so forth. The immediacy of the imperative of unemployment, which disproportionately affects women, and the failure so far to arrest it thus far, call for unique special measures which may in the long run, perhaps after a special dispensation, no longer be necessary.

Before doing fieldwork for this research, I and probably many other South Africans, who often wonder how a young immigrant from Bangladesh comes into a country that is unfamiliar, sets up a stall selling small electronic appliances such as cellular phones and laptop chargers, and within a short period time becomes a profitable business person. Many South Africans, mired in long-term unemployment who later turn into discouraged work-seekers, would be forgiven for thinking that the young man is a genius who possesses "miraculous" business acumen. After my research, and having been made aware of the wonder of the almost unparalleled scale that is Yiwu, I now know that the Bangladeshi young man, like the Chinese trader south of Johannesburg, simply went to Yiwu or bought wholesale from someone that did.

As a significant beginning, not a comprehensive fix-all solution for dealing with the unemployment imperative, South Africa therefore needs to undergo a paradigm shift. By embracing Yiwu, South Africans will be able to cut through the numerous middle men and realize considerable profit themselves for good which trade matrix data demonstrates they and the world consume in matching patterns. This in turn will increase their returns of scale and have an incremental effect on employment, for they themselves will participate in warehousing and wholesale distribution at the top of the trade value chain.

From the data presented, South Africa is a country which has developmentally been left behind by other emerging economies in whose midst economic indices otherwise suggest it belongs. It has a unique trade matrix, one that is more diverse than Africa and the world in comparison. Yet most indices point to a country that should have had an economic take-off by now but instead remains mired in endemic challenges. This fundamental developmental lag characterized by poverty, inequality, and unemployment this section has sought to address relegate what should be an advanced emerging economy into the realm of (developing) countries still struggling with the most basic of services.

In her challenge to the South African government to take certain developmental potential serious, April compared Yiwu to the province of Limpopo, whose economic condition hardly corresponds to its vast potential.

The Limpopo province, a potential SEZ (special economic zone) territory has, unlike Yiwu, a lot of natural advantages, and yet remains one of the poorest provinces in the country. Limpopo has . . . mineral deposits that include platinum group metals, iron ore, chromium, diamonds, antimony, phosphate and copper, as well as mineral reserves like gold. More than 45 percent of the more than R2 billion annual turnover of the Johannesburg Fresh Produce Market comes from Limpopo. The province produces mangoes, papayas, tomatoes, potatoes, etc. While both Limpopo and Yiwu are landlocked, unlike Yiwu, Limpopo has very good access to the world. the Maputo development Corridor links directly with the port of Maputo in Mozambique. . . . In essence, the Yiwu market scenario raises further questions as to why South Africa has not been able to ensure that its informal economy is strategically utilized to participate in the creation of economic growth.[33]

This challenge by April is developmental, and it may be met only through an immediate and sustained commitment by the government—through speedy and measurable action—to building structural mechanisms for a developmental state as well as education. Yiwu and Zhejiang may well hold a lot of promise for partially addressing the latter, but the achievement of the former still rests with South Africans entirely.

The humanitarian development paradigm holds that human fulfillment plays an important if not consequential role in individual human beings being efficient stewards of their own well-being. It remains within the realm of a caring government in South Africa to foster confidence among its population, especially the unemployed, discouraged women and youth who long for an economic breakthrough. Formal education need not be a precondition for participating in international trade. A majority of the African women traders I interviewed in Yiwu said they had not done much formal education after high school. Yet because of confidence in their efforts, they are able to travel for thousands of miles, not to be a "big" entrepreneur but simple to make good economies of scale, which they do.

In the short term, South Africans looking for base subsistence cannot be expected to make household merchandise and derive as much profit in excess of products from sources such as Yiwu. If there is something that needs to be fixed in this dynamic, it cannot be fixed by South Africa alone; but in the meantime, as an integral part of its developmental returns from the accelerated rate of trade and cooperation with China, South Africa can join and rise in the value chain beginning at the source.

## NOTES

1. Chinese Scholar, interview by author, Jinhua, September 17, 2014.
2. "Quarterly Labor Force Survey," *Statistics South Africa*, accessed December 23, 2019, http://www.statssa.gov.za/?page_id=1866&PPN=P0211&SCH=7891.
3. Ibid.
4. Ibid.
5. Ibid.
6. Ibid.
7. Ibid.
8. "Trade Reports," *Department of Trade and Industry of the Republic of South Africa*, accessed July 02, 2020, http://tradestats.thedti.gov.za/ReportFolders/reportFol ders.aspx?sCS_referer=&sCS_ChosenLang=en.
9. Londiwe Buthelezi, "It's Time for Africa to Add Value to Exports to China—Davies," *Business News*, September 16, 2013; Lamido Sanusi, "Africa Must Get Real about Chinese Ties," *Financial Times*, March 11, 2013.
10. "Economic Trends," *UNCTAD*, accesses June 2, 2020, https://unctadstat.u nctad.org/wds/ReportFolders/reportFolders.aspx.
11. Ibid.
12. Ibid.
13. Ibid.
14. Ibid.
15. Ibid.
16. "Trade Reports," *Department of Trade and Industry of the Republic of South Africa*, accessed February 15, 2020, http://tradestats.thedti.gov.za/ReportFolders/repo rtFolders.aspx?sCS_referer=&sCS_ChosenLang=en
17. "Indicators," *World Bank*, accessed December 23, 2019, https://data.world-bank.org/indicator.
18. Ibid.
19. Ibid.

20. Ibid.

21. Ibid.

22. Du Rusheng, *Chinese Economists on Economic Reform—Collected Works of Du Runsheng* (New York: Routledge, 2013), 143.

23. Adam M. Bodomo, "From Guangzhou to Yiwu: Emerging Facets of the African Diaspora in China," *International Journal of African Renaissance* 5, no. 2 (2010): 283–4.

24. "Yiwu Municipality," accessed November 11, 2020, http://english.yw.gov.cn/english_1/e_sw/e_sc/e_scjs/201104/t20110410_28124.htm.

25. Gene Cooper, *The Market and Temple Fairs of Rural China: Red Fire* (New York: Routledge, 2013), 32.

26. Interview with Ghanaian trader, September 21, 2014.

27. Interview with Kenyan trader, September 20, 2014.

28. Interview with Zimbabwean trader, September 20, 2014.

29. Chinese scholar, interview by author, Jinhua, September 16 and 17, 2014.

30. "Incentives, CIS," *Ministry of Small Business Development of South Africa*, accessed November 11, 2020, http://www.dsbd.gov.za/about-dsbd.html.

31. "Programs," *Ministry of Small Business Development of South Africa*, accessed November 11, 2020, http://www.dsbd.gov.za/?page_id=1218.

32. Yazini April, "Understanding Aspects of China's Governance and Economic Growth," *Africa Insight* 41, no. 4 (2012): 120.

33. Ibid., 116–117.

## Chapter 7

# Prospects for a Developmental State in the Time of China

For a while in the 1990s, at the zenith of neoliberalism and structural adjustment programs, in whose prescriptions seemed embedded the sentiment that government is antithetical to efficient economic principles, the idea of state intervention in the economy was considered "unorthodox." This orthodoxy which dominated economic development and planning, particularly following the crisis of the Asia tigers, saw the idea of the developmental state, which had been embraced before, lose its "shine" as even prominent development economists joined the wave and denounced as "suspect," "monocausal" explanations stressing the role of the developmental state.[1] This, however, did not last.

Following the financial crisis of 2008 and 2009, whose roots were traced to the unregulated state of the Western economies including the United States, many observers began to look at what role state intervention could have played in averting the crisis. Indeed, in almost all economies a series of state intervention in their economies began: the British government nationalized the Royal Bank of Scotland; and the US government effectively nationalized Chrysler and the Bank of America, among others. These interventions, so went the proponent's argument, were meant to stabilize these organizations since they were deemed "too big to fail." In other words, there was an abiding, strategic, indeed public interest, in seeing that these giants of Western capitalism did not fall on their own sword of market fundamentalism—a tenet which, had it been heeded in their case, would have dictated that they fold and accept their failure as a result of the market forces punishing as they always do (their) proverbial "inefficiency." While it was not necessarily the spark, this state intervention in nations constituting the core of the Washington Consensus cannot be underestimated as having been a catalyst to the flurry of literature on state intervention that has pervaded scholarship since then—especially concerning the developmental state of developing countries. If rich nations, erstwhile opponents of any state intervention in the economy, could intervene to the point of taking over whole giant commercial companies, many of which ostensibly could take the fair share of responsibility for their dire straight, why not developing states whose ends were decidedly more dire and far more often concerned with matters of real "life and death?"

If active, timely and strategic intervention of the state in the running and regulation of economic activity virtually constitutes the developmental state, this chapter looks at the developmental state as attempted by China and South Africa. I draw on the ideas of the seminal 1982 study of the Japanese developmental state by Chalmers Johnson, entitled *MITI and the Japanese Miracle*, not as an exploration of the study itself but as a conceptual framework from which "Four Essential Elements" of a developmental state have been extracted. First, to compare the fortunes (and misfortunes) of South Africa and China's developmental states, and second, to identify certain features in the Chinese developmental state that pose a "point-of-caution" as far as South Africa's itself (and its development) is concerned and which need addressing as the relations between these two nations continue to blossom.

As has been demonstrated in previous chapters, while China's relations with South Africa are relatively new compared to other African countries, they have grown dramatically since the two nations established relations in January 1998 after South Africa turned away from Taiwan. In 1998 trade with China amounted to only 3 percent of South Africa's total trade. However, by 2014, it was 15.5 percent, exceeding South Africa's trade with the United Kingdom, the United States, and Japan put together. By 2011, when South Africa joined BRICS with the invitation of China, the volume of trade between the two countries had reached US$103 billion, and China had become South Africa's largest trading partner. These and other indices of the extent of China's involvement in South Africa form the urgent context in which an analysis of South Africa's developmental state is strengthened if it does not ignore international factors and players, principal among these being China.

## THE DEVELOPMENTAL STATE IN
## SOUTH AFRICA'S HISTORY

Two scholars, one South African, another British, Ben Turok and Ha-Joon Chang proffer the definition that a developmental state is where a "state has a more independent or autonomous, political power, as well as control over the economy" which it achieves through industrial policy. They make a distinction between the "classical" "developmental state"—like Japan—and current aspiring ones like China and South Africa, emphasizing that the latter states can and should learn from the former but should not copy it wholesale.[2] But as for South Africa, the history is also important.

The history of any semblance of a developmental state in South Africa, like many facets of life, revolves around race. Characterized as an "outpost of global capital," South Africa's race-based displacement of the black majority precedes the 1948 apartheid state.[3] So far-reaching and extensive was state intervention in the economy on behalf of whites—this time Afrikaners that in the 1940s, the Afrikaans term *"reddingsdaad* (act of rescue)" was used to refer to a state-led campaign to introduce Afrikaners into the economy for their own development.[4] Certain elements that have come to be associated with a latter-day developmental state existed in South Africa since the 1961 Union that made South Africa a republic. Only they were for the white minority.

The instances are numerous. After World War II, the "Nationalist regime systematically intervened in the economy;" with the help of the "oligopolist mining finance," the government built up "a military-industrial complex;" the state spent on "industry, infrastructure and the military in the context of low wages" to guarantee high returns for international investors; and, the "racist state capitalism" further collaborated to accelerate the penetration of neighboring economies and ensured the apartheid state maintained some, certainly not all, elements we would come to associate with a developmental state, while sustaining itself with low black wages.[5] This "apartheid state with developmental characteristics" found wide appeal among the white minority electorate such that white politicians explicitly called for "state interference and state control on a large scale."[6] Out of this emerges a picture of a state that had fundamental developmentalist elements only as long as it was *not* democratic—in other words, until power had to be transferred to the black majority.

This state intervention in the economy existed until its end in the early 1990s. This environment, therefore, constitutes the structural embers of what had been an interventionist state, which greeted the new leaders of post-apartheid South Africa, and would have a consequential and restraining effect for years to come.

## THE FOUR ESSENTIAL ELEMENTS OF A DEVELOPMENTAL STATE

### Talented Bureaucracy

Chalmers Johnson's, the father of the "developmental state" concept, states that the first essential element for a developmental state is the "existence of

a small, inexpensive, but elite state bureaucracy staffed by the best manage-
rial talent available in the system."[7] Its duty is to come up with the following
three things: first, "industrial structure policy" (the identification of industries
to be developed); second, "industrial rationalization policy" (to come up with
the best way to develop the industries selected to be developed); and third, to
come up with ways and start to "supervise competition" in sectors that have
been designated as strategic.[8] The assumption, of course, is that "market-
conforming" means will be used.

In China, there exists a highly capable bureaucracy not just in the state
apparatus but also on a parallel level within the Communist Party. Thus
for every office in government, there is within the Communist Party an
equally—if not more—capable "shadow" officer to monitor the performance
of government outcomes. In his influential tome, *When China Rules the
World: The End of the Western World and the Birth of a New Order*, China
expert Martin Jacques traces this fluidity within the Chinese bureaucracy to
Chinese people's millennia-old experience not with elected but with imperial
power. Indeed, he argues that "the legitimacy of the Chinese state" and, as a
corollary, bureaucracy, "rests on the fact that it is seen by the people as the
representative and embodiment of Chinese civilization," which makes China
a "civilizational-state."[9] This has imbued the country with a highly competent
state mechanism "probably superior to any other state-tradition in the world,"
together with other Asian nations in the region including Japan, who are
"time-compression societies . . . habituated to rapid change."[10] Therefore, this
condition has enabled China's developmental state to be able to dominate in a
field where a bureaucracy's ability to adapt to quick change is a proceed asset.

But the evidence paints a different picture for South Africa. At the beginning of 2013, up to 365,750 positions in the government, the core of the
bureaucracy, remained open, some having stood unfilled for years.[11] Worse
yet, the Office of the President had up to 143 vacancies. The National
Planning Commission, tasked with designing the roadmap for the developmental state, had 54 unfilled vacancies.

## Bureaucratic Latitude

South Africa has a unique negative political condition for the developmental
state in terms of state autonomy: its energy-mineral conglomerates, with
unusually globalized links and capabilities for firms from a developing
country. This reduces the range of things a state can do without facing major
opposition from the capitalists.[12]

The second essential element of a developmental state is that there is a
"political system in which the bureaucracy is given sufficient scope to take
initiative and operate effectively."[13] The implication is that the other organs

of the state have their roles transformed into the function of being "safety valves" to guard against complete system failure but never to encumber the developmental work being carried out by the empowered bureaucracy.

For China, a one-party state where there is a vague if not superficial distinction between where the state begins and the Communist Party ends, this may be plausible. However, in more rural locales, where the Party official may have more power than a bureaucrat and inclined to practice it against developmental ends, a more complex picture emerges. For South Africa, once again, the challenges seem more easily noticeable than possible solutions. The number of unfilled positions in government remains a significant signifier of a developmental state whose capacity, as represented by human resources alone, is still far into the future. It may well be that South Africa is a victim of its own success with democracy and the separation of powers in that there *is* a distinction between the state and parties, and there is a diversity of and distinction between political parties. This means that party loyalty is likely to factor into bureaucratic decisions that should not be about politics. In this instance, the amount of possible latitude with policy pales.

## Market-Conforming State Intervention

In contrast to deliberate control in strategic industries, the [Chinese] state introduces competition in ways that relinquish control over industries that are less important to national security, that make little contribution to the national technology base, and where the domestic industry is more competitive.[14]

The "perfection" by the state of the manner in which it intervenes in the economy is the third essential element.[15] This may happen in various ways including: the creation of government finance companies; making sure that government banks have as much influence as private ones; widespread-yet-specific use of tax incentives; and contracting out some government duties to strategically placed private institutions.

The first manner by which this element can be operationalized is especially resonant in South Africa where the government does not have a large bank that is similar in operation to the commercial ones. Moreover, the government of South Africa does not have a central bank; only a "reserve" bank (as in the United States) which is not only privately owned but has significant ownership in the hands of non-South Africans. China, on the other hand, has the "big four banks" (Bank of China, Agricultural Bank of China, China Construction Bank, and Industrial and Construction Bank) all of which are state-owned. As an indicator of China's developmental trajectory in this regard, not only are these four banks economic players in China but they also dominate the global economy. In 2009, the Construction Bank of China, for instance, was the fifth largest company in the world by capitalization.[16] This type of intervention into a world conventionally considered the preserve of private capital requires a highly competent state management apparatus, one that South Africa seems far from obtaining.

## Pilot Organization

The last essential element is to have a "clearinghouse" for the developmental state using an agency that is able to coordinate different plans from various constituencies of the bureaucracy and to channel them into the specific ends of economic development as planned. In essence, an organization modeled after Japan's Ministry of International Trade and Industry (MITI). Johnson argues that such an agency must "combine at least planning, energy, domestic production, international trade, and a share of finance," the key being the "indirect control" of government funds and the effective bypassing of what is often the constraining Treasury department.[17] At its most effective, this organization also has its own think tank, thus is able to control the creation of knowledge as far as the direction of the developmental state is concerned.

After the elections of 2009 the National Planning Commission (NPC) was established in South Africa. Also, two "super-ministries" were created, one for planning and another for evaluation. The task of the former was to chair the NPC which was tasked with coming up with a development plan for the country. Many observers were optimistic about these initiatives from Zuma and saw it as a victory for what had been a developmental push by the trade unionists within the ruling coalition in the run-up to the election. Their optimism was short lived. The person soon announced as the minister to chair the NPC was none other than Trevor Manuel, who had been Finance Minister since 1996 and who had presided over the most neoliberal period in South Africa, one which many observes decry as having been a lost opportunity to build a developmental state. By pouring "old wine" into "new bottles," the Zuma administration was unable to adhere to the overarching requirement for bureaucracies that want to create such a state—that it be dynamic and responsive to the changing environment.

## WHAT THE FUTURE HOLDS

South Africa's inequality is among the highest in the world. It goes against not only what is expected from a developmental standpoint but is not sustainable for the stability of the country itself. On the other side stands China, the enormous, highly capable, efficient, and experienced "civilization-state" whose practice of statecraft goes back millennia. The Chinese state is aggressive in how it exacts market regulation within its borders. In a globalized world, these have far-reaching consequence that must be understood to be addressed.

To retain and enhance central authority over industry, the state manages competition to limit the number of players and reformulates old rules and writes new ones concerning market entry and business scope with sector-specific goals in mind. Departing from the developmental state model, the Chinese government ensures the enhancement of state authority in these industries first and foremost, and then from there it pursues industrial development that achieves security and economic goals.[18]

The ends of such an approach, whose first manifestation begins at home where local demand for locally produced good increases, is borne out by David, who posited in his *The Conversation on Economic Development* that what contributed to Japan's "phenomenal" rate of growth in the 1970s were the economies of scale "stemming from the growth in domestic demand, which, in turn, enhanced Japanese competitiveness in foreign markets."[19]

On the future of a developmental state, Professor Fine takes a dim view of South Africa's prospects. He argues that the country has a "long way to go if it is to do more than aspire to be a developmental state. Indeed, South Africa was much closer to developmental state status in the past than it is now."[20] Evans, however, acknowledges the difficulty of building a developmental state in South Africa, a land where capital and land remain disproportionately distributed. However, he argues that this unique situation should be accepted as the dynamic context in which a "twenty-first-century developmental state" can be built, but only if it has "all the capacities of the twentieth-century version and others in addition."[21] Therefore, the success of South Africa's developmental state will be determined by whether or not it can amass a "capable, cohesive" bureaucracy," itself a "key to giving the state the level of autonomy it needs to pursue a coherent national project" like the twentieth century was.[22]

However, in the twenty-first century, the state must account for and engage with more than just the private sector. It must engage with civil society. It will be successful because it has the potential to achieve three returns: first, "it is not a welfare strategy that neglects growth;" second, it will have structural features that "link high growth with broadly shared returns—in part because it is a naturally labor-intensive;" and third, it will have "a light ecological footprint."[23]

## WHAT IT WILL TAKE FOR AN ENDOGENOUS DEVELOPMENTAL STATE

Whether a developmental state is within reach for South Africa, all evidence seems to point to the decision makers themselves. For an internationally integrated economy like South Africa, with vast and powerful vested interests that desire the opposite of a developmental state, there is a political price to be paid by the leaders, indeed a social one by the people. There is also on the horizon a bigger one for the stability of the country if a developmental state is not braved. A choice between the two unpleasant states seems to be the only choice.

However, inasmuch as other states sought to move beyond the ideal of the original model of it, Chalmers Johnson's "capitalist developmental state," South Africa will also have to move beyond a simply "democratic developmental state." Through its home-grown tenets—not least of all is Ubuntu—it must seek to increase its policy autonomy space, enough to aim for a "strategic developmental state" instead, one premised on a "strategic humanomic paradigm" of development. Such a paradigm admits the Humanitarian (Ubuntu) ideal for development as a complement not only to the democratic one but also to the market-oriented (capitalist) global reality. Hence a strategic humanomic paradigm, one which takes into cognizance not only South Africa's global political ambitions as a rising power in the global South, but also accepts that the achievement of a developmental state itself has to take place as an imperative for the country's strategic position.

A diversification of its economic basket, therefore, lies at the center of this and China's role in it will be a defining if not determining one. Hence it must be comprehensively studied. These converging imperatives between China and South Africa, together with the changing dynamics in the way the global economy is run and the players dominating it, have led to a vitality and a proliferation of new insights concerning the state's role not just in development but also in the economy, thus producing converging paradigms on the developmental state itself.

As the center of gravity continues to shift from West to East, and China continues to rise in economic and political pre-eminence, there are diverse implications for Africa.

While multipolarity may imply more room for individual African countries to maneuver, this will depend on the ability of African countries to articulate a long-term development vision that would enable the continent to break free of Western-led (or G8-dominated) diktak. The rise of BRICS itself does not produce desired "policy space." National efforts in "strategic integration" into the world markets, complemented by strategic tactical alliance with BRIC, the G20 and other multilateral initiatives, are likely to create the necessary space for African countries to maneuver and chart their own path of development.[24]

Therefore, an empirical and theoretical contribution to African Studies and IPE literature on relations between African (aspiring) developmental states and China, a (risen) developmental state, is the end of this study.

## "Narrative Dissonance?"—Between Planning and Implementation

To achieve development and human progress in any society, Professor Wilfred David argues, requires three types of resources, which are often "interwoven with concrete economic and social practices."[25] The first of these, which is found at the economic level, is to "allocate resources" like "raw materials, means of production, finished goods, and money;" that emanate from "ownership rights and entitlement systems that enable or disable human capabilities."[26] In the arena of politics and public management, there are "authoritative resources"- and they allow policy-making and policy-implementing elites to exercise deterministic "control over the socially constituted world in terms of people's life chances, spatio-temporal positioning, and relations with other human beings."[27]

## What Is the Second Resource?

The third resource is "stored information" and is the "most influential resource" at the disposal of wielders of power, who use it to obtain or increase their "economic, social, and political power in space and time."[28] This section looks at time series data of important policy documents as well as speeches of leaders in South Africa in order to assess the extent to which policy-making elites have used these resources over time, and how or if the manner in which they have used them has affected the deferral of a developmental state or not. This is done across three various levels: the political party level, the cabinet level, and the presidency level. The hope is that from the data will emerge an indicator of a source for the developmental as it relates to how, primarily, the information resource has been exercised by political leaders in the country.

## Political Party Level

During the time that South Africa has enjoyed diplomatic relations (established in 1998) with China only one party, the ANC, has dominated the South African polity through electoral victories. Therefore, only the ANC is engaged here. In 1992, the ANC produced a document, "Ready to Govern: ANC Policy Guidelines for a Democratic South Africa," outlining its desire for a "developmental state."[29] While the term "developmental" is mentioned seven times, at no point in the 28,000-word document is it mentioned as relating to economic matters, but it is associated with vague references such as declaring that "local government must be developmental."[30] This reveals a certain apprehension toward the developmental state that has been a feature of the South African policy-making nexus—not just since the democratic era but also before. It may demonstrate a possession of information resources at an early time, regarding the feasibility of the developmental state that may well have been withheld from the general populace who, through the advent of democracy, would almost automatically herald a developmental state.

The ANC holds its national conference every five years. In the data provided, three documents produced at every ANC conference were analyzed to find out how many times the word "developmental" occurs or is mentioned in them. Then an analysis was undertaken of the annual State of the Nations Addresses (given by the president) and the Budget speeches of the year immediately following the ANC conferences to study the occurrence of the word "developmental" there. The reason for looking at these together is that, as the ruling party, it is safe to assume that resolutions which are taken at its conferences, in order for them to find any "traction" or implementation, must also be found at the cabinet/presidency level; where the cabinet/president principals, in almost all cases of the ANC, are present or participate in political party level formulations of the documents anyway.

The ANC documents are the Conference Resolutions, the Strategies and Tactics, and the Conference Declarations. An important point must be born in mind regarding these documents. The Conference Resolutions are crafted at the end of the conference and are supposed to guide policy the ANC will implement through the government. The Conference Declarations are crafted to express the agreed policy consensus with broader alliance partners, and the Strategies and Tactics are crafted before the congress to guide what should be discussed and resolved during its duration. The data indicates that from as early as 1996, at the 50th congress, resolutions have featured the word "developmental" at least 20 times; since 2002, the Strategies and Tactics documents also increased its feature of the word. This may demonstrate that at a party level, the ANC has shown consistency in communicating the wishes of the majority of its supporters, and by extension the majority of voters, that the developmental state is a desired policy.

However, in all these years in which the developmental state was discussed and adopted as a policy to be implemented, strikingly, not once did either the State of the Nation address or the Budget speech immediately following the congress mention it. Even more striking is that the same political principals who governed the adoption of the documents, and the docuuments' plans for a more developmental trajectory, would be the the same who as state—no longer party—actors, ignore the concept altogether a year later.

## Cabinet Level

Another realm in which the occurrence of "developmental" is instructive of how political elites use the "information resource" is at the cabinet level. An

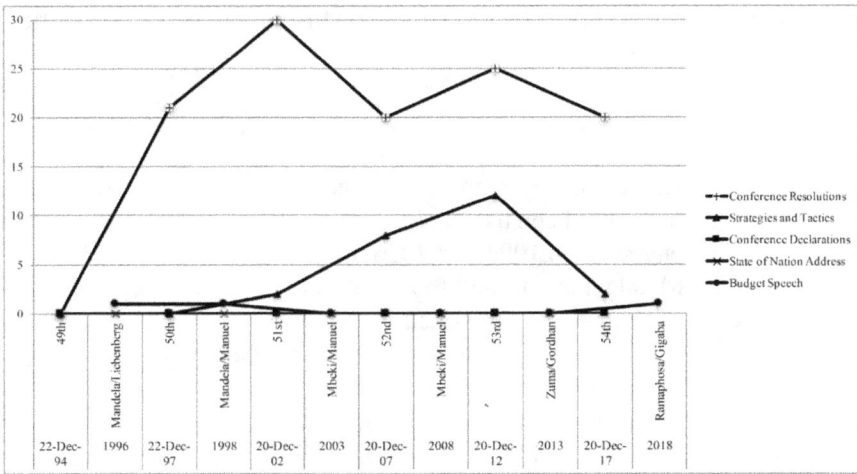

**Figure 7.1 Number of Times "Developmental" Is Mentioned in Important ANC Congress Documents and the South Africans Government's Speeches, 1994–2018.** *Source*: "African National Congress Archive," accessed March 20, 2021, http://www.anc.org.za/54th-national-conference.

analysis of time series data was undertaken where the number of times "developmental" features in the annual budget speeches of the minister of finance.

According to the data, the most times "developmental" has been mentioned in a budget speech is five times in 1997. After that, the most it has been mentioned is in the 2009 and 2015 budget speeches. This is important because of the financially consequential nature of not only the speech but also the

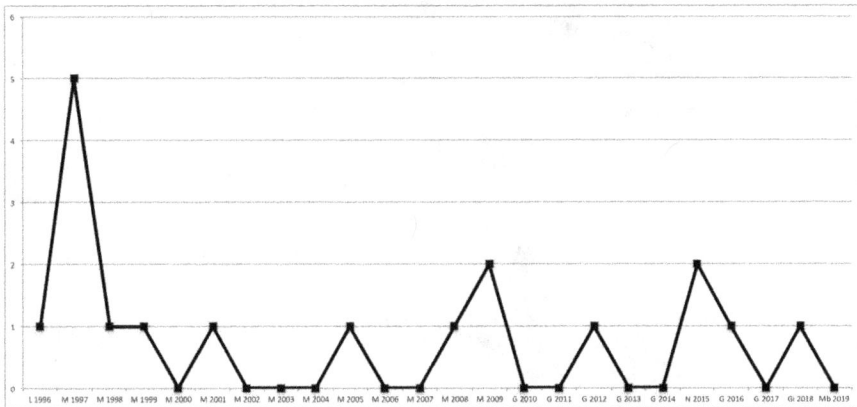

**Figure 7.2 Number of Times "Developmental" Is Mentioned in State of the Nation Speech, 1997–2019.** *Source*: "State of the Nation Address," Government of South Africa, accessed March 20, 2021, https://www.gov.za/search?search_query=sona.

role of the minister as a distributor, and by extension proprietor, of political resources.

## Executive Level

Another set of data that has been analyzed concerns the number of times the term "developmental" has been used in State of the Nation addresses in South Africa's Parliament between 1994 and 2016. Interestingly, between 1994 and 1998, President Mandela mentioned the word only once; between 1999 and 2008, President Thabo Mbeki mentioned it only in three speeches for a total of six times, the first time being in 2004, six years after taking the presidency. Tellingly, President Jacob Zuma, between 2009 and 2012, has mentioned "developmental" in all his State of the Nation speeches, for a total of seven times—equal to Mbeki and Mandela combined!" But if this was any sign of a rise in the mention of the word, the following speeches put this hope to rest—President Zuma has not mentioned "developmental" since then.

## Other Mentions—The National Development Plan

In 2012 the National Development Plan was published. It is a thoroughgoing document containing mainly prescriptions for the country's development since 1994. It differs from the documents discussed above in that the 15-chapter document had a whole section entitled, "Building a Capable Developmental State," where the term "developmental" occurs no less than 51 times.[31] This indicates, however anecdotally, the constrained way in which South Africa's developmental goals have often found expression, and, lately, a changing environment. But the extent to which these references, in all the

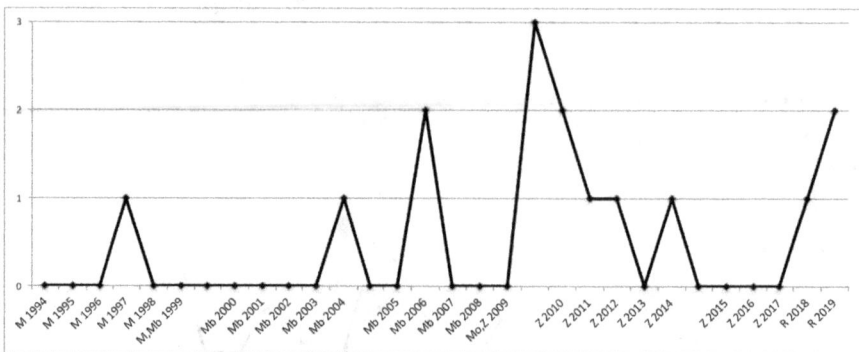

**Figure 7.3 Number of Times "Developmental" Is Mentioned in the Minister of Finance's Budget Speech, 1996–2019.** *Note:* M = Mandela; Mb = Mbeki; Mo = Montlanthe; Z = Zuma; R = Ramaphosa. *Source:* "National Budget," Government of South Africa. accessed March 20, 2021, https://www.gov.za/national-budget-0#.

documents, specifically address or expand on development promises more to be added to the conversation for future studies.

This data analyzed, it is argued here, demonstrates what may be called a "narrative dissonance." The developmental state narrative occurs frequently at political party level, ostensibly where the people's aspirational wishes are expressed. But between the congresses and the time the policy makers, the same people, make it to their offices in Pretoria, and the consequential State of the Nation and Budget speeches are given in Cape Town, an intervention demonstrably takes place. As the data shows, this has happened since the early years of the democratic era. If there exist obstacles which intervene in narrative and plans becoming implemented actions, therefore developmental outcomes, the next sections discuss certain aspects of the South African economy which are worthy to consider as playing a contributing factor to the chasm between lofty plans and deferred implementation toward a developmental state.

## ATTENUATED CONTACTS REDUX?

### Capital

South Africa is among the most integrated economies in the world system. Some Chinese scholars note that this is the singular most important feature that makes South Africa important to China. Indeed, Chinese scholars have mentioned how this state of affairs makes South Africa unique but crucial to China's relations with the continent.

But an analysis of data on market capitalization may suggest that certain aspects of being highly integrated into the global economy may, however unwittingly, present a barrier to South Africa's developmental aspirations.

Market capitalization ("the market value of a company's outstanding shares"[32]) as a percentage of the GDP, for instance, which was 267 percent in 2015, shows a country for whom global opinion which affects market shares is an existential concern (Figure 52). South Africa's market capitalization as a percentage of the GDP was also far higher than China's.

This status quo, which at the same time may show a country that is well integrated into the mainstream economy, also exposes South Africa more disproportionately to volatility of capital. Most importantly, this volatility exposure is made worse by the ease of capital movement, thanks to relatively liberal capital controls.

### Agriculture

Another area in which barriers to progress toward a developmental state manifest themselves in South Africa is in agriculture. South Africa is a country

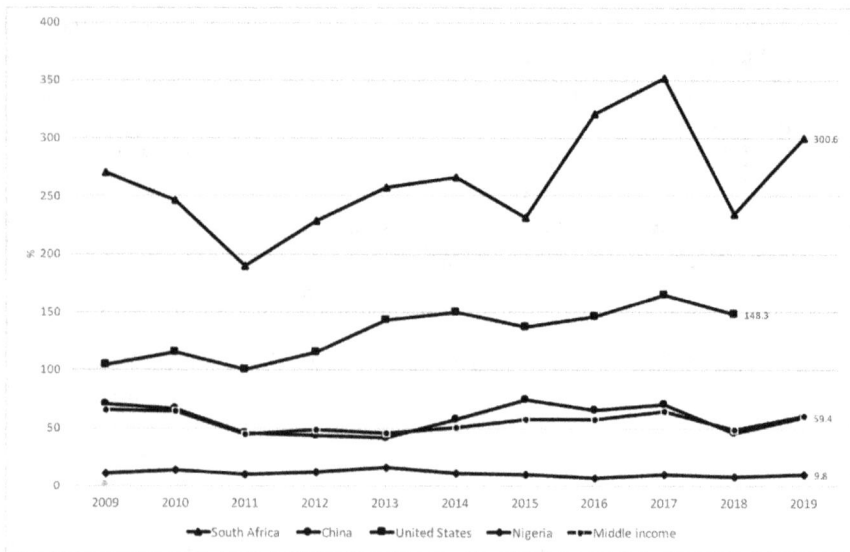

**Figure 7.4   Market Capitalization of Listed Domestic Companies as Percentage of GDP.**
*Source*: "World Bank development Indicators," World Bank, accessed March 20, 2021,
https://data.worldbank.org/indicator.

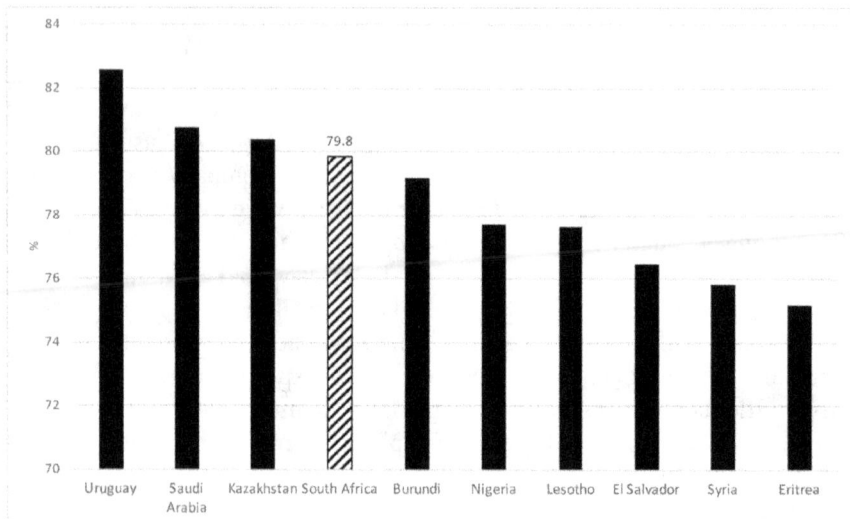

**Figure 7.5   Countries with Largest Agricultural Land as Percent of Land Area,
2013.** *Source*: World Data Bank, http://data.worldbank.org/indicator/AG.LND.AGRI.ZS
(accessed January 17, 2016).

that is well-endowed with many resources, including land. The country has the fourth-largest agricultural land as a percentage of land area in the world.

However, regardless of its endowment, the data demonstrates that South Africa has at best not taken advantage of this endowment in land by increasing its agricultural production. To analyze this neglect of the agricultural sector as a significant economic activity, countries are ranked by the percentage of value-added agriculture as a percentage of their GDP in 2013. South Africa, which has agricultural land larger than all the countries analyzed, was ranked last in value-added agriculture as a percentage of its GDP.

This seeming neglect of agriculture is explained by an analysis of different economic activities as a whole. Again, there is a demonstration of how much South Africa has not taken advantage of agriculture. Also, this data demonstrates that the services industry has risen, standing at 68 percent of the GDP, an increase from 63 percent in 1998. Both South Africa's concentration on services as a large part of its economic activity, together with

**Table 7.1   Value-Added Agriculture as Percent of GDP and Agricultural Land as Percent of Land Area**

| Country/Region | Agriculture, value added (% of GDP) | | | | | Agricultural land as % of land area |
|---|---|---|---|---|---|---|
| | 2006 | 2016 | 2017 | 2018 | 2019 | 2016 |
| Mozambique | 24.0 | 22.9 | 25.0 | 24.5 | 24.0 | 63.5 |
| Pakistan | 21.6 | 23.2 | 22.9 | 22.9 | 22.0 | 47.8 |
| Nigeria | 24.7 | 21.0 | 20.8 | 21.2 | 21.9 | 77.7 |
| India | 16.8 | 16.4 | 16.4 | 15.4 | 16.0 | 60.4 |
| *Sub-Saharan Africa* | *16.2* | *15.1* | *15.2* | *14.4* | *15.3* | 43.7 |
| Egypt, Arab Rep. | 13.2 | 11.8 | 11.5 | 11.2 | 11.0 | 3.8 |
| *Middle income* | *9.4* | *8.6* | *8.3* | *7.8* | *7.9* | 38.1 |
| Malaysia | 8.6 | 8.5 | 8.6 | 7.5 | 7.3 | 26.3 |
| Argentina | 6.9 | 6.3 | 5.5 | 6.1 | 7.2 | 54.3 |
| *China* | *10.6* | *8.1* | *7.5* | *7.0* | *7.1* | *56.2* |
| Namibia | 9.8 | 6.3 | 7.1 | 7.0 | 6.6 | 47.1 |
| Turkey | 8.2 | 6.2 | 6.1 | 5.8 | 6.4 | 49.8 |
| Brazil | 4.4 | 4.9 | 4.6 | 4.4 | 4.4 | 33.9 |
| *World* | *3.8* | *3.5* | *3.4* | *4.0* | *3.6* | *37.4* |
| Russian Federation | 3.9 | 3.8 | 3.6 | 3.4 | 3.4 | 13.3 |
| Saudi Arabia | 2.9 | 2.7 | 2.5 | 2.2 | 2.2 | 80.8 |
| *South Africa* | *2.3* | *2.2* | *2.4* | *2.2* | *1.9* | *79.8* |
| European Union | 1.7 | 1.6 | 1.7 | 1.7 | 1.6 | 41.1 |
| Germany | 0.7 | 0.7 | 0.8 | 0.8 | 0.8 | 47.7 |
| United Kingdom | 0.6 | 0.6 | 0.7 | 0.6 | 0.6 | 71.7 |

*Source*: "World Bank development Indicators," World Bank, accessed March 20, 2021, https://data.worldbank.org/indicator.

its excessively capitalized economy, are just a few barriers to South Africa becoming a developmental state. Perhaps beyond any narrative dissonance and inconsistencies in rhetoric, these barriers, barely visible or considered by a regular citizen, are the most entrenched barriers militating against South Africa realizing a developmental state.

In chapter 1, early contacts between China and South Africa were characterized as an attenuated encounter that took place when both the Chinese and Africans had little to no agency over their socio-politico-economic condition. Later on in the twentieth century, while there may have been significantly more agency, the contact between Chinese people and the vast majority of Africans in South Africa continued to be attenuated by apartheid. After the birth of the "new" South Africa in 1994, China and South Africa did not establish diplomatic relations until 1998. Although it had been expected that the recognition of China would be a fait accompli as soon as the ANC assumed power, as most even within the ANC had hoped, it was not so. A combination of political opposition coming from opposition parties, which continued until the end of the Government of National Unity, meant that South Africa continued not to have relations with the PRC for four years. Behind the opposition had been the significant business interest which began during the apartheid era. Even after liberation, relations between China and South Africa continued to be attenuated by business interests, sometimes more than the aspirations of the masses of the South African people.

But South Africa has since enjoyed an acceleration of relations that have seen the two countries develop a "comprehensive strategic partnership." But the extent to which South Africa will derive a developmental outcome from this high level of relations will be determined by the extent to which attenuating factors in the relationship are avoided or removed. South Africa's neoliberal and liberal economic management model is one such attenuating factor. By allowing South Africa to function as a progressive economy while turning away from some of the basic tenets of a developmental state, including value-added agriculture, while endowed with so much of it, its model puts South Africa farther away from a developmental state than had been envisaged before this research began.

## TOWARD AN ENDOGENOUS
## DEVELOPMENTAL STATE

The combination of factors which militate against the developmental state in South Africa may seem overwhelming when considering a possible way forward. South Africa's aspiration to achieve a developmental state, like its relations with China over the last century, has been attenuated by deep capital interests, many of which have become entrenched. As a consequence, any scholar considering a developmental state in South Africa must first consider the volatility of the economy which comes with any tinkering with economic policy. The integrated nature of the South African economy to the world capital markets, together with the country's liberal laws, compounds this problem even more because there is a perennial disincentive for any prudent South African leader to bravely implement a structural re-adjustment toward a developmental state. The market backlash would be swift.

## Reasons for Hope

It was always going to be difficult for South Africa to achieve a developmental state. Allowing for the barriers already discussed, there are other barriers embedded in the era in which South Africa obtained liberation and then sought to effect a developmental state. First, South Africa became free in the 1990s at the zenith of the neoliberal perspective on all matters economic. As such, there was little maneuvering room for the new leaders; all they sought was economic stability and they found it in the Washington Consensus orthodoxy. By so doing they, perhaps unwittingly, pushed back the prospects for a developmental state even farther.

Secondly, unlike the countries of East Asia like Japan and South Korea, there was no overriding geopolitical motivation for the Western countries to brook a South African deviation from the economic norm. Scholars of the developmental states of East Asia have noted how, in the case of South Korea, the "transformation of the state and the economic development strategy" was "larger than South Korea alone" and can be explained by a "specific, domestic, regional, and global conjunctural situation."[33] Gills calls this a *structural opportunity* whereby "a convergence of interests that directly encompassed economic, social, and political forces" militated for South Korea as well as Japan to go against the grain and focus on export-oriented industrialization.[34] According to this argument, the possibility that other countries like South Africa could replicate the East Asian example to build a developmental state, in the present epoch, are undermined.

But rather than be a reason for despondency, this argument itself is the reason for South African hope. First, Gill's explanation does not account for other developmental states like Malaysia, which not only achieved a developmental state but also transformed their society's racially stratified economies, a feat South Africa should wish to replicate. The second reason is epochal and concerns the subject of this study, China. The current environment where China, together with other emergent economies, such as India and Brazil, have risen in economic profile and relative power may well constitute South Africa's own epochal "structural opportunity," akin to that which befell East

Asian countries in the 1960s. As discussed in chapter 3, the present period of changing dynamics where developmental wherewithal is no longer confined to the developed north should give more hope for a developmental state for South Africa. The very existence of the BRICS bank, of which South Africa is a member, is reason enough for hope. However, no epochal convergence of international forces, however favorable to South Africa's aspirations, will substitute for what seems to be a dearth of will for brave, forward-looking, endogenous conceptions of what type of developmental state South Africa exactly wants. That duty belongs to South Africa's political elites themselves.

## Creating an Identity

In his characterization of China as a civilization-state, Jacques juxtaposes this surety of self with that of other developing countries. He argues that

> Form many developing countries, the process of modernization has been characterized by a crisis of identity, often exacerbated by the colonial experience, a feeling of being torn between their own culture and that of the West, linked to an inferiority about their own backwardness. The Chinese certainly felt a sense of humiliation, but never the same kind of overwhelming and demeaning inferiority: they have always had a strong sense of what it means to be Chinese and are very proud of the fact.[35]

For South Africa to conceive of an endogenous developmental state in order to take full advantage of the global dynamics as they currently obtain, it will have to ask itself a question: If China is a civilization-state, what is South Africa? It is argued here that the answer to South Africa's conception of what type of a developmental state it wishes, which, beyond vague diagnostic plans it has hitherto not answered, will go a long way to imbue the country with a strong sense of identity. None of the countries cited above that have successfully achieved a developmental state has done it without a strong unifying identity. South Africa has not done this with the sustained, requisite, seriousness it deserves. Thus it may be that South Africa's biggest challenge may not be in the realm of securing developmental finance but in what epistemological, conceptual sense of self will be the centrifugal force for its development. This may prove more difficult than all the economic planning in the world.

As a point-of-departure, there are certain "sub-questions" that may help start a conversation in this regard in order to answer the main question. In the doctrine of *Ubuntu*, what concepts can be extracted and translated into practice to build an identity for a developmental state? What constitutes work as far as South Africa is concerned? Is working a 40-hour week desirable for South Africa's developmental state? Should South Africa adjust its work hours in winter to start later so that the masses of the people can get to work safer and then be re-adjusted when summer returns? Is South Africa an African country, and if it is, what in its developmental policy plan will reflect this? In answer to these questions will be found the building blocks for an endogenous developmental state. It is in South Africa's responses, through prescient and sustained scholarly inquiry, that the country will be better able to take advantage of the "window of opportunity" currently existing for it to achieve developmental goals.

## NOTES

1. Steve Chan et al., "Look beyond the Developmental State," in *Beyond the Developmental State: East Asia's Political Economies Reconsidered* (Basingstoke, UK: Macmillan, 1998), 8.

2. Ben Turok, Ha-Joon Chang and João Carlos Ferraz, *Development in a Divided Country Vol. 5* (Auckland Park, South Africa: Jacana Media, 2011), 230, xii.

3. Ann Seidman and Neva Seidman Makgetla, *Outposts of Global Capitalism: Southern Africa in the Changing Global Economy* (London: Zed Press, 1980), 89.

4. Walter E. Williams, *South Africa's War Against Capitalism* (New York: Praeger, 1989), 106.

5. Ibid.

6. Stanley Greenberg, *Race and State in Capitalist Development: Comparative Perspectives* (New Haven, CT: Yale University Press, 1980), 385.

7. Chalmer Johnson, *MITI and the Japanese Miracle* (Stanford, CA: Stanford University Press, 1982), 314–15.

8. Ibid.

9. Martin Jacques, *When China Rules the World: The End of the Western World and the Birth of a New Order* (New York: Penguin, 2012), 574.

10. Ibid.

11. New Age, "365 000 Vacant Positions," accessed November 11, 2015, http://www.thenewage.co.za/mobi/Detail.aspx?NewsID=21916&CatID=1025.

12. Ha-Joon Chang, "How to 'Do' A Developmentalist State: Political, Organizational, and Human Resource Requirements for the Developmental State," in *Constructing A Democratic Developmental State in South Africa: Potentials and Challenges*, ed. Omano Edigheji (Cape Town: Human Sciences Research Council Press, 2010), 88.

13. Johnson, *MITI and the Japanese Miracle*, 315–16.

14. Roselyn Hsueh, *China's Regulatory State*, 255.

15. Johnson, *MITI and the Japanese Miracle*, 317–19.

16. *Financial Times* "Top 500 List," accessed November 11, 2015, http://media.ft.com/cms/419e021c-fecd-11de-91d7-00144feab49a.pdf.

17. Johnson, *MITI and the Japanese Miracle*, 319–20.

18. Hsueh, *China's Regulatory State*, 255.

19. Wilfred David, *The Conversation on Economic Development: Historical Voices, Interpretations, and Reality* (Armonk, NY: M.E. Sharpe, 1997), 53.

20. Ben Fine, "Can South Africa be a Developmental State?" 169.

21. Peter B. Evans, "Constructing the 21st Century Developmental State," 38.

22. Ibid, 46.

23. Ibid, 52.

24. T. Shaw, *China, India and (South) Africa: What International Relations in the Second Decade of the Twenty-First Century?* (New York: Routledge, 2013), 20.

25. Wilfred David, *The Humanitarian Development Paradigm: Search for Global Justice* (Lenham, MD: University Press of America, 2004), 67.

26. Ibid.

27. Ibid.

28. Ibid.

29. African National Congress, "Ready to Govern: ANC Policy Guidelines for a Democratic South Africa," accessed November 11, 2015, http://www.anc.org.za/show.php?id=227.

30. Ibid.

31. Office of the Presidency of the Republic of South Africa, "National Development Plan 2030," accessed November 11, 2013, http://www.npconline.co.za/pebble.asp?relid=25.

32. "Market Capitalization Defined," *Investdopedia*, accessed February 18, 2016, http://www.investopedia.com/articles/basics/03/031703.asp.

33. Barry Gills, "The International Origin of South Korea's Export Orientation," in *Trancending the State-Global Divide: A Neostructuralist Agenda in International Relations*, ed. Ronen P. Palan and Barry Gills (Boulder, CO: LynneRienner, 1994), 203.

34. Ibid.

35. Martin Jacques, *When China Rules the World: The End of the Western World and the Birth of a New Global Order* (New York: Penguin Books, 2009), 251.

# Conclusion

On February 15, 2018, Cyril Ramaphosa was sworn in as the new president of South Africa. His first five international trips were all within Africa (to Angola, Botswana, Mozambique, Zimbabwe, and Rwanda). Like his predecessor, Jacob Zuma, his first overseas visit was to the United Kingdom. On the one hand, the visit to African countries is indicative of the importance South Africa has attached to crafting its own ascendance within the continent to help address its developmental imperatives at home. The visit to the United Kingdom, on the other hand, may indicate a resilient South African compunction with upsetting relational dynamics with "traditional" partners in the West while seeking a breakthrough under Ramaphosa, even as it deepens far-reaching strategic relations with China.

Later on, in July 2018, Chinese president, Xi Jinping, did pay a four-day visit to South Africa. A few weeks later, the British prime minister, Theresa May, also visited South Africa on August 28, 2018. The visit lasted a day. Three days later, on August 31, Ramaphosa began a nine-day visit to China. In Beijing he spoke of South Africa's desire that relations with China as well as the Forum on China-Africa Cooperation (FOCAC) be "strategic," and that they bring about "dignity, work, opportunity and economic security" in order for South Africans to "see and feel the benefits of this strategic cooperation."[1]

It may be tempting to view these events as illustrative of a dilemma still facing South Africa in its international relations. However, this book has argued that on the whole, a marked inability to match China's overtures by the West is beginning to emerge. Whether it is at the symbolic level of country visits and their duration or at multilateral levels such as Beijing's successful lobby for South Africa's membership in BRICS, a closer partnership with China has embedded itself in a systematic way in South Africa's foreign policy-making nexus. This close, coordinated partnership has not only become a mainstay of foreign policy in Pretoria, but it has also taken a strategic significance—whether the president is an openly pro-Beijing Zuma or Ramaphosa, the billionaire who had been expected to tread a more Western-centric path. In this book, it has been argued that, ironically, it is a Western reticence when it comes to investment capital, as well as the lack of structural reforms of multilateral institutions that have magnified the strategic appeal of closer relations with China for a South Africa pressured by developmental problems.

Compared to most of its neighbors in the region, the Republic of South Africa's diplomatic relations with the People's Republic of China are quite new and, contrary to the expectations of many at the time, were established quite late (on January 1, 1998) after the country achieved liberation. Earlier in the book it was argued that it took four years to establish formal relations because the Mandela administration, indeed the great statesman himself failed to appreciate Chinese history and the country's extreme sensitivity on the issues of Taiwan. The roots of this problem lay in Taiwan's aggressive lobbying of ruling-party and opposition politicians alike, apartheid South Africa's long-standing strategic relations with Taiwan, and how the negotiated nature of South Africa's transition to democracy meant the Mandela government had to live with apartheid commitments for a while. These combined to turn what was expected to be a straightforward decision to recognize the PRC into a drawn-out fiasco.

This and numerous other instances in the history between these two countries, going back centuries, demonstrate what we have called *attenuated* contacts between the Chinese and the (South) African people. Throughout most of the 1990s *apartheid* attenuated contact through business interests. Previous contact was attenuated by apartheid rule and opposition to it; before, that it was attenuated by the Sino-Soviet split, which forced liberation movements to pick sides; even further before that, it was attenuated by colonial rule, which brought indentured Chinese to work in the mines and caused friction between them and Africans. The current South Africa-China relations, therefore, constitute the least attenuated contact that has ever taken place between the Chinese and (South) Africans.

We have also pointed out earlier in the book how South Africa under Mbeki enjoyed a high profile in the multilateral arena, remained cooperative with the Western-centric neoliberal order, and placed much trust in multilateral institutions. This saw South Africa attend the yearly G8 summits as an "invited nonmember." Mbeki's "African renaissance" agenda proposed a more Western-centric, growth-driven New Partnership for Africa's Development (NEPAD), among other "African solutions to African problems." It, however, failed to marshal enough capital even as it elicited widespread enthusiasm within the continent. Instead of a "renaissance," an African "de-naissance" took place instead whereby Africa saw a decrease in FDI even as investment grew in other developing economies of the world. Increasingly, NEPAD found itself pitted against FOCAC. The latter bore more investment capital, had little to no conditionalities, and was on a bi-lateral level of cooperation. This state-of-affairs where a South African fidelity to the neoliberal world order was seen as unrequited left Mbeki's Pretoria with little choice but to explore further cooperation with Beijing, even as Mbeki still openly nursed unease about deepening relations. But for this reticence, South Africa-China relations may well have reached "comprehensive strategic partnership" level sooner.

If the necessity of closer South Africa-China relations was not compelling enough for the Mbeki administration, we have argued that two events were. First, the 2008 global recession saw a decimation of demand for South African exports to "traditional" Northern economies, a gap which Beijing swiftly filled, saving thousands of jobs in South Africa. Secondly, Mbeki was removed as president in 2008 and Jacob Zuma eventually assumed the presidency in 2009. We identify these two events as having decidedly turned Pretoria toward Beijing, setting the country on an inexorable path to the comprehensive strategic partnership that was formalized in 2013. They also set in motion China's successful lobby for South Africa to be accepted as a member of BRICS in 2010.

Similar to the South African reticence to sever ties with Taiwan in 1997, which was followed by a rash of Chinese investment and aggressive lobbying, the Chinese push for South Africa's BRICS membership is identified as a recurrent pattern of a trademark Chinese diplomacy or statecraft. In 1997 Beijing helped the Mandela administration save face for having miscalculated how untenable a "Two Chinas" scenario was; in 2008 Beijing helped South Africa save face when faced with serious economic effects from the 2008 recession while at the same time overcoming the reticence of the Mbeki years, and effectively quieted oft-heard talk of a "neo-colonialist" China in Pretoria.

This change in the global dynamics where emerging economies were increasingly finding their voice on matters of global economic governance, as well as seeking bigger decision-making positions, found better appreciation under Zuma. The data on South Africa's increased participation in FOCAC, G20, and later BRICS, and a cessation of participation in G8 "outreach" meetings, suggests this. The Zuma administration, therefore, stands out as having been responsible for the most comprehensive transformation of South Africa's economic diplomacy through the strategic comprehensive partnership, and for having achieved membership into the exclusive BRICS bloc, both monumental achievements half-driven by events beyond South Africa itself. While this may be a latter-day attenuation of South

Africa-China relations, it is one with a markedly more agency than previous instances.

Because of how entrenched unemployment is in South Africa, any strategy to address it must involve both long-term and rapid, measurable short-term initiatives. This book has proposed that sponsoring South African women co-ops to go to Yiwu International Trade City to order inventory themselves, and re-sell it in South Africa ought to be incorporated into South Africa's small enterprises strategy. While this may not help in reversing the long-standing trade deficit South Africa has with China, data demonstrates that South Africa is not an exception in the regards, nor is it an exception in the matrix of its imports. Therefore, to decisively deal with unemployment, South Africa must take advantage of the global environment as it is, especially in the short term. The research on the success of pilot programs for small enterprises motivates for this approach as is our conclusion that a large number of small enterprises involved in commodities trade, when they are Chinese in South Africa, they did not receive extensive training in business. They simply went to Yiwu and took advantage of economies of scale. These are promising prospects for South African women to participate and also take advantage of the economies of scale by going to Yiwu themselves, like many traders encountered from other countries like Zimbabwe.

In the long term, however, it is proposed that South Africa's strategy must include sending its young people to study at Zhejiang, with the intention of learning about the feasibility for a "South Africa Yiwu," a trade hub-city trading in value-added products unique to the country. Indeed, data suggests that not only is South Africa's matrix full of potential products for such a scheme but also they have high demand and ready Chinese market and would form a dual export-import strategy for South African small enterprises that is regulated through bilateral mechanisms.

The quest for a developmental state in South Africa was also examined with a view of deepening partnership with Beijing. An important distinction has been made between stated desires for a developmental state and the implementation of policy toward its achievement. Since 1994, a documentary survey of policy statements (of the ruling ANC and the government) and budget speeches indicates a *policy dissonance* between state policy objectives at the party level and actionable objectives at the executive level. Data on mention of the term "developmental" in the ANC's conference resolutions is instructive: 20 times in the 52nd congress (2007), 25 times in the 53rd (2012), and 20 times in the 54th (2017). But in the finance minister's budget speeches of the same respective time periods, "developmental" is mentioned zero, one, and zero times. The same number of mentions are also found in the State of the Nation speech by the president in the same respective time periods.

When dealing with a capable state such as China, it is this policy dissonance which we conclude constitutes the Achilles' heel in South Africa's prospects for realizing a developmental state using the wherewithal extracted from deeper partnership with Beijing. The instability and uncertainty such dissonance causes not only limit the scope of South Africa-China relations but also continue to elicit an increasingly vocal discussion concerning it among the Chinese officials.[2] It may be argued that a need exists for South Africa to strengthen its mechanisms for monitoring developmental policy, one that makes a distinction between stated and implemented plans.

## TOWARD A QUADRILINEAR MODEL FOR
## SOUTH AFRICA-CHINA RELATIONS

From the beginning, this study has proceeded on the premise that a need exists for South Africa to find lasting solutions to its developmental impasse and ensure continued social stability that will be unsustainable in the long run if the socioeconomical status quo persists. Central to any solution is the need to increase policy autonomy enough to allow the South African government sufficient agency to restructure aspects of the economy to make them developmental, and doing so without adversely affecting economic growth. This study has sought to de-mystify the Chinese role in this context.

To this end, we need to reimagine the analytical spaces from an African scholar or practitioner perspective. A comprehensive way of looking at (South) Africa–China relations, one that takes into consideration the varying scope of interactions that often cut across disciplinary lines—in academia—as well as sectorial ones—in political economy—will avoid what may be called a "narrative dilution." This is when the tone of the narrative in one sphere of South Africa-China engagement affects the tone of the narrative in another sphere.

Many Africans who have had experience with China have had varying experiences with different players at different times, that is, their interactions took place in different spheres. Many of the misunderstandings that have taken place between people-to-people interaction have left negative impressions. They have often gone on to "dilute" the overall impression of that person to all things Chinese. If an African trader in Guangzhou has an unfortunate incident with a Chinese trader, later on that person is most likely to have a negative impression of a Chinese government initiative or their (African) country's cooperation with China or a negative impression of a Chinese company somewhere in Africa.

To promote mutual understanding between China and South Africa, as well as between China and Africa at large, we propose a quadrilinear model for analyzing what the blossoming field of relations is. The idea is to compartmentalize general interactions between South Africa and China at different spheres with the hope that this will constitute an analytical tool for scholars and practitioners alike.

China-South Africa relations may be viewed as constituting interactions between four general entities, which interact in the following manner: sphere I, Chinese government—South African government (in the international relations realm); sphere II, South African government-Chinese nationals; sphere III, South African nationals—Chinese government (in China); and sphere IV, South African nationals-Chinese nationals (in South Africa). This model is not for analysis of China-South Africa interactions alone; it may be modified to apply to any other African country.

Sphere I is about relations between the countries' governments and their bi- as well as multilateral interactions. It is about the strategic relations and how each government's decisions or policies affects the other. A determination about each of the country's ascendance or relative power is made at this sphere of analysis. Sphere II concerns interactions taking place between the South African government and the Chinese nationals, whether domiciles in South Africa or visiting. South African government policy on issues such as immigration, or policy on Chinese fishing vessel restrictions in South Africa, for instance, is analyzed at this sphere. Sphere III is the reverse of the previous sphere. It is about interactions between South African nationals and the Chinese government, whether the former are visiting or domiciled in China. A Chinese government policy or general treatment of African foreigners in China, for instance, would be analyzed in this sphere. Sphere IV is about South African nationals and Chinese nationals. Person-to-person interactions,

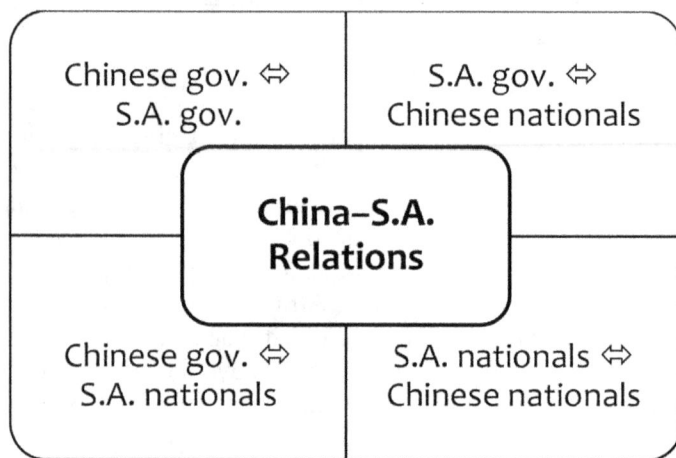

Figure C.1   Quadrilinear Model of South Africa-China Relations. *Source:* Author.

which are an enormous part of how most narratives are mutually formed about the other by Chinese and South Africans, are what this sphere helps analyze.

One hopes that this model will help African Studies as well as South African foreign policy-makers to be cognizant of the various compartments of South Africa-China relations, replete with their inherent complications, challenges, and opportunities. By doing so, a "China policy" will be easier to make because different factors and players will be accounted for. With the deepening of relations between these two societies must come a deepening of analytical tools to inform fruitful discussion, indeed debate on the South Africa-China relations. Making a clear distinction between government-to-government, people-to-government, and people-to-people spaces in which interaction take place, we will better account for problem areas in relations and avoid conclusions about one area of relations affecting occlusions about another. Ultimately, it is the abiding hope of this study that this and similar models of looking at China's relations with South Africa will improve mutual understanding between the peoples of these countries, leading to even better relations in the future not just between the governments but the people as well.

## NOTES

1. "Remarks on the China-Africa High Level Dialogue," Department of International Relations and Cooperation, President Cyril Ramaphosa during the China-Africa High Level Dialogue with Business Representatives Forum on China-Africa Cooperation, September 03, 2018, Beijing, China, accessed September 16, 2020, http://www.dirco.gov.za/docs/speeches/2018/cram0903.htm.

2. Alexander Winning and Joe Bavier, "Ramaphosa is 'Last Hope' for South Africa, Chinese Diplomat Says," *Reuters*, July 29, 2019, accessed February 23, 2021, https://www.reuters.com/article/safrica-china-idINKCN1UO1Y7.

# Appendix 1

## *Statement by President Nelson Mandela on South Africa's Relations with the Greater China Region*

November 27, 1996

The guiding principle in South Africa's position towards the Greater China region has always been that South Africa wishes to have cordial relations with both the People's Republic of China and the Republic of China on Taiwan. This principle has been based on the strong economic relations that South Africa maintains with both the People's Republic of China and with Taiwan. This principle will continue to guide South Africa's relations with the Greater China region.

On assumption of office, we stated that we have inherited a situation with South Africa recognizing the Republic of China on Taiwan, but that these relations could not be abandoned overnight. I, and the South African Government, have enormous appreciation for the contribution that the Government of the Republic of China has made through the commitment of the Government sector in the economic development Africa. The Republic of China, further, made a generous and much appreciated contribution to South Africa's transition to democracy and I would like to pay special to Ambassador I-Cheng for his personal endeavors in this regard.

In its international relations, South Africa has become an active participant within the ambit of the OAU and the Non-Aligned Movement, as well as within the UN system. A permanent continuation of diplomatic recognition of the Republic of China on Taiwan is inconsistent with South Africa's role in international affairs.

I had the opportunity to meet with the representatives of the Republic of China and the People's Republic of China yesterday. I expressed the hope that within the next twelve months it would be possible to achieve a smooth transition, acceptable to both the People's Republic of China and the Government of the Republic of China on Taiwan, in terms of which South Africa recognizes the People's Republic of China, but continues to conduct constructive relations with Taiwan.

Issued by: Office of the President

Source: South African Government Information Office

# Appendix 2

## Joint Communiqué between the Government of the People's Republic of China and the Government of the Republic of South Africa on the Establishment of Diplomatic Relations

January 1, 1998

1. The Government of the People's Republic of China and the Government of the Republic of South Africa, in conformity with the interests and desire of the two peoples, have decided upon mutual recognition and the establishment of diplomatic relations at ambassadorial level as from January 1, 1998.
2. The Government of the People's Republic of China and the Government of the Republic of South Africa agree to develop the friendly relations and cooperation between the two countries on the basis of the principles of mutual respect for sovereignty and territorial integrity, mutual non-aggression, non-interference in each other's internal affairs, equality and mutual benefit and peaceful coexistence.
3. The Government of the Republic of South Africa recognizes that there is but one China in the world, the Government of the People's Republic of China is the sole legal government representing the whole of China and recognizes China's position that Taiwan is an inalienable part of China.
4. The Government of the People's Republic of China and the Government of the Republic of South Africa agree, on the basis of the principle of reciprocity and in accordance with the relevant provisions of the Vienna Convention on Diplomatic Relations, to provide each other with all the

necessary assistance for the establishment and performances of the functions of diplomatic missions in their respective capitals and to exchange ambassadors as soon as possible.

For the Government of
The People's Republic of China
Mr. Qian Qichen

For the Government of the
Republic of South Africa
Mr. Alfred Nzo

# Appendix 3

## *Pretoria Declaration on the Partnership between the People's Republic Of China and the Republic of South Africa*

April 25, 2000

We,[1] the Heads of State of the People's Republic of China and the Republic of South Africa, having gathered in Pretoria on this Twenty-Fifth Day of April in the Year Two Thousand, hereby declare that we:

Recall the ties of friendship and the principles that have brought together the peoples of China and Africa over many years, as articulated 45 years ago at the Bandung Conference and also 4 years ago at the Headquarters of the Organization of African Unity, when the 5 principles of Sino-African relations were conceptualized as:

Sincere Friendship
Equality and Sovereignty
Common Development on the Basis of Mutual Benefit
Increased Consultation and Cooperation in International Affairs
Cooperation in the Establishment of a New International Political and Economic Order;

Commit ourselves anew to the spirit of partnership and constructive dialogue between China and South Africa, and to the position that there is but one China in the world and Taiwan is an inalienable part of China, as articulated in the Joint Communiqué on the Establishment of Diplomatic Relations, and express appreciation for the noble ideals embodied in the philosophy of the African Renaissance;

Take cognizance of the moral imperative for developing countries to strengthen capacity for cooperation and mutual support in the international economic milieu;

169

Note with satisfaction the strong growth in political, economic, scientific, technological and cultural relations between our countries, and dedicate ourselves to the further development of these relations on the basis of mutual benefit and in a way that will support and strengthen each other;

Recognize that both China and South Africa share many objectives with regard to key multilateral issues and on the urgent need for the reform of the international multilateral political, economic and financial architecture to reflect new global realities.

Now, therefore we undertake that:

Firstly, the Governments of China and South Africa will endeavor to further enhance the existing partnership between them by calling into being, through this Declaration, a high-level Bi-National Commission.

This Bi-National Commission will meet regularly at mutually convenient times and levels. This Bi-National Commission will aim to guide and coordinate all government-to-government relations between China and South Africa, and to consult on matters of mutual interest in the bilateral and multilateral spheres. As such, due cognisance is taken of the existing agreements and arrangements on Bilateral Consultations and Joint Commissions and that this Bi-National Commission will, in principle, safeguard and incorporate those earlier agreements and arrangements.

Both Governments hereby also commit themselves to constructive dialogue, the creation of wealth for their peoples, the safeguarding of their national sovereignty, safety and integrity through the proceedings of the Bi-National Commission. Both Governments also agree that the modalities for the operation of this Bi-National Commission will be confirmed through the Diplomatic Channel and that the first meeting of the Commission will be held at an early date;

Secondly, the Governments of China and South Africa will, within the context of South-South Cooperation, endeavor to develop, strengthen and diversify their economic relationship to the mutual benefit of their peoples, by removing obstacles impeding negatively on their bilateral trade, investment, service, and commercial relations. The two Governments will work hard to primarily encourage and support closer cooperation between enterprises of the two countries in the development of natural resources, especially in the areas of mining and manufacturing;

Thirdly, the Governments of China and South Africa will cooperate constructively and effectively in the promotion of a new Sino-African relationship on the basis of equality and mutual benefit, by supporting the African continent in its efforts to seek peace, stability and development and by promoting the interests of Africa through multilateral fora such as the G-77 and China, and the structures of the United Nations; and

Fourthly, the Governments of China and South Africa will support each other in efforts to create a new international political and economic order. The two sides maintain that in this future New Order, the diversity of the world should be respected; the principles of sovereign equality and non-interference in the internal affairs of other countries should be upheld; no country should dominate others; the negative effects of globalization—especially on developing nations—should be reduced and restricted; and harmony, democracy, justice and equality in international relations should be actively pursued and fully promoted.

This Declaration publicly states our common guiding vision for the future and the fundamental principles for the forging of even closer and stronger relations between the People's Republic of China and the Republic of South Africa.

This Declaration is signed at Pretoria, on this Twenty-Fifth Day of April in the Year Two Thousand, in the Chinese and English languages, both being equally authentic.

PRESIDENT OF THE
PEOPLE'S REPUBLIC
OF CHINA
Mr. Jiang Zemin

PRESIDENT      OF      THE
REPUBLIC OF SOUTH AFRICA

Mr. Thabo Mbeki

## NOTE

1. Ministry of International Relations and Cooperation of the Republic of South Africa, "Pretoria Declaration on the Partnership between the People's Republic of China and the Republic of South Africa," accessed November 14, 2019, http://www.dfa.gov.za/docs/2013/chin0326.html.

# Bibliography

"Africa Must Be Free!" *Renmin Ribao* (Beijing). April 15, 1961.

"Africa's New Number One." *The Economist*. April 12, 2014; "China is Now EU's Biggest Trading Partner; Overtakes US." *The Star*. Accessed October 6, 2020, https://www.thestar.com.my/aseanplus/aseanplus-news/2020/10/05/china-is-now-eu039s-biggest-trading-partner-overtakes-us

"African Countries' Support of China in History." *The Global Times*. April 14, 2020. Accessed August 21, 2020. https://www.globaltimes.cn/content/1185568.shtml

"After the Fall." *The Economist*. November 13, 2008.

"Black Business Criticizes Ruling on Chinese South Africans." *Mail and Guardian*. June 02, 2008.

"BRICS Create Development Bank, 'Mini-IMF'." *The Times of India*. June 16, 2014.

"Counting their Blessings." *The Economist*. December 30, 2009.

"Dalai Lama Visits Tutu and Mandela." *Hobart Mercury* (Australia). August 23, 1996.

"Hallo, China—Or Is It Taiwan?" *The Economist*. September 14, 1996.

"Hello Dalai Lama." *San Jose Mercury*. August 20, 1996.

"India Cuts Exposure to US Government Securities at $77.5 Billion in October." *The Times of India*. December 21, 2014.

"Interview with Oliver Tambo." *Noticias* (Maputo). August 5, 1983.

"Kangningbo." *My Old Maps*. Accessed August 21, 2020. http://www.myoldmaps.com/late-medieval-maps-1300/236-yoktae-chewang-honil/236-kandingo.pdf

"Lifting One-child Policy Echoes People's Will." *Global Times*. October 30, 2014.

"Mbeki Warns Africa on Relationship with China." *Mail and Guardian*. December 13, 2006.

"Nelson Mandela in My Eyes." *Beijing Review*. December 19, 2013.

"NEPAD and Its Relevance to Zimbabwe." *Financial Gazette* (Harare). October 23, 2003.

"Outcry over Foreign Reporter's Treatment." *Mail and Guardian*. May 1, 1996.

"Premier Sun Visits Four African Countries." *Taiwan Review*. May 1, 1980.

"Residents Without *Hukou* Pin Hopes on New Policy." *China Daily*. December 3, 2015.

"Second in Line." *The Economist*. August 11, 2010.

"Statement by President Nelson Mandela on South Africa's Relations with the Greater China Region." *South African Government Information*. Accessed August 21, 2020. http://goo.gl/zlfx3S

"The Freedom Charter." *Wits Historical Papers*. Accessed September 20, 2020. http://www.historicalpapers.wits.ac.za/inventories/inv_pdfo/AD1137/AD1137-Ea6-1-001-jpeg.pdf

"Trade Reports." *Department of Trade and Industry of the Republic of South Africa*. Accessed September 4, 2020. http://tradestats.thedti.gov.za/ReportFolders/reportFolders.aspx?sCS_referer=&sCS_ChosenLang=en

Abegunrin, Olayiwola. *Africa in Global Politics in the Twenty-First Century: A Pan-African Perspective*. New York: Palgrave Macmillan, 2009.

Adekunle, Julius, O. "East African States." In *Africa Volume 1: African History Before 1885*, edited by. Falola, Toyin, 191–206. Durham, NC: Carolina Academic Press, 2000.

Africa-EU Partnership. Accessed August 21, 2020. https://africa-eu-partnership.org/en/our-events/1st-africa-eu-summit

Africa-EU Partnership. Accessed September 16, 2020. http://www.africa-eu-partnership.org/en/3rd-africa-eu-summit

African National Congress. "Ready to Govern: ANC Policy Guidelines for a Democratic South Africa." Accessed November 11, 2020. http://www.anc.org.za/show.php?id=227

African Union. Accessed August 21, 2020. https://au.int/ar/summit/2ndafricaindia. Ministry of Foreign Affairs of Japan. "TICAD." Accessed August 21, 2020. https://www.mofa.go.jp/region/africa/ticad/index.html

Anderlini, Jamil and Lucy Hornby. "China Overtakes US as World's Largest Goods Trader." *Financial Times*. January 10, 2014.

Andrews, Edmund. "Leaders of G-20 Vow to Reshape Global Economy." *The New York Times*. September 25, 2009.

Anti-Taylor, William. "China through African Eyes." *Race & Class* 5, no. 4 (1964): 48–51.

April, Yazini. "Understanding Aspects of China's Governance and Economic Growth." *Africa Insight* 41, no. 4 (2012): 106–22.

Baogang, Guo. *China's Quest for Political Legitimacy: The New Equity-Enhancing Politics*. Lanham, MD: Lexington Books, 2010.

Bayne, Nicholas. "The Decline of the G8 and Lessons for the G20." In *The New Economic Diplomacy: Decision-Making and Negotiation in International Economic Relations*, edited by Nicholas Bayne, Stephen Woolcockeds. Farnham, 220–37. Farnham, UK: Ashgate, 2011.

BBC. "25th Africa-France Summit." Accessed August 21, 2020. https://www.bbc.co.uk/worldservice/africa/2010/06/100601_afriquefrancesummit.shtml

Bodomo, Adam M. "From Guangzhou to Yiwu: Emerging Facets of the African Diaspora in China." *International Journal of African Renaissance* 5, no. 2 (2010): 283–89.

Bosrstelmann, Thomas. *Apartheid's Reluctant Uncle: The United States and Southern Africa in the Early Cold War.* New York: Oxford University Press, 1993.

Boyd, R. G. *Communist China's Foreign Policy.* New York: Praeger, 1962.

Brautigam, Deborah. *The Dragon's Gift: The Real Story of China in Africa.* New York: Oxford University Press, 2009.

BRICS. "Summits." Accessed April 19, 2020. https://infobrics.org/news/summits/

Bright, Rachel K. *Chinese Labor in South Africa, 1902–10: Race, Violence, and Global Spectacle.* New York: Palgrave Macmillan, 2013.

Bunting, Brian. *Moses Kotane, South African Revolutionary.* London: Inkululeko Publishing, 1975.

Buthelezi, Londiwe. "It's Time for Africa to Add Value to Exports to China—Davies." *Business News.* September 16, 2013.

Callinicos, Lulu. *Oliver Tambo: Beyond the Engels Mountains.* Claremont, South Africa: David Phillip, 2004.

Campbell, Horace. "China in Africa: Challenging US Global Hegemony." *Third World Quarterly* 29, no. 1 (2008): 89–105.

Castells, Manuel. "Four Asian Tigers with a Dragon Head: A Comparative Analysis of State, Economy, and Society in the Asian Pacific Rim." In *States and Development in the Asian Pacific Rim*, edited by Jeffrey Henderson and Richard P. Appelbaum. London: Sage Publications, 1992.

Chan, Steve et al. "Look Beyond the Developmental State." In *Beyond the Developmental State: East Asia's Political Economies Reconsidered.* Basingstoke, UK: Macmillan, 1998.

Chang, Ha-Joon. "How to 'Do' A Developmentalist State: Political, Organizational, and Human Resource Requirements for the Developmental State." In *Constructing A Democratic Developmental State in South Africa: Potentials and Challenges*, edited by Omano Edigheji. Cape Town: Human Sciences Research Council Press, 2010.

Chinese scholar, Interview with author. September 16, 2014.

Chinese scholar. Interview by author. Jinhua, September 16 and 17, 2014.

Chinese scholar. Interview by author. Jinhua, September 17, 2014.

Chinese scholar. Interview by author. September 16, 2014.

Chinese scholar. Interview with author. Jinhua, September 16, 2014.

Chinese scholar. Interview with author. Jinhua, September 17, 2014.

Chinese scholar. Interview with author. September 29, 2014.

CIA World Facebook. Accessed November 11, 2020. https://www.cia.gov/library/publications/the-world-factbook/

Cohen, William B. *The French Encounter with Africa: White Response to Blacks, 1530–1880.* Bloomington, IN: Indiana University Press, 2003.

Collier, Paul. *Exodus: How Migration is Changing the World.* New York: Oxford University Press, 2013.

Cooper, Gene. *The Market and Temple Fairs of Rural China: Red Fire.* New York: Routledge, 2013.

David, Wilfred. *The Conversation on Economic Development: Historical Voices, Interpretations, and Reality.* Armonk. New York: M.E. Sharpe, 1997.

David, Wilfred. *The Humanitarian Development Paradigm: Search for Global Justice*. Lenham, MD: University Press of America, 2004.

De Santiago, Alphonse and Georges Musset, ed. *Cosmographie de l'Europe en 1544*. Paris, 1904. December 23, 2019. http://www.statssa.gov.za/?s=documented&sitem=publications

Deng Xiaoping. "Maintain the Tradition of Hard Struggle." Excerpt from a talk with President Yoweri Museveni of the Republic of Uganda on March 23, 1989. Accessed September 23, 2020, https://dengxiaopingworks.wordpress.com/2013/03/18/maintain-the-tradition-of-hard-struggle/

Deng, Xiaoping. "We Can Develop Market Economy Under Socialism." *The Selected Works of Deng Xiaoping*. Accessed September 16, 2020. https://goo.gl/4TXjSC

Department of International Relations and Cooperation. "Remarks on the China-Africa High Level Dialogue." President Cyril Ramaphosa during the China-Africa High Level Dialogue with Business Representatives Forum on China-Africa Cooperation, September 03, 2018, Beijing, China. Accessed September 16, 2020. http://www.dirco.gov.za/docs/speeches/2018/cram0903.htm

Department of Trade and Industry of the Republic of South Africa. "Trade Reports." Accessed November 11, 2020. http://tradestats.thedti.gov.za/ReportFolders/reportFolders.aspx?sCS_referer=&sCS_ChosenLang=en

Dhjab, Jalaj Dhiab. "Black Iraqis: Scarred Memory and Recovered Identity." In *Minorities in Iraq: Memory, Identity and Challenges*, edited by Salloum, Sa'ad, 102–11. Beirut, Baghdad: Masarat for Cultural and Media Development, 2013.

Dreyer, Edward L. *Zheng He: China and the Oceans in the Early Ming Dynasty, 1405–1433*. Upper Saddle River, NJ: Pearson, 2006.

Du, Rusheng. *Chinese Economists on Economic Reform—Collected Works of Du Runsheng*. New York: Routledge, 2013.

Duyvendak, J. J. L. *China's Discovery of Africa*. London: Arthur Probsthain, 1949.

Edigheji, Omano. "Constructing a Democratic Developmental State in South Africa: Potentials and Challenges." In *Constructing A Democratic Developmental State in South Africa: Potentials and Challenges*, edited by Omano Edigheji. Cape Town: Human Sciences Research Council Press, 2010.

Edoho, Felix M. "Globalization and the Marginalization of Africa: Contextualization of Africa-China Relations." *Africa Today* 58, no. 1 (2004): 103–24.

Ellis, Stephen and Tsepo Sechaba. *Comrades Against Apartheid*. Bloomington, IN: Indiana University Press, 1992.

Evans, Peter B. "Constructing the 21st Century Developmental State." In *Constructing A Democratic Developmental State in South Africa: Potentials and Challenges*, edited by Omano Edigheji. Cape Town: Human Sciences Research Council Press, 2010.

Fei, Xi. "Xingcha Shenglan" (Arresting Views from a Raft Guided by Stars). In *Shuofang Beisheng* (Complete Historical Records of the North), vol. 3, edited by Quitao He, 4.4a–b. Shanghai: Guji Chunbanshe, 1999.

Feinstein, Charles H. *The Economic History of South Africa: Conquest, Discrimination and Development*. New York: Cambridge University Press, 2005.

Filesi, Teobaldo. *China and Africa in the Middle Ages.* London: Routledge, 1972.

Fine, Ben. "Can South Africa be a Developmental State?" In *Constructing A Democratic Developmental State in South Africa: Potentials and Challenges,* edited by Omano Edigheji. Cape Town: Human Sciences Research Council Press, 2010.

Fleminger, David. *Mapungubwe Cultural Landscape.* Pinetown, South Africa: 30° South Publishers, 2008.

FOCAC. Accessed August 21, 2020. http://www.focac.org/eng/ljhy_1/dyjbzjhy_1/CI12009/

Ford, Christopher A. *The Mind of Empire: China's History and Modern Foreign Relations.* Lexington, KY: University of Kentucky Press, 2010.

Foreign Office of the United Kingdom. "UK-Africa Summit 2020." Accessed August 21, 2020. https://www.gov.uk/government/topical-events/uk-africa-investment -summit-2020

Fouche, Leo, ed. *Mapungubwe Ancient Bantu Civilization on the Limpopo: Reports on Excavations at Mapungubwe (Northern Transvaal) from February 1933 to June 1935.* Cambridge: Cambridge University Press, 1937.

Freifedler, Jack. "For Third Straight Month, China Cuts US Debt Holdings." *China Daily.* June 17, 2014.

Fuchs, Walter. "Was South Africa Already Known in the 13th Century?" *Imago Mundi: The International Journal for the History of Cartography* 10, no. 1 (1953): 50.

G20 Information Center. "G20 Summits." Accessed April 19, 2020. http://www.g20. utoronto.ca/summits/index.html

Gavin, Lewis. "China's Success is Limited." *Financial Mail.* December, 10, 2010.

George T. "China's Failure in Africa." *Asian Survey* (1966): 46–468.

Gilbert, Robert. *The Unequal Treaties: China and the Foreigner.* Arlington, VA: University Publications of America, 1976.

Gills, Barry. "The International Origin of South Korea's Export Orientation." In *Transcending the State-Global Divide: A Neostructuralist Agenda in International Relations,* edited by Ronen P. Palan and Barry Gills. Boulder, CO: Lynne Rienner, 1994.

Greenberg, Stanley. *Race and State in Capitalist Development: Comparative Perspectives.* New Haven, CT: Yale University Press, 1980.

Harris, Karen L. "Sugar and Gold: Indentured Indian and Chinese Labor in South Africa." *Journal of Social Science* 25 (2010): 147–58.

How, Tan Tarn. "Taiwan Under Attack for Muscling in on the World Scene." *The Strait Times* (Singapore). August 28, 1996.

Hu, Jintao. "Enhance China—Africa Unity and Cooperation To Build a Harmonious World." Speech at University of Pretoria, South Africa. Accessed August 21, 2020, http://www.dirco.gov.za/docs/speeches/2007/jintao0207.htm

Hucker, Charles O. "Preface." In *Chinese Government in Ming Time,* edited by Charles Hucker. New York: Columbia University Press, 1969.

Interview with Ghanaian trader, September 21, 2014.

Interview with Kenyan trader, September 20, 2014.

Interview with South Africa diplomat. Beijing. September 25, 2014.

Interview with Zimbabwean trader, September 20, 2014

Jacques, Martin. *When China Rules the World: The End of the Western World and the Birth of a New Order.* New York: Penguin, 2012.

Johnson, Chalmer Johnson. *MITI and the Japanese Miracle.* Stanford, CA: Stanford University Press, 1982.

Johnson, R. W. "China Offers £11bn Investment." *The Times.* September 3, 1996.

Kahn, Joseph. "China Opens Summit for African Leaders." *The New York Times.* November 2, 2006.

Kasrils, Ronnie. *Armed and Dangerous: My Undercover Struggle Against Apartheid.* Oxford: Heinemann, 1993.

Kauffman, Carol. "Patterns of Contact: Designs from the Indian Ocean World: A Curator's View." *The East African Review* 51 (2016): 151–60.

Keet, Dot. "South-South Strategic Bases for Africa to Engage China." In *The Rise of China and India in Africa: Challenges, Opportunities and Critical Interventions,* edited by Fantu Cheru and Cyril Obi, 21–33. London; New York; Uppsala, Sweden: Zed Books; Nordic Africa Institute, 2010.

Kirton, John. "From G8 2003 to G13 2010? The Heiligendamm Process's Past, Present, and Future." In *Emerging Powers in Global Governance: Lessons from the Heiligendamm Process,* edited by Andrew F. Cooper and Agata Antkiewicz, 45–82. Ontario: Wilfrid Laurier University Press, 2010.

Lampton, David M. *The Three Faces of Chinese Power: Might, Money, and Minds.* Berkeley: University of California Press, 2008.

Lapper. Richard. "Furore as South Africa Bans Dalai Lama from Peace Conference." *Financial Times,* March, 24, 2009.

Le Blanc, Vincent. *Voyages Famieux de Vincent le Blanc.* Paris, 1649.

Levine, Steven. "Perception and Ideology in Chinese Foreign Policy." In *Chinese Foreign Policy—Theory and Practice,* edited by Thomas Robinson and David Shambaugh, 37–46. Oxford: Clarendon Press, 1995.

Lewis, Gavin. "China's Success is Limited." *Financial Mail.* December 10, 2010.

Li, Anshan, et al. *FOCAC: Twelve Years Later: Achievements, Challenges, and the Way Forward.* Beijing: Peking University, 2012.

Li, Anshan. "African Studies in China: A Historiographical Survey." *African Studies Review* 48, no. 1 (April 2005): 59–87.

Li, Anshan. "China and Africa: Policy and Challenges." *China Security* 3, no. 3 (Summer 2007): 69–93.

Lipton, David. "South Africa: Facing the Challenges of the Global Economy." Speech at the International Monetary Fund. May 8, 2013. Accessed September 16, 2020. https://www.imf.org/external/np/speeches/2013/050813.htm

Low, Alfred D. *The Sino-Soviet Dispute: An Analysis of the Polemics.* Cranbury, NJ: Associated University Presses, 1976.

Mahbubani. Kishore. *The New Asian Hemisphere: The Irresistible Shift of Global Power to the East.* New York: Public Affairs Book, 2008.

*Mail and Guardian.* "Carroll: Mine Violence Caused by Legacy of Apartheid." December 05, 2012.

Mandela, Nelson. *Long Walk to Freedom: The Autobiography of Nelson Mandela.* Boston: Little, Brown and Company, 1994.

Mason, Warren. "What is New in Neostructuralism?" In *Transcending the State-Global Divide: A Neostructuralist Agenda in International Relations*, edited by Ronen P. Palan and Barry Gills, 1–22. Boulder: Lynne Rienner, 1994.

Mazama, Ama. *Africa in the 21st Century: Toward a New Future*. New York: Routledge, 2007.

Mbeki, Thabo. "Address at Tsinghua University." Speech in Beijing, China. Accessed September 21, 2020. http://www.dirco.gov.za/docs/speeches/2001/mbek1211.htm

Mbeki, Thabo. "Reconciliation and Nation Building: Statement of Deputy President Thabo Mbeki at the Opening of the Debate in the National Assembly." Cape Town. May 29, 1998. Accessed October 8, 2020. http://www.dfa.gov.za/docs/speeches/1998/mbek0529.htm

Mbeki, Thabo. "The African Renaissance, South Africa and The World." *United Nations Archive*. Accessed September 16, 2020. http://archive.unu.edu/unupress/mbeki.html

McGregor, Richard. "Sino-African Summit Ends With Swipe At Critics." *Financial Times*. November 6, 2006.

Middle East Institute. "Iran Invests Time and Energy in Africa." Accessed August 21, 2020. https://www.mei.edu/publications/iran-invests-time-and-energy-africa

Mingst, Karen. "Group of Eight." *Encyclopedia Britannica*. Accessed August 21, 2020. https://www.britannica.com/topic/Group-of-Eight

Ministry of Foreign Affairs of South Africa. "President Mbeki to lead South African Delegation to China-Africa Co-operation Summit." Accessed September 16, 2020. http://www.dfa.gov.za/docs/2006/chin1030.htm

Ministry of Foreign Affairs of Taiwan. *The Republic of China Yearbook*. Taipei: Government Information Office, 1996.

Ministry of Foreign Affairs of the People's Republic of China. "Joint Communiqué Between the Government of the People's Republic of China and the Government of the Republic of South Africa on the Establishment of Diplomatic Relations." Accessed August 21, 2020. http://www.fmprc.gov.cn/mfa_eng/wjdt_665385/2649_665393/t15813.shtml

Ministry of Foreign Affairs of the People's Republic of China. "Joint Communiqué between the Government of the People's Republic of China and the Government of the Republic of South Africa on the Establishment of Diplomatic Relations." Accessed September 16, 2020. http://www.fmprc.gov.cn/mfa_eng/wjdt_665385/2649_665393/t15813.shtml

Ministry of Foreign Affairs of the PRC. "China's Africa Policy." Accessed June 23, 2020. https://www.fmprc.gov.cn/zflt/eng/zgdfzzc/t481748.htm

Ministry of Foreign Affairs of the PRC. "President Jiang Zemin's Visit to Six African Countries." Accessed June 21, 2020. https://www.fmprc.gov.cn/mfa_eng/ziliao_665539/3602_665543/3604_665547/t18035.shtml

Ministry of Foreign Affairs of Turkey. "Turkey-Africa Partnership Summit." Accessed August 21, 2020. http://africa.mfa.gov.tr/default.en.mfa

Ministry of Small Business Development of South Africa. "Incentives, CIS." Accessed November 11, 2020. http://www.dsbd.gov.za/about-dsbd.html

Ministry of Small Business Development of South Africa. "Programs." Ministry of Small Business Development of South Africa. Accessed November 11, 2020. http://www.dsbd.gov.za/?page_id=1218

Mirsky, Jeannette. *The Great Chinese Travellers*. New York: Pantheon, 1964.

Monson, Jamie. *Africa's Freedom Railway*. Bloomington, IN: Indiana University Press, 2009.

Moore, D. M. "The South African Air Force in Korea: An Assessment." *Military History Journal* 6, no. 3 (June 1984): 88–94.

National Assembly of the Republic of South Africa. *Hansard of the National Assembly of the Republic of South Africa*, vol. 11 (1996).

New Partnership for Africa's Development (NEPAD). "History." http://www.nepad .org/history

Nigeria's Success Due, in Part, to SA's Success." *Financial Mail*. April 10, 2014.

Office of the Legislative Analyst of the State of California. "California's Economy." Accessed September 16, 2020. http://goo.gl/NJEXnh

Office of the President of Russian Federation. "Joint Statement of the BRIC Countries' Leaders." Accessed September 16, 2020 http://archive.kremlin.ru/eng/ text/docs/2009/06/217963.shtml

Ouyang Xiu, Song Qi, et al., *Xin Tangshu* (New Tang History). Taipei: Dingwen Shuju, 1976.

Park, Yoon Jung. *A Matter of Honor: Being Chinese in South Africa*. Lanham, MD: Lexington Books, 2009.

Pfister, Roger. *Apartheid South Africa and African States: From Pariah to Middle Power, 1961–1994*. New York: Tauris Academic Studies, 2005.

Pilling David. "Asia Emerges from Global Crisis with Growth Intact." *Financial Times*. September 9, 2010.

Potter, Joshua. "Chinese-East Africa Trade Before the 16th Century." *Ufahamu: A Journal of African Studies* 5, no. 2 (1974): 113–34.

Prinsloo, Linda Nigel Wood, Maggi Loubser, Sabine M. C.Veryn and Sian Tiley. "Re-Dating of Chinese Celadon Shards Excavated on Mapungubwe Hill, a 13th Century Iron Age Site in South Africa, Using Raman Spectroscopy, XRF and XRD." *Journal of Raman Spectroscopy* 36, no. 8 (August 2005): 806–16.

Raine, Sarah. *China's African Challenges*. New York, NY: Routledge, 2009.

Ramos, Joseph and Osvaldo Sunkel. "Towards a Neostructuralist Synthesis." In *Development from Within: Towards a Neostructuralist Approach for Latin America*, edited by Osvaldo Sunkel. Boulder, CO: Lynne Rienner, 1993.

Reinert, Erik S., Yves Ekoue Amaizo and Rainer Kattel. "The Economics of Failed, Failing, and Fragile States." In *Towards New Developmentalism*, edited by Shahrukh Raki Khan and Jens Christiansen, 59–90. New York: Routledge, 2011.

Richardson, Peter. "Chinese Indentured Labor in the Transvaal Gold Mining Industry, 1904–1910." In *Independent Labor in the British Empire: 1834–1920*, edited by Kay Saunders, 260–91. London: Croom Helm, 1984.

Rodzinski, Witold. *The Walled Kingdom: A History of China from Antiquity to the Present*. New York: The Free Press, 1984.

Roy, Joyashree et al. "Developing Pathway." In *Global Environmental Changes in South Asia: A Regional Perspective*, edited by A. P. Mitra and C. Sharma, 14–53. Berlin: Springer, 2012.

Sanusi, Lamido. "Africa Must Get Real About Chinese Ties." *Financial Times*. March 11, 2013.

Schrecker, John E. *The Chinese Revolution in Historical Perspective*. New York: Greenwood Press, 1991.

Scott Thomas. *The Diplomacy of Liberation*. New York: Taurus Academic Studies, 1996.

Segatti, Aurelia. *Contemporary Migration to South Africa: A Regional Development Issue*. Washington DC: World Bank Publishing, 2011.

Seidman, Ann and Neva Seidman Makgetla. *Outposts of Global Capitalism: Southern Africa in the Changing Global Economy*. London: Zed Press, 1980.

*Shanjiang* (Classic of Mountains and Seas). Shanghai: Shanghai Shudian, 1989.

Shaw, T. *China, India and (South) Africa: What International Relations in the Second Decade of the Twenty-First Century?* New York: Routledge, 2013.

Shelton, Garth. "China and South Africa- Common Interests and Global Objectives." In *Perspective on South Africa-China Relations*, edited by Funeka Yazini April and Garth Shelton, 11–25. Pretoria: Africa Institute of South Africa, 2014.

Shinn, David.and John Eisenman. *China and Africa: A Century of Engagement.* Philadelphia: University of Pennsylvania Press, 2012.

Shu, Zhan. "China and Africa: The Chinese and the African Dream." In *Perspective on South Africa-China Relations*, edited by Funeka Yazini April and Garth Shelton, 107–17. Pretoria: Africa Institute of South Africa, 2014.

Shubin, Vladimir. *The Hot "Cold War."* Scotsville, South Africa: University of Kwazulu-Natal Press, 2008.

Shwarz, EJL. "The Chinese Connections with Africa." *Journal of Royal Asiatic Society of Bengal (Calcutta)* 5 (1938): 175–93.

Sisulu, Elinor. *Walter and Albertina Sisulu: In our Lifetime*. Claremont, South Africa: David Phillip Publishers, 2002.

Smith, Gordon S. "G7 to G8 to G20: Evolution in Global Governance." *CIGi G20 Papers*. Accessed September 16, 2020. https://www.ciaonet.org/attachments/1845 8/uploads

Snow, Phillip. *The Star Raft: China's Encounter with Africa*. London: Weidenfeld and Nicolson, 1988.

South African scholar. Interview author. November 12, 2014.

Spence, Jonathan. "Confucian Ways." *BBC Reith Lectures*. Accessed August 21, 2020, http://www.bbc.co.uk/radio4/reith2008/transcript1.shtml

Statistics South Africa. "Documented Immigrants into South Africa." Accessed December 23, 2019. http://www.statssa.gov.za/?s=documented&sitem=publications

Statistics South Africa. "Quarterly Labor Force Survey." Accessed December 23, 2020. http://www.statssa.gov.za/?page_id=1866&PPN=P0211&SCH=7891

Tang, Frank. "China Set To Break Key Economic Barrier Despite Trade War." *South China Morning Post*. January 1, 2020.

Taylor, Ian. "The Ambiguous Commitment: The People's Republic of China and the Anti-Apartheid Struggle in South Africa." *Journal of Contemporary African Studies* 18, no. 1 (2000): 91–106.

Taylor, Ian. *China and Africa: Engagement and Compromise.* New York: Taylor & Francis, 2006.

Taylor, Ian. *The Forum on China-Africa Cooperation (FOCAC).* New York: Routledge, 2011.

Thom, H. B., ed. *Journal of Jan van Riebeeck Volume 1: 1651–1655.* Cape Town: A.A. Balkema, 1952.

Tiejun Cheng and Mark Selden. "The Origins and Social Consequences of China's Hukou System." *The China Quarterly* 139, no. 1994 (1994): 644–68.

Tiley, Sian. *Mapungubwe: South Africa's Crown Jewels.* Johannesburg: Sunbird Publishing, 2004.

Turok, Ben, Ha-Joon Chang and João Carlos Ferraz. *Development in a Divided Country Vol. 5.* Auckland Park, South Africa: Jacana Media, 2011.

Tyalor, Ian. *China and Africa: Engagement and Compromise.* New York: Taylor & Francis, 2006.

UN-Wider. "World Income Inequality Database." Accessed December 23, 2019. https://www.wider.unu.edu/project/wiid---world-income-inequality-database

UNCTAD. "Economic Trends." Accessed June 2, 2020. https://unctadstat.unctad.org/wds/ReportFolders/reportFolders.aspx

UNCTAD. "Foreign Direct Investment." Accessed June 2, 2020. https://unctadstat.unctad.org/wds/ReportFolders/reportFolders.aspx?sCS_ChosenLang=en

UNCTAD. "Output and Income." Accessed June 2, 2020. https://unctadstat.unctad.org/wds/ReportFolders/reportFolders.aspx?sCS_ChosenLang=en

UNESCO. "Mapungubwe Cultural Landscape." Accessed August 21, 2020. http://whc.unesco.org/en/list/1099/

United Nations Population Division. "World Population Prospects." *World Bank Open Data.* Accessed December 23, 2019. https://data.worldbank.org/indicator/SM.POP.NETM

van Dijk, Meine. Peiter. "Introduction: Objectives of and Instruments for China's New Presence in Africa." In *New Presence of China in Africa,* edited by Meine Peiter van Dijk, 1–23. Amsterdam: University Press, 2010.

Vom Hau, Matthias, James Scott and David Hulme. "Beyond the BRICs: Alternative Strategies of Influence in the Global Politics of Development." *European Journal of Development Research* 24, no. 2 (2012): 187–204.

Wang, Dayuan. *Daoyi Zhulie* (Annals of Island Barbarians). Taipei: Dingwen Shuju, 1975.

Wei, Liang-Tsai. *Peking Versus Taipei in Africa: 1960–1978.* Taipei: Asia and World Institute, 1982.

Wilensky, Julie. "The Magical Kunlun and 'Devil Slaves': Chinese Perceptions of Dark-skinned People and Africa before 1500." *Sino-Platonic Papers* 122 (July 2002): 1–51.

Williams, Walter E. *South Africa's War Against Capitalism.* New York: Praeger, 1989.

Winning, Alexander and Joe Bavier. "Ramaphosa is 'Last Hope' for South Africa, Chinese Diplomat Says." *Reuters*. July 29, 2019. https://www.reuters.com/articl e/us-safrica-china/ramaphosa-is-last-hope-for-south-africa-chinese-diplomat-says -idUSKCN1UO1XG

World Bank. "Indicators." Accessed December 23, 2019. https://data.worldbank.org /indicator

World Food Program. "China Emerges as World's Third Largest Food Aid Donor." Accessed September 16, 2020. http://www.wfp.org/node/534

Worstfold, Basil. *The Reconstruction of the New Colonies under Lord Milner Volume I*. London: Keegan Paul, Trench, Tubner and Company, 1913.

Wu, Yujiang. *Mozi Jiaozhu* (Collated commentaries on Mozi). Chongqing: Duli Chubanshe, 1944.

Wyatt, Don J. *The Blacks of Premodern China*. Philadelphia: University of Pennsylvania Press, 2010.

Yat-sen, Sun, *San Min Chu-I* (The Three Principles of the People) trans. by Frank W. Price. Taipei: Sino-American Publishing, 1953.

Yiwu Municipality. Accessed November 11, 2020. http://english.yw.gov.cn/english _1/e_sw/e_sc/e_scjs/201104/t20110410_28124.html

Yu, George T. *China's Africa Policy: A Study of Tanzania*. New York: Praeger Publishers, 1975.

Yu, George, T. *China and Tanzania: A Study in Cooperative Interaction*. Berkeley: Regents of the University of California, 1970.

Zhang, Tingyu et al. *Mingshi* (Ming History). Beijing: Zhonghua Shuju, 1974.

Zhongui, Zhu. "Political Changes in Africa." *Contemporary International Relations* 3, no. 2 (1993): 1–14.

# Index

Abegunrin, Olayiwola, 8, 76
Adekunle, Julius, 20
Afri-Asian Peoples' Solidarity
Organization (AAPSO), 46
Africa-China relations: incompatibility,
8; from Ming to Qing era, 24–35; the
'spirit of Bandung' and, 43; the UN
and early, 50–52
African National Congress (ANC):
in Bandung, 41; Beijing visits by
Tambo, 45, 48, 54; developmental
state pronouncements by, 145–46;
founding, 35; Mao and doubts
about ANC armed struggle, 42;
narrative dissonance in, 145–49;
PAC formation and rivalry with, 43;
Taiwan aid to post-apartheid, 55; UN
observer status, 51
African renaissance, 67–68
African traders in China, 125–27
Afro-Asian Conference. *See* Bandung
Conference
Afro-Asian-Latin American
People's Solidarity Organization
(AALAPSO), 46
Afro-Asian People's Permanent Writers
Bureau (AAPWB), 46
agriculture: developmental state
prospects and, 149–52; percentage

of South African land for, 150–51;
percentage of value-added GDP
from, 151
allusive contacts between Chinese and
Africans, 17–30
ANC. *See* African National Congress
Anti-Taylor, William, 63–64
apartheid: the developmental state
under, 138–39; and early Sino-
African studies, 22–24
April, Yazini, 131
attenuated contacts between Chinese
and Africans, 30–58
attenuated contacts redux: capital
constraints, 149

Bandung Conference, 41–43
Baogang, Guo, 9
Bayne, Nicholas, 89
Bhoola, Ismail, 42
Bi-National Commission for China-
South Africa coordination, 69
Bobali, 20–21
Bodomo, Adam, 124
Botha, Pik, 55
Brautigam, Deborah, 53
BRICS: and South Africa-China
relations, 10; South Africa's
participation in *vs.* G-8, 88–92

# About the Author

**Phiwokuhle Mnyandu** holds joint teaching positions in the Department of African Studies and the Department of World Languages and Culture at Howard University. He is the co-author of *Introduction to African Humanomics: Economics and the Human Good*, as well as coeditor of *Pan African Spaces: Essays on Black Transnationalism*. He speaks Zulu, English, Shona, and French. He currently lives in the Washington, DC area with his wife and three children.

www.ingramcontent.com/pod-product-compliance
Lightning Source LLC
Chambersburg PA
CBHW050651280326
41932CB00015B/2858